The Researcher's Guide:
Film, Television, Radio and Related Documentation Collections in the UK

7th Edition

Editor: Sergio Angelini

British Universities Film & Video Council

British Universities Film & Video Council
77 Wells Street, London W1T 3QJ
Tel: 020 7393 1500 Fax: 020 7393 1555
e-mail: ask@bufvc.ac.uk

First published 1981 as *The Researcher's Guide to British Film & Television Collections*
Second edition 1985
Third edition 1989
Fourth edition 1993
Fifth edition 1997
Sixth edition 2001 as *The Researcher's Guide: Film, Television, Radio and Related Documentation Collections in the UK*
Seventh edition 2006

ISBN 0–901299–76–6

Front cover picture: Marilyn Monroe. Image courtesy of ITN Source/British Pathe

Back cover picture: cel from ANIMAL FARM (1954). Image courtesy of The Halas & Bachelor Collection Ltd.

Typesetting and layout by Columns Design
Printed in Great Britain by Latimer Trend and Company

Contents

Foreword

Murray Weston

This is the seventh edition of this book, now in its twenty-fifth year. As Sergio Angelini, its latest editor, notes in his introduction, the first edition was produced by Elizabeth Oliver in 1981, when the British Universities Film Council (as we were then called) undertook to compile a researcher's guide to film and television collections, partly to cope with the growing number of footage researchers who were using the Council's Information Service. The guide has grown from the 120 collections listed in 1981 to 644 in this latest incarnation, which now encompasses radio and related documentation collections, and which comes in a new compact form which we hope will prove all the more useful to researchers both academic and commercial who we know have valued this publication over the years and come to trust each new edition.

We can produce this edition with its shorter summaries thanks to our corresponding database, the Researcher's Guide Online (http://www.bufvc.ac.uk/rgo), which provides the researcher with more extensive descriptions, collection details, illustrations and live web links. The RGO is constantly updated, and now comes with the facility for collection owners to be able to add new records or amend existing ones.

The RGO is one among several BUFVC online resources which are designed to bring moving image and sound resources to the attention of UK higher education, for learning, teaching and research. They range from general resources such as the RGO and the Moving Image Gateway, to specialised research services such as the British Universities Newsreel Database, to the vast Television and Radio Index for Learning and Teaching (TRILT), offering access to information on programme content both pre- and post-transmission, and now linked to the ordering system of the BUFVC's Off-Air Recording Back-up Service. Users can find more on our range of databases on page 215 of this guide.

Although the BUFVC focuses much of its activity on the online delivery of content and data, we remain committed to publishing authoritative printed reference works. We are indebted to Sergio Angelini for his hard work in producing this guide, and to the support of his colleagues in the BUFVC's Information Service. We must also thank all those archives and collections which supplied us with up-to-date information, and whose commitment to making moving image and sound materials available for research access we warmly welcome. There is much to discover here – we hope that the guide opens up for all of its readers a world of research opportunities.

Murray Weston *is the Director of the British Universities Film & Video Council*

Introduction – 25 years of *The Researcher's Guide*

Sergio Angelini

During the second weekend of October 2005, all the major news agencies covered the South Asia earthquake. Within minutes, reports of the devastation were available as images and sound through a multiplicity of outlets – television, radio, the internet and mobile phones being merely the most prominent. Much of the material that was most widely seen was generated not just by professional news companies but also by amateurs making first person accounts using domestic camcorders and mobile phones.

On a smaller scale, that same weekend in the UK also saw coverage of the damage caused by yet another fire at Southend Pier, first built in 1830 and 1.34 miles in length by 1929, and the complete destruction of the archives of the Aardman Animation company in Bristol when the building behind it went ablaze. Aardman, the creators of *Wallace and Gromit*, have been the pre-eminent 3D animation production company in the UK for the last thirty years. The coincidence of these three events occurring during the same weekend, and the intense UK media response to them, brings in to relief the issues surrounding the use of many different types of moving images and sound, their availability to the public, their value and role in the media marketplace, and the extent to which such material is being properly archived for future generations. This is an issue that will become ever more relevant as the ability to deliver media online becomes even simpler and easier to access. Audio-visual material has never been so readily available nor so technologically malleable, but the sheer range of sources can of itself be problematic for both the information specialist and the student.

7th edition of the *Guide*

Ever since its inception in 1981, when its editor Elizabeth Oliver referred to it as 'in the nature of an experiment', this publication has had the challenging task of straddling the world of the commercial film and television researcher and the education community. This present volume provides details of nearly 650 collections in the UK relating to moving image and sound, ranging from national and regional film archives to specialist collections in academic institutions. We have tried to include a wide variety of resources and so accommodate a reasonably broad spectrum of user needs, but inevitably not everything that is included here will be of direct relevance to production companies, while some of the commercial entities listed provide services well out of the financial reach of most students and lecturers. Nevertheless, we hope that there will be more than enough in this volume to suit both the professional film and television researcher and the academic community at large.

'Archive' is a term that has considerably expanded its meaning and resonance in the last quarter of a century. Production companies nowadays regularly use the term to refer to footage or sound material simply made for other productions, irrespective of how long ago. The possibilities inherent in digitisation mean that material is much more widely available than ever before, though there is no denying that the cost of licensing that material has grown at a vastly accelerated rate in the last two–and-a-half decades. The recent arrival of podcasting and advanced multimedia telephony has seen a rapid growth in ancillary markets for all kinds of 'archive' material. The British Universities Film & Video Council keeps abreast of these developments through its various service activities and publications, both on paper and online, as the emergence of new formats and new delivery media result in broader implications for the education community's relationship to audio-visual materials in teaching and learning. The *Guide* has itself been available on the internet as the Researcher's Guide Online (RGO) since May 2001 and a great many of the entries that appear in this book were updated electronically via the RGO by the organisations themselves. As is customary, we have where possible provided access information and descriptions as supplied to us by the individuals and institutions concerned.

Replevin

Increasingly rapid changes in technology mean that even research methods can quickly become outmoded. 'Replevin', for instance, was once a much-used part of Anglo-French law denoting a form of legal recovery of goods, but what was important once is now mostly a word used by people setting acrostics. In 1970 when Len Deighton published his historical novel *Bomber*, Anthony Burgess warmly received it as a work that 'could only have been written with an electronic retrieval system', but the technology would undoubtedly seem archaic by today's standards. In fact, since then the electronic age has also ensured that certain kinds of primary research materials, such as written correspondence, manuscripts with hand-written comments/changes and so on, are no longer going to be available in the same way. The need properly to document, and catalogue materials that are now being generated is crucial and questions of effective access to these materials flows directly from this.

The perils of technological obsolescence were crystallised in the furore over the BBC's 1986 Domesday project, when the Digital Preservation Coalition highlighted the fact that much of the data on their LaserDiscs was no longer accessible barely fifteen years later. The Coalition set out its findings and recommendations in its February 2006 report, *Minding the Gap: Assessing Digital Preservation Needs in the UK*, though the various 'push-pull' effects of the commercial sphere and the special access and use of media materials for education in the UK are likely to have more direct impact in the near future without some kind of state intervention.

Googling

Telephony is probably the most important audio-visual tool in the world, as it incorporates the internet and 'Next Generation' imaging and sound technology, which was startlingly used to supply first-hand accounts (actively sought by broadcasters) following the 7/7 attack in London. Aardman have recently signed a deal to deliver new content to phones and BBC Worldwide has recently made licensing deals to deliver complete episodes of DOCTOR WHO, RED DWARF and LITTLE BRITAIN that way too.

The onslaught of new technologies has reached such fever pitch of late that it has left many dazed and confused, and in some cases there is clearly cause for concern. The BBC's five-month TV on-demand trial concluded in February 2006. Its iPlayer allows broadband users to download programmes up to seven days after their initial transmission, but these cannot be copied or otherwise archived. This may have serious implications for educational users who would like to access programme online, while even those institutions currently able to make copies of programmes under the Educational Recording Agency's licensing scheme may be affected if programmes are repeated less often as a result of 'view again' services. The education community in the UK is already able to access high quality digital materials online via such projects as Film and Sound Online (formerly Education Media Online) and Newsfilm Online, projects which are exclusively delivering thousands of hours of downloadable documentary materials.

As the events of autumn last year prove, even in this age of digital redundancy, there is still much being lost through accidents and natural disasters. Moreover, it might seem that such video-file sharing services as YouTube are providing greater and faster access to audio-visual material, but much of it is badly or misleadingly catalogued and ignores copyright implications. The job of the information professional is to help the user understand what they really want and help them get it - the aim of this publication is similarly to provide a roadmap to the material that may potentially be available to researchers in the UK interested in materials relating to moving images and sound.

There is thus much to look forward to as the digital age continues to develop and prosper and a concomitant satisfaction and even a little pride in being able still to offer this latest, fully revised and up-to-date edition of *The Researcher's Guide*, a full quarter of a century after the publication of its first edition.

Acknowledgements

During the long gestation of this new edition a great many friends and colleagues generously lent their expertise and advice. I am particularly indebted, first and foremost, to those editors that came before me: Elizabeth Oliver, Daniela Kirchner and, most especially, the indefatigable James Ballantyne, whose work from previous editions permeates the entirety of this volume. My colleagues at the BUFVC, Cathy Grant, Luke McKernan, Marianne Open, Marilyn Sarmiento and Jo Yates, have all made valuable contributions to the content and shape of this text.

Sergio Angelini is the BUFVC's Library and Database Manager

Using the Researcher's Guide

This book is a guide to film, television, radio, and related documentation collections in the UK and Ireland that are of interest to both academic and commercial researchers. Some oral history collections are also included. It is intended as a handy reference guide, and is designed to be used in tandem with the fuller web version, the Researcher's Guide Online (RGO), available without charge at http://www.bufvc.ac.uk/rgo (*see below*).

The following fields are provided for each record:

Number Each entry is numbered, and subject terms in the index point to the collection number. The collections are listed alphabetically, for the UK and then for the Republic of Ireland.

Name The current name of the organisation (some recent changes of name are given afterwards in parentheses).

Address

Email

Web For particularly long web addresses we have replaced these with truncated TinyURL addresses (a free service available from http://www.tinyurl.co.uk). The original addresses can be found on the RGO.

Telephone   Fax

Contact The name given at the time of writing the entry.

Access Details are given of the visitor access provided by the collections. Users should be aware that many commercial collections do not offer visitor access, particularly to non-commercial users; also, some of the smaller archives will be limited in their opening hours and the services that they can provide. It is always advisable to ring or write ahead of any planned visit. Information on access for the disabled is also provided, where available.

Description The collection descriptions are shortened from those provided in the RGO. The descriptions give a general guide to contents and services, but users can always look online for fuller versions, particularly for details of film, video and sound materials.

Following the main guide, there is a listing of some of the major **research organisations and services** in the UK, both academic and commercial, and a listing of the **BUFVC's own research services**.

The **subject index** is not a full listing of all the subjects covered by all the collections. Many of the major collections, including national film archives, television companies and stock shot libraries will cover almost every subject. Numbers refer to the number of the entry for that collection in the *Guide*, not page numbers.

Every effort has been made to ensure that records in the Researcher's Guide are accurate and up-to-date. Please inform us of any errors, omissions or amendments required to the details cited in the text. Email us at rgo@bufvc.ac.uk.

Researcher's Guide Online

The Researcher's Guide Online (RGO) is the online version of this reference work. The RGO has entries on over 640 film, television, radio and related documentation collections in the United Kingdom and Ireland, and is being constantly updated and amended. The RGO enables users to define searches by collection title, subject, index term, personality and medium. Entries on the RGO are more detailed than those given in this book, and there are more illustrations.

Collection owners can add or update their own records through the RGO's online form. Adding or updating records is a simple process, and all such amendments are moderated by staff at the BUFVC's Information Service, so your records will be secure.

The RGO is a freely-available online resource.

The original development of the RGO was funded through the Research Support Libraries Programme.

http://www.bufvc.ac.uk/rgo

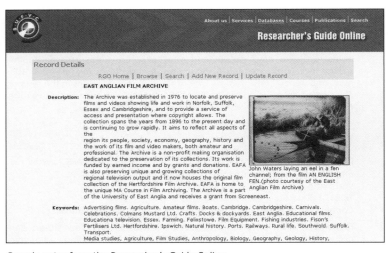

Sample entry from the Researcher's Guide Online

Film, television, radio and related documentation collections – United Kingdom

1   100–102 CENTURY FM

Century House, PO Box 100, Gateshead NE8 2YX
Email: http://www.100centuryfm.com/contactus.asp
Web: http://www.centurynortheast.com
☎ 0191 477 6666 **Fax:** 0191 477 5660
Contact: Paul Jackson, Century Group Programme Controller

Holds legal requirement plus special news items and programmes which are kept for in-house use, e.g. in compiling end of year review. Now part of GCap Media, a company born following the merger of Capital Radio and the GWR Group.

2   104.7 ISLAND FM

12 Westerbrook Street, Sampsons, Guernsey GY2 4QQ
Email: Damien@islandfm.Guernsey.net
Web: http://www.islandfm.com
☎ 01481 242000 **Fax:** 01481 249676
Contact: Damien St. John, Programme Controller

Radio station covering Guernsey and Alderney in the Channel Islands. It holds forty-two days' output and also keeps Christmas days and some special local and extended programmes. It provides a mixture of music, news and general information. One of the first radio stations in the region. The first air date was on 15 October 1992. The initial licence is due to expire on 14 October 2008.

3   105.4 CENTURY FM

Laser House, Waterfront Quay, Salford Quays, Manchester M5 2XW
Email: ande.macpherson@centuryfm.co.uk
Web: http://www.1054centuryfm.com
☎ 0161 400 0105 **Fax:** 0161 400 1105
Contact: Ande Macpherson, Century Group Programme Controller

Radio station holding legal requirement plus special news items and programmes which are kept for in-house use, e.g. in compiling end of year review. Now part of GCap Media, a company born following the merger of Capital Radio and the GWR Group.

4   107 OAK FM

7 Waldron Court, Prince William Road, Loughborough,
Leicestershire LE11 5GD
Email: studio@oak.fm
Web: http://www.oak.fm
☎ 01509 211711 **Fax**: 01509 246107
Contact: Don Douglas, Station Manager

Radio station. Holds forty-two days' output only to meet legal requirement.

5   107.3 TIME FM

2–6 Basildon Road, London SE2 0EW
Email: mark@timefm.com
Web: http://1073.timefm.com
☎ 020 8311 3112 **Fax**: 020 8312 1930
Contact: Mark Reason, Operations Director

Radio station. Holds three months' output of all radio recordings only. Formerly Fusion 107.3 and before that FLR 107.3. Is now part of Sunshine Radio.

6   2CR FM

5 Southcote Road, Bournemouth, Dorset BH1 3LR
Email: graham.mack@musicradio.com
Web: http://2crfm.musicradio.com/homepage.jsp
☎ 01202 259259 **Fax**: 01202 255244
Contact: Graham Mack, Programme Manager/Controller

Radio station. Holdings: 2CR FM – key clips of its BREAKFAST SHOW (weekdays 06.00–09.00) and all logger tapes of output for up to sixty days.

7   95.8 CAPITAL FM

30 Leicester Square, London WC2H 7LA
Email: info@capitalradio.co.uk
Web: http://www.capitalfm.com
☎ 020 7766 6000 **Fax**: 020 7766 6100
Contact: Jeff Smith, Programme Controller
Access: No public access

Capital Radio took to the airwaves in October 1973, the UK's second commercial radio station. The radio station holds three months' output to meet legal requirement. Other programmes have gone to the British Library Sound Archive (qv), including early programmes from the start of Capital FM. The Capital Group's central library is based in London. A music library is maintained.

8   96 TRENT FM

29–31 Castle Gate, Nottingham NG1 7AP
Email: dick.stone@musicradio.com
Web: http://trentfm.musicradio.com/homepage.jsp
☎ 0115 952 7000 **Fax**: 0115 912 9333
Contact: Dick Stone, Programme Controller

Radio station serving the Nottinghamshire region. Launched in 1975 as Radio Trent, it was renamed Trent FM in 1988. Since the summer of 2005 it has been part of the GCap Media group. Holdings include general local interest – news items are also kept.

9   97.4 VALE FM

Longmead, Shaftesbury, Dorset SP7 8QQ
Email: studio@valefm.co.uk
Web: http://www.valefm.co.uk
☎ 01747 855711 **Fax**: 01747 855722
Contact: Anne Holmes, Sales

Since it began broadcasting in 1995, Vale FM has become an integral part of the community with a popular mix of music, news, information and interactive competitions. Local news kept for one year only.

10   ABERDEEN UNIVERSITY LIBRARY

Queen Mother Library, Meston Walk, Old Aberdeen, Aberdeen, Grampian AB24 3UE
Email: j.a.beavan@abdn.ac.uk
Web: http://www.abdn.ac.uk/diss/library
☎ 01224 272553 **Fax**: 01224 273956
Contact: Jennifer Beavan, Site Services Manager, Arts & Divinity Section

The collection of films on video reflects the interests of a number of departments within the University's Faculty of Arts & Divinity; Film Studies (within English), Hispanic Studies (Spanish and Latin American), French and German. In particular Film Studies focuses on American, European and Irish-Scottish films.

11   THE ADVERTISING ARCHIVES

45 Lyndale Avenue, London NW2 2QB
Email: info@advertisingarchives.co.uk
Web: http://www.advertisingarchives.co.uk/index.php
☎ 020 7435 6540 **Fax**: 020 7794 6584
Contact: Suzanne Viner
Access: Due to space constraints we are not open to visitors at this time

The Advertising Archives was established in 1990 by Larry and Suzanne Viner. The collection comprises over one million catalogued images and includes: television advertising; British television stills dating from the very first transmitted advert to the latest campaigns; thousands of cinema posters.

12   AFRICAN VIDEO CENTRE

7 Balls Pond Road, London N1 4AX
☎ 020 7732 4224 **Fax**: 020 7249 6886
Contact: Magnus Macauley
Access: Mon–Sat, 10.30–21.30

A small family-run business, specialising in sale/hire of video cassettes by, for or about black persons. Only items released on video format available.

13   AIRTIME TELEVISION

PO Box 258, Maidenhead, Berkshire SL6 9YR
Email: martin@airtimetv.co.uk
Web: http://www.airtimetv.co.uk
☎ 0870 8503047 **Fax**: 01628 474016
Contact: Martin White
Access: Available by appointment

Founded in 1991, initially to provide pooled television news coverage from Heathrow airport. An initial supply contract with ITN was followed by agreements with many other broadcasters. Heathrow news is still the core of the business but the company now does many other things – with corporate video production and the supply of archive footage taking on particular importance. In 2002 we opened an office in Pinewood Studios, a stone's throw from Heathrow but also the centre of the British film production industry and in 2004 moved to a new bureau in Heathrow's Terminal 1. In 2003 we signed a long-term agreement with ITN for the marketing of archive footage.

14   ALAN PATEMAN FILM ARCHIVE COLLECTION

6 Brookfield Gardens, Carlisle, Cumbria CA1 2PJ
Email: alanpateman@freenetname.co.uk
Web: http://www.Pateman-Organization.co.uk
☎ 01228 527141
Contact: Alan Pateman
Access: By arrangement only

The collection includes material on countries and regions including: Australia, France, India, Egypt, USA, Germany, China, Soviet Union, UK, Sweden, Rhodesia, Bermuda, Corsica, Italy, Mexico, Borneo, Costa Rica and others. Subjects include politics, newsreels, comedians, animation and trick photography, westerns, Mack Sennett, sports, River Thames, car manufacturers, ships, railways, aircraft, music hall, royalty, world wars, film stars, firefighting, mining, propaganda, Nazis, speed attempts, dancing, holiday camps, advertising, fashion, animals, ENSA, oil, horse-racing, glamour-adult nude from 1915. Recent additions include: well-filmed 16mm colour amateur footage: 1959 African Congo; 1960 Austria; 1962/4 Australia, New Zealand and Tasmania; 1963/4 Norway and Denmark; 1963 France, Egypt and Holy Land.

15 ALEXANDER KEILLER MUSEUM

Avebury, Marlborough, Wiltshire SN8 1RF
Web: http://www.english-heritage.org.uk
☎ 01672–539250
Contact: Curator
Access: Free access for researchers

Material from archaeological excavations carried out at Windmill Hill, Avebury, in 1925, directed by Alexander Keiller (1889–1955). The investigation of Avebury Stone Circles was largely the work of Alexander Keiller in the 1930s. He put together one of the most important prehistoric archaeological collections in Britain and this can be seen in Avebury Museum.

16 ALEXANDRA PALACE TELEVISION SOCIETY ARCHIVE

Email: apts@apts.org.uk
Web: http://www.apts.org.uk
Contact: Simon Vaughan
Access: Can be given, subject to certain copyright restriction

The Alexandra Palace Television Society has been in existence since 1993 and during that time has steadily increased the number of items within the Archive. From an initial 400 items the Archive currently stands at nearly 5,000 individual items. At present there are over fifty hours of audio tapes, usually recorded in group sessions, of three or more. Mostly they contain reminiscences of working live at Alexandra Palace and various television practices during the formative years of the television service and during the late 1940s and early 1950s. Archive films from the pre-war era give an insight into the type of programming that was available to the small quantity of pioneer viewers. Post-war programmes show how the television service developed during the years of expansion.

17 ALPHA 103.2

Radio House, 11 Woodland Road, Darlington, Co Durham DL3 7BJ
Email: studio@alphafm.co.uk
Web: http://www.alpha1032.com
☎ 01325 255552 **Fax**: 01325 255551
Contact: Steve Phillips, Programme Manager

Radio station. Holds forty-two days' output – local DARLINGTON LINE weekly programme.

18   AMBLESIDE ORAL HISTORY GROUP ARCHIVE

Ambleside Public Library, Kelsick Road, Ambleside, Cumbria LA22 0BZ
Email: http://www.aohg.org.uk/email.html
Web: http://www.aohghistory.f9.co.uk
☎ 015394 32507
Access: Library opening hours: Mon & Wed 10.00–17.00, Tue & Fri
10.00–19.00, Thu & Sun closed all day, Sat 10.00–13.00

Ambleside Oral History Group was founded in 1976 and has created an archive of over 300 interviews, on almost every subject related to life in Ambleside, Cumbria, and its surrounding area, in the Lake District of England, beginning with memories from the 1880s. The archive exists in both hard copy and electronic form. Essentially it consists of recordings and indexed transcripts of interviews. Transcripts are available in printed form and also as digital files on computer, searchable by topic or keyword. Recordings of interviews can be heard by prior arrangement.

19   ANGLESEY COUNTY RECORD OFFICE

Swyddfa'r Sir, Glanhwfa Road, Llangefni, Isle of Anglesey LL77 7TW
Email: archives@anglesey.gov.uk
Web: http://anglesey.gov.uk
☎ 01248–752083
Contact: Anne Venables, Archivist
Access: Mon-Fri 09.00–13.00 and 14.00–17.00

Very small collection consisting of items of local history interest, including oral history materials.

20   ANGLIA RUSKIN UNIVERSITY

East Road, Cambridge CB1 1PT
Email: a.r.a.wood@apu.ac.uk
Web: http://www.anglia.ac.uk
☎ 01223 363 271 Ext: 3562 **Fax**: 01245 494199
Contact: Andrew Wood, Head of Media Production
Access to general public for reference use only

The library collection at Cambridge holds approximately 4,000 tapes – off-air recordings on all subjects, plus British and European films. It also houses a specialist collection of documents and facsimile documents, as well as audio-visual materials, on the history of the French Resistance in World War II. Formerly known as Anglia Polytechnic University.

21 AP ARCHIVE

The Interchange, Oval Road, Camden Lock, London NW1 7DZ
Email: info@aparchive.com
Web: http://www.aparchive.com
☎ 020 7482 7886 **Fax**: 020 7413 8348
Contact: Véronique Foucault, Library Manager
Access: By appointment

News and entertainment footage from around the world including exclusive and iconic shots from history up to the present day. AP Archive is the moving image archive of Associated Press, the world's oldest and largest newsgathering organisation. The library also represents other collections including ABC America, ABC Australia, Vatican Television, the Grinberg collection, WWF and broadcasters like CCTV China and KRT in North Korea. Formerly known as APTN Library.

22 ARCHIFDY CEREDIGION ARCHIVES

County Office, Marine Terrace, Aberystwyth, Wales SY23 2DE
Email: archives@ceredigion.gov.uk
Web: http://archifdy-ceredigion.org.uk
☎ 01970–633697 / 8
Contact: Helen Palmer, County Archivist
Access: Not available without consent of the owner

The Archives collects, preserves and makes available to the public all sorts of records about the history of Ceredigion, which is the county formerly known as Cardiganshire. Ceredigion Archives was originally established in 1974 as the third office of the Dyfed Archives Service. It was then known as the Cardiganshire Area Record Office. In 1996 at local government re-organisation the record office was re-launched as Ceredigion Archives. It remains one of the smaller county record offices. Official and private documents relating to the history of the county are held here.

23 ARCHITECTURAL ASSOCIATION SCHOOL OF ARCHITECTURE PHOTO LIBRARY

36/37 Bedford Square, London WC1B 3ES
Email: valerie@aaschool.ac.uk
Web: http://www.aaschool.ac.uk/photolibrary/index.shtm
☎ 020 7887 4066
Contact: Valerie Bennett
Access: 10.00 to 17.00 Mon-Fri (latest time for viewing videos 16.00)

The Photo Library holds approximately 150,000 slides of both historical and contemporary buildings, 25,000 slides of AA student work and several valuable archives of black-and-white photographs. The collection is primarily for use within the School. It also operates as a commercial photo library, lending slides for publication in books and journals worldwide. The Photo Library is also responsible for the AA's video archive. This important collection, including material from the late 1960s, is based primarily on lectures and events presented at the AA, but the library has also started to collect videos of important feature and art house films. All videos must be viewed *in situ*.

24   ARCHIVE FILM AGENCY

49 South Croxted Road, London SE21 8AZ
Email: archivefilmagency@mail.com
☎ 020 8670 3618 **Fax**: 020 8670 3618
Contact: Bob Geoghegan, Director

The collection ranges from material from the first film experiments to documentaries of early 1960s. A good percentage is non-fiction, documentary and newsfilm of the 1910s, 1920s and 1930s, mostly British and American with a small amount in colour. The archive also holds non-fiction material shot in Birmingham and Yorkshire. The remainder comprises fiction films, feature films and shorts from the 1920s and 1930s, mainly British and American, with a small percentage of Italian and French. Advertising, amateur, science and education short films form part of the collection.

25   ARKive

Wildscreen, Anchor Road, Harbourside, Bristol BS1 5TT
Email: harriet.nimmo@wildscreen.org.uk
Web: http://www.arkive.org
☎ 0117 915 7100 **Fax**: 0117 915 7105
Contact: Harriet Nimmo, Wildscreen Chief Executive
Access: Normal working hours, plus occasional evening screenings

ARKive is a specialist digital library of wildlife and environmental images and recordings. It includes: 1) top wildlife programmes from around the world, and a large collection of historical films on the changing genre of wildlife film-making; 2) a representative selection of moving images, stills and sound recordings of endangered species; 3) a collection of filmed interviews with pioneering wildlife film-makers and others associated with the industry; 4) a library of books and journals associated with the history and techniques of wildlife film-making; 5) a database of the location and copyright details of all known collections of wildlife and environmental images and recordings.

Nick Garbutt / naturepl.com

Crowned lemur (*Eulemur coronatus*)

26   ARROW FM

Priory Meadow Centre, Hastings, East Sussex TN34 1PJ
Email: studio@arrowfm.co.uk
Web: http://www.arrowfm.co.uk
☎ 01424 461177 **Fax**: 01424 422662
Contact: Peter Quinn, Programme Director

Radio station. Holdings: Normal forty-two days' output. Very small collection of material of local interest and news collections kept.

27   ARTS COUNCIL FILM AND VIDEO LIBRARY

c/o Concord Video & Film Council, Rosehill Centre, 22 Hines Road, Ipswich, Suffolk IP3 9BG
Email: sales@concordvideo.co.uk Web: http://www.concordvideo.co.uk
☎ 01473 726012 **Fax**: 01473 274531
Access: By arrangement

The Arts Council film and video collection was established in 1981 and is the largest collection of documentaries on the arts in Great Britain. It represents twenty years of Arts Council commitment to the production of high quality arts programmes with an enduring value to education. Educational distribution now handled by Concord Video & Film Council (qv).

28   ASTON UNIVERSITY
LIBRARY & INFORMATION SERVICES

Aston University, Aston Triangle, Birmingham B4 7ET
Email: library@aston.ac.uk
Web: http://www.aston.ac.uk/lis
☎ 0121 359 3611 Ext 4398 **Fax**: 0121 359 7358
Contact: N.R. Smith, Director
Access: Reference use only

Small collection of videos in Short Loan Collection.

29   AUSTIN SEVEN FILM LIBRARY

9 Arden Road, London N3 3AB
☎ 020 8349 0770 **Fax**: 020 8346 2998
Contact: Joseph Henri Spalter
Access: Available by arrangement

Most of the films are 16mm copies of films made by Austin Car Ltd in the 1930s for showing in the cinema and car show-rooms. They were presented to the Austin Seven Club Association when the 16mm library was closed. In addition there are films made in the 1920s and 1930s on 16mm, 8mm and Super-8mm, and film shot in the 1950s-1980s of Austin Seven Club events. Most of the collection is also on Video VHS, U-matic lo-band and some on Hi-8 video.

30 B-LINE PRODUCTIONS

135 Sydney Road, London N10 2ND
Email: info@b-lineproductions.co.uk
Web: http://www.b-lineproductions.co.uk
☎ 020 8444 9574 **Fax**: 020 8365 3664
Contact: Annie Moore

The company specialises in programming for the family audience, ranging from series on alternative therapies, cats, a six-part cake decorating series, to a series on mother-and-baby related subjects.

31 THE BAIM COLLECTION LIMITED

c/o 52 Warwick Crest, Edgbaston, Birmingham B15 2LH
Email: richard.jeffs@baimfilms.com
Web: http://www.baimfilms.com
☎ 0121 455 8840 **Fax**: 0121 455 8841
Contact: Richard Jeffs
Access: By telephone or e-mail application

Harold Baim was a prolific producer of short films from 1946 to 1983. There are over one hundred 35mm short films in the collection originally made for release in the British cinema. The collection also holds two feature films. Nearly all of the surviving films are in colour and more than fifty of the titles are available on Beta SP. The collection holds unique images of Britain as well as a number of international travel films. These films provide general programme makers, entertainment producers, historians and documentary makers with affordable illustrative colour material.

Baim Collection

The English Riviera – Holidays in the 50s

32 BALINESE TELEVISION PROJECT ARCHIVE

c/o Dr Mark Hobart, Media & Film Studies Programme, SOAS, University
of London, Thornhaugh Street, London WC1H 0XG
Email: inquiries@bajra.org
Web: http://www.soas.ac.uk
☎ 020 7898 4415 **Fax**: 020 7898 4699
Contact: Mark Hobart

This video collection is a comprehensive archive of programmes on Balinese
culture, broadcast on Indonesian state television (TVRI) since September
1990. The project is a collaborative venture between STSI (the Indonesian
Academy of Performing Arts) and SOAS (the School of Oriental and African
Studies). The project has some 750 hours of theatre and dance as well as
300 hours on general culture. Sales: 155 hours is available with
transcriptions on CD-ROM in MPEG1 for purchase as three sets. Set 1:
Classical Balinese Theatre and Dance (forty-nine hours). Set 2: Modern
Balinese/Indonesian Theatre and Culture (sixty-two hours). Set 3: Modern
Indonesian Society, Culture and Economy (forty-three hours). Twenty-six
hours of particularly valuable and useful materials has been remastered in
MPEG2 on DVD in both PAL and NTSC. Copies are available at a charge for
educational institutions.

33 BARBICAN LIBRARY

Barbican Centre, Silk Street, London EC2Y 8DS
Email: barbicanlib@corpoflondon.gov.uk
Web: http://www.barbican.org.uk
☎ 020 7638 0569 **Fax**: 020 7638 2249
Contact: John Lake, Librarian

The Barbican Library is the City of London's leading lending library with
books, spoken word recordings, videos, DVDs, CD-ROMs, music CDs and
scores available for loan. There are particular strengths in music, arts,
children's and financial sections as well as Internet access, self-service
photocopying, listening facilities and a practice piano.

34 BARNARDO'S FILM & PHOTOGRAPHIC ARCHIVE

Barnardo's, Tanners Lane, Barkingside, Ilford, Essex IG6 1QG
Email: stephen.pover@barnardos.org.uk
Web: http://www.barnardos.org.uk/who_we_are/history/
photo_archive.htm
☎ 020 8498 7345 **Fax**: 020 8550 0429
Contact: Stephen Povers, Photographic Resources Officer
Access: Mon-Fri 09.30–16.30. Staff are available to assist. Access for
disabled

Barnardo's image archive dates back to the early 1870s, and is a unique and
rich resource of images that depicts British family life, street scenes, poverty
and Barnardo's history of childcare in the Victorian period. The collection
comprises 150 films dating back to 1905 regarding the social history of the
20th century, focussing on children, child-care and education. The
collection includes material relating to emigration and the war years.
Dating back to 1874, the archive contains 500,000 images and 300 films of
the visual history of the organisation, including our work overseas in
Canada and Australia.

Barnardo's Photographic Archive

Ragged boy and girl

35　BATH SPA UNIVERSITY COLLEGE

Sion Hill Library, 8 Somerset Place, Bath BA1 5HB
Email: h.rayner@bathspa.ac.uk
Web: http://www.bathspa.ac.uk
☎ 01225 875648 **Fax**: 01225 427080
Contact: Helen Rayner, Campus Librarian
Access: Non-members of the College must make an appointment

The Library and Information Services are housed on two sites: Newon Park Campus and Sion Hill Campus. Both libraries include a video collection of roughly the same size, but numbering over 500 videos in all. A small percentage of these are off-air recordings. Sion Hill Library's book collection relates to film, video, television and radio, mostly at undergraduate level.

36   BBC 7

Room 1010, BBC Broadcasting House, London W1 1AA
Email: http://www.bbc.co.uk/feedback/
Web: http://www.bbc.co.uk/bbc7
Contact: Mary Kalemkerian, Programme Manager

Digital radio channel that broadcasts programmes from the BBC's archives.

37   BBC ASIAN NETWORK

Epic House, Charles Street, Leicester LE1 3SH
Email: mike.curtis@bbc.co.uk
Web: http://www.bbc.co.uk/asiannetwork
☎ 0116 202 1563 **Fax**: 0116 253 2004
Contact: Mike Curtis

The radio station is working on its archive at the moment. Holdings: a limited news archive for the last two years, and sixteen half-hour programmes based on immigrant experiences in the UK from *The Century Speaks* series (copies of these are held in the British Library Sound Archive, qv.)

38   BBC BRISTOL NEWS LIBRARY

Broadcasting House, Whiteladies Road, Bristol BS8 2LR
Email: jan.abbott@bbc.co.uk
Web: http://www.bbc.co.uk/bristol/news.shtml
☎ 0117 973 2211 **Fax**: 0272 744114
Contact: Jan Abbott, News Librarian
Access: The Library's first responsibility is to the regional production teams. All enquiries from outside of the BBC should be directed to BBC Worldwide, 80 Wood Lane, London W12 0TT. Tel: 020 8576 2000

Regional television began in the late fifties and the Library was set up in 1979 to cope with the vast backlog. Newsfilm is available from 1957 when the area covered by Bristol was England south-west of a line from Gloucester to Brighton. Later, smaller sites at Southampton and Plymouth reduced the regional area.

39   BBC EAST RECORDED MATERIALS LIBRARY

BBC East, The Forum, Millennium Plain, Norwich NR2 1BH
Email: nora.wilson@bbc.co.uk
Web: http://www.bbc.co.uk/england/lookeast
☎ 01603 284358 **Fax**: 01603–764303
Contact: Nora Wilson, Recorded Materials Librarian
Access: No access

BBC East began transmissions in 1959 but a librarian was only appointed in 1979. Little material exists from before 1976. BBC East produces news bulletins throughout the day, a daily regional news programme, a weekly thirty-minute programme on various subjects and a weekly parliamentary programme. News and features material exists on film (negative and colour master), and 1-inch, $\frac{3}{4}$-inch and $\frac{1}{2}$-inch videotape. The library also has a collection of Beta stock shots. BBC East has been transmitting from a server since October 2003. Footage is archived from the server onto DVcam. All U-matic ($\frac{3}{4}$-inch) tapes have been transferred to DVcam. We do not make VHS viewing copies.

40   BBC GMR

PO Box 951, Oxford Road, Manchester M60 1SD
Email: gmr@bbc.co.uk
Web: http://www.bbc.co.uk/england/gmr
☎ 0161 200 2000 **Fax**: 0161 236 5804
Contact: Steve Taylor, Editor

Very small private and in-house radio collection of major Manchester news. Coverage of 2002 Commonwealth Games archived. Other material is deposited with the North West Sound Archive (qv).

41   BBC INFORMATION AND ARCHIVES

BBC Television Centre, Wood Lane, London W12 7RJ
Email: research-central@bbc.co.uk
Web: http://www.bbcresearchcentral.com
☎ 020 8225 7193 **Fax**: 020 8576 7020
Contact: Research Team
Access: Weekdays, 09.30–18.00 for external enquiries

BBC Information and Archives comprises the BBC's libraries, programme archives and information centres. The programme archives and collections of recorded and printed music are regarded as the most extensive in the world. Holdings include BBC Television and Radio programmes and News in broadcast master format, with film or VHS cassette access copies for television and DAT or cassette copies of radio programmes. The BBC Photograph Archive contains over four million stills. The Gramophone Collection is one of the largest in the UK and there is a considerable sheet music collection. The Programme Collections date from 1936 for television and from 1922 for radio.

42   BBC INFORMATION & ARCHIVES: BBC SOUTH WEST PLYMOUTH TELEVISION NEWS LIBRARY

Seymour Road, Plymouth, Devon PL3 5BD
Email: plymouth.library@bbc.co.uk
Web: http://www.bbc.co.uk/devon
☎ 01752 234559 **Fax**: 01752 234596
Contact: Paula Griffiths, Senior Librarian
Access: BBC production staff only. External requests directed to BBC Worldwide

The collection comprises local material from 1962 to date plus local feature/documentary programmes from the same period. Not all material was kept in the early years. The South West region covers Devon, Cornwall and the Channel Islands and some bordering areas.

43 BBC INFORMATION & ARCHIVES: BELFAST RESEARCH CENTRE

Ormeau Avenue, Belfast, Northern Ireland BT2 8HQ
Email: fiona.johnston@bbc.co.uk
Web: http://www.bbc.co.uk/northernireland
☎ 028 9033 8323 **Fax**: 028 9033 8329
Contact: Fiona Johnston, Library Services Co-ordinator
Access: Restricted access now provided for external production company researchers. Anyone wishing to purchase BBC NI footage can contact BBC NI directly – contact: Paul McKevitt on tel: 028 9033 8046

The Research Centre provides a multi-media research service to BBC NI programmes and network productions.

44 BBC INFORMATION & ARCHIVES: BIRMINGHAM

The Mailbox, Birmingham B1 1RF
Email: garry.campbell@bbc.co.uk Web: http://www.bbc.co.uk/birmingham
☎ 0121 567 6384 **Fax**: 01231 432 8736
Contact: Garry Campbell, Information and Archives Manager
Access: The service exists primarily for BBC staff. Members of the public and independent companies wishing to view or purchase material should go through the BBC Public Enquiry Unit or BBC Worldwide

Information and Archives provides a service primarily to BBC Regional and Network programme-making departments covering both radio and television that are based in Birmingham. This includes MIDLANDS TODAY, the daily local news programme, and the weekly MIDLANDS REPORT and MIDLANDS AT WESTMINSTER. Network programme departments located in Birmingham include: Television: lifestyle and features (COUNTRYFILE, GARDENERS' WORLD, COAST) and television drama (DOCTORS, DALZIEL AND PASCOE); Radio: a range of programmes including THE ARCHERS, SILVER STREET, COSTING THE EARTH, OPEN COUNTRY, THE CRITICAL LIST and BEST OF JAZZ.

45 BBC INFORMATION & ARCHIVES: BRISTOL RESEARCH CENTRE

BBC Broadcasting House, Whiteladies Road, Bristol BS8 2LR
Email: alan.baker@bbc.co.uk
Web: http://www.bbc.co.uk/bristol
☎ 0117 973 2211 **Fax**: 0117 923 8879
Contact: Alan Baker, Information & Archives Manager
Access: BBC production staff only. External researchers directed to BBC Worldwide

The Research Centre provides a multimedia research service which incorporates specialist natural history research. Service is primarily for network documentary and feature programmes, the Natural History Unit, regional television and network radio productions. The collection (1960 to present) comprises viewing, safety, archive/insert and rushes material for network television features and regional news on a variety of formats – 16mm, 1-inch, Beta-SP, D3, DigiBeta, DV and VHS. Sound: $\frac{1}{4}$-inch, DAT, CD. All BBC Network transmission material is archived at BBC Information & Archives – Television Archive, Windmill Road, London.

46 BBC INFORMATION & ARCHIVES: LEEDS NEWS LIBRARY

BBC TV, Broadcasting Centre, Woodhouse Lane, Leeds LS2 9PX
Email: leeds.library@bbc.co.uk
Web: http://www.bbc.co.uk/leeds
☎ 0113 244 7218 **Fax**: 0113 243 9390
Contact: Jane Sheehan, Research Librarian
Access: Limited. Access for disabled. Ground floor location; ramp and WC

Collection based on regional magazine programmes from its commencement in 1968, regional feature and documentary programmes and supporting material. The region includes Yorkshire and parts of Nottinghamshire, Derbyshire and Lincolnshire.

47 BBC INFORMATION & ARCHIVES: MANCHESTER RESEARCH CENTRE

New Broadcasting House, Oxford Road, Manchester M60 1SJ
Email: heather.powell@bbc.co.uk
Web: http://www.bbc.co.uk/manchester
☎ 0161 244 4391 **Fax**: 0161 244 4376
Contact: Heather Powell, Manager Information and Archives, North
Access: The library exists primarily to serve BBC staff broadcasters on site

The library primarily provides a service to BBC regional and network programme-making departments including radio, television and online based in Manchester. This includes the daily local news magazine NORTHWEST TONIGHT and the weekly INSIDE OUT and POLITICS PROGRAMME. Regional programmes: all transmitted news items, programmes and rushes produced on tape have been retained since 1984. Selected earlier newsfilm has been deposited at the North West Film Archive (qv). Network programmes: Master film and tape programmes are stored at the BBC's Information & Archives premises in London. Some duplicates are held on site in Manchester together with rushes material.

48 BBC INFORMATION & ARCHIVES: NEWCASTLE NEWS LIBRARY

Broadcasting Centre, Barrack Road, Newcastle Upon Tyne NE99 2NE
Email: lesley.fraser@bbc.co.uk
Web: http://www.bbc.co.uk/tyne
☎ 0191 244 1217 **Fax**: 0191 221 0796
Contact: Lesley Fraser, Research Librarian
Access: No access to public

The library was formed in 1973 to serve regional news and magazine programmes, but was not properly organised until 1977 when more news stories were retained. It covers north east England (from North Yorkshire to Berwick) and northern Cumbria.

49 BBC NATURAL HISTORY UNIT FILM AND SOUND LIBRARY

Broadcasting House, Whiteladies Road, Bristol BS8 2LR
Email: alan.baker@bbc.co.uk
Web: http://www.bbc.co.uk/sn
☎ 0117 974 2416 (Film) 0171 974 2415 (Sound) **Fax**: 0117 970 6124
Contact: Alan Baker, Senior Librarian NHU Libraries
Access: By arrangement via BBC Worldwide Library Sales for commercial film enquiries. Non-commercial enquiries via Librarian

The library has been an integral part and growth area of the Natural History Unit since its formation in 1957. It is a production media library servicing the entire Corporation for data and materials in the field of wildlife, ecological and environmental subjects. There is also an associated sound library covering wildlife atmospheres and specific sounds. With the exception of selected archive material, the library holds work material of film output from the Natural History Unit, cumulatively since 1968. The rate of expansion matches the Unit's output – currently about sixty hours film and tape programmes per year, plus associated rushes.

50 BBC RADIO CORNWALL

Phoenix Wharf, Truro, Cornwall TR1 1UA
Email: radio.cornwall@bbc.co.uk
Web: http://www.bbc.co.uk/england/radiocornwall
☎ 01872 75421 **Fax**: 01872 40674
Contact: Pauline Causey, Editor
Access: The collection is private – for use by BBC production staff only

Material held to meet legal requirement, plus large news stories, large features, interviews and special news items. A small archive of local interest programmes/news items, social events, disasters, is held. All news scripts are archived.

51 BBC RADIO CUMBRIA SOUND ARCHIVE COLLECTION, CUMBRIA RECORD OFFICE

Cumbria Archive Service, Cumbria Record Office, The Castle, Carlisle, Cumbria CA3 8UR
Email: carlisle.record.office@cumbriacc.gov.uk
Web: http://www.cumbria.gov.uk/archives
☎ 01228 607285 **Fax**: 01228 607299
Contact: David M. Bowcock, Assistant County Archivist

Collection deposited by BBC Radio Cumbria (formerly BBC Radio Carlisle). The Sound Archive is mostly reel-to-reel tape but also some cassette. Coverage early 1970s onwards with a little pre-1970s material.

52 BBC RADIO DERBY

PO Box 104.5, Derby DE1 3HL
Email: radio.derby@bbc.co.uk
Web: http://www.bbc.co.uk/england/radioderby
☎ 01332 361111 **Fax**: 01332 290794
Contact: Mike Bettison

Two months' output kept plus major local news stories.

53 BBC RADIO DEVON

Broadcasting House, Seymour Road, Mannamead, Plymouth PL3 5YQ
Email: radio.devon@bbc.co.uk
Web: http://www.bbc.co.uk/radiodevon
☎ 01752 260323 **Fax**: 01752 234599
Contact: John Lilley, Editor

Holdings kept as per legal requirement. Digital recordings have also been made, covering the last five/six years, of about four-five news stories per week – held on minidisc and CD. This material is held specifically for the use of the Radio Devon Newsroom for annual review programmes, etc. In addition, there is a large radio archive in Exeter, the contents of which have not yet been logged.

54 BBC RADIO GLOUCESTERSHIRE

London Road, Gloucester GL1 1SW
Email: radio.gloucestershire@bbc.co.uk
Web: http://www.bbc.co.uk/gloucestershire/radio/index.shtml
☎ 01452 308585 **Fax**: 01452 309491
Contact: Bob Lloyd Smith, Editor

News items are kept if they are considered to be of special historical or local interest.

55 BBC RADIO GUERNSEY

Broadcasting House, Bulwer Avenue, St Sampson's GY2 4LA
Email: radio.guernsey@bbc.co.uk
Web: http://www.bbc.co.uk/england/radioguernsey
Contact: Rod Holmes, Editor

Material kept to meet legal requirement, but does hold items recorded for *The Century Speaks: BBC Millennium Oral History Project.*

56 BBC RADIO HUMBERSIDE

Queens Court, Hull, East Yorkshire HU1 3RH
Email: radio.humberside@bbc.co.uk
Web: http://www.bbc.co.uk/england/radiohumberside
☎ 01482 323232 **Fax**: 01482 621458
Contact: Simon Pattern, Editor
Access: BBC access restrictions apply

News and programme archive 1971 to present day (includes demise of fishing industry).

57 BBC RADIO LANCASHIRE

20–26 Darwen Street, Blackburn BB2 2EA
Email: radio.lancashire@bbc.co.uk
Web: http://www.bbc.co.uk/england/radiolancashire
☎ 01254 262411 **Fax**: 01254 680821
Contact: John Clayton, Editor

Local news features are kept on minidisc (on discretion). Oral history sound recordings also kept. Some material other than news is kept but not filed. Regional studies may keep own items. In the past the North West Sound Archive (qv) received many items from Radio Lancashire and other radio stations throughout Lancashire. Producers keep personal archives as well. Since digitisation, the producer decides what to keep.

58   BBC RADIO LEEDS

Broadcasting House, Woodhouse Lane, Leeds LS2 9PN
Email: radio.leeds@bbc.co.uk
Web: http://www.bbc.co.uk/england/radioleeds
☎ 0113 224 7300 **Fax**: 0113 242 0652
Contact: Richard Whitaker, Editor

Material is kept to meet general legal requirement. Local interest news and programmes, as well as *The Century Speaks: BBC Millennium Oral History Project programmes*, are also held.

59   BBC RADIO MERSEYSIDE

55 Paradise Street, Liverpool, Merseyside L1 3BP
Email: mick.ord@bbc.co.uk
Web: http://www.bbc.co.uk/england/radiomerseyside
☎ 0151 708 5500 **Fax**: 0151 794 0988
Contact: Mick Ord, Editor
Access: Mon-Fri, 9.00–17.00

At 12.30pm on 22 November 1967 a specially-composed jingle by Gerry Marsden announced the arrival of BBC Radio Merseyside, the country's third and largest local radio station. BBC Radio Merseyside was one of a series of eight local stations set up in various parts of England with the stated intention of providing an intimate localised service. BBC Radio Merseyside's editorial area embraces the whole of Merseyside (Liverpool, Bootle, Birkenhead, Southport, St. Helens etc.) much of North Cheshire (Chester, Warrington, Runcorn, Widnes, Ellesmere Port) and West Lancashire (Skelmersdale, Orrell, Burscough, Ormskirk).

60   BBC RADIO NEWCASTLE

Broadcasting Centre, Barrack Road, Newcastle Upon Tyne NE99 1RN
Email: graham.moss@bbc.co.uk
Web: http://www.bbc.co.uk/england/radionewcastle
☎ 0191 232–4141 **Fax**: 0191 261 8907
Contact: Graham Moss, Editor
Access: The collection is private – for in-house use by BBC production staff only

Material to meet legal requirement. There is a thirty-year archive of news items, items of major interest and interviews.

61   BBC RADIO NORTHAMPTON

Broadcasting House, Abington Street, Northampton NN1 2BH
Email: david.clargo@bbc.co.uk
Web: http://www.bbc.co.uk/england/radionorthampton
☎ 01604 239100 **Fax**: 01604 230709
Contact: David Clargo, Managing Editor
Access: Private access – for use of BBC production staff only

Local news stories going back eighteen years are held at the discretion of news editors. A lot of audio of breakfast shows is kept. All interesting stories (three-four minutes) of local interest, interviews with local celebrities, etc are held.

62   BBC RADIO OXFORD

269 Banbury Road, Oxford OX2 7DW
Email: steve.taschini@bbc.co.uk
Web: http://www.bbc.co.uk/england/radiooxford
☎ 01865 889021 **Fax**: 08459 311555
Contact: Steve Taschini, Executive Editor
Access: Private access – for the use of BBC production staff only

All output is held for three months. Major local news items are also kept.
In addition, there is a music library.

63   BBC RADIO SHROPSHIRE

2–4 Boscobel Drive, Shrewsbury SY1 3TT
Email: radio.shropshire@bbc.co.uk
Web: http://www.bbc.co.uk/england/radioshropshire
☎ 01743 248484 **Fax**: 01743 271702
Contact: Tim Pemberton, Editor

BBC Shropshire's radio archives include news and local interest stories,
interviews and a variety of programmes. Holds items recorded for *The
Century Speaks: BBC Millennium Oral History Project*.

64   BBC RADIO STOKE

Cheapside, Hamley, Stoke-on-Trent, Staffordshire ST1 1JJ
Email: sue.owen@bbc.co.uk
Web: http://www.bbc.co.uk/england/radiostoke
☎ 01782 208080 **Fax**: 01782 289115
Contact: Sue Owen, Editor
Access: The archive is an internal facility and not really available to
outsiders. A charge would be made for any exceptions

Various and many radio programmes from the last thirty-two years are held.

65   BBC SCOTLAND, INFORMATION & ARCHIVES

BBC, Queen Margaret Drive, Glasgow G12 8DG
Web: http://www.bbc.co.uk/scotland
☎ 0141 338 2880 **Fax**: 0141 337 6460
Contact: Noreen Adams, Manager, Information & Archives
Access: Limited access available for commercial and non-commercial
requests. Charges may apply. Contact as above. Limited wheelchair access

Television came to Scotland in 1952. Very little BBC Scotland output
survives from the 1950s. Since the 1960s, a representative sample of output
from drama, light entertainment, current affairs, sports, music and arts,
Gaelic and religious programmes has been held either in Scotland or in the
main BBC Library in Brentford. Written enquiries only.

66   BBC SOUND ARCHIVE

The British Library, Sound Archive, 96 Euston Road, London NW1 2DB
☎ 020 7412 7676 **Fax**: 020 7412 7441
Email: sound-archive@bl.uk
Web: http://www.bl.uk/collections/sound-archive/bbc.html

The BBC Sound Archive has selectively retained copies of broadcasts down the years with its holdings reflecting the trends and interests of different generations. While the emphasis today is on comprehensive coverage of chosen areas this has not always been the case. Between 1964 and 2000 the Sound Archive recorded thousands of radio and, from the late 1980s, television programmes off-air. The programmes reflected the interests of subject curators and are therefore particularly strong in the areas of music, drama and literature, oral history and wildlife sound. Currently, live major news sequence programmes, live music sessions and concerts, drama, arts, features, events, light entertainment, science and education programmes are automatically selected and archived.

67   BBC SOUTH RECORDED MATERIALS LIBRARY

Broadcasting House, Havelock Road, Southampton, Hampshire SO14 7PU
Email: sunil.bali@bbc.co.uk
Web: http://www.bbc.co.uk/england/southtoday
☎ 023 80 374247/8 **Fax**: 023 80 374247
Contact: Sunil Bali, Recorded Materials Librarian
Access: Contact the Librarian

BBC TV South has been serving Southern England (roughly sixty miles around Southampton) since 1961. Film has been used and kept since then, but only selectively covers the 1960s period. Holdings include SOUTH TODAY news items (magazine format) and opt-out programmes (thirty-minute non-fiction features shown locally only, although some repeated nationally).

68   BBC SPORTS LIBRARY

Room 5078, Television Centre, Wood Lane, London W12 7RJ
Email: Stephen.Whitehead@bbc.co.uk
Web: http://news.bbc.co.uk/sport/default.stm
☎ 020 8225 6025 **Fax**: 020 8225 6673
Contact: Steve Whitehead, Senior Librarian
Access: All requests for research and access should go through BBC Sports Sales, Room A3057, BBC Worldwide Ltd, 80 Wood Lane, London W12 0TT. tel: 020 8433 2573. fax: 020 8433 2939

The Library was set up in 1975 by the BBC's TV Sports Department in order to centralise and help control the Corporation's vast use of videotape. Retention policies, in the past determined by the Producer in Charge of Videotape for each individual programme, have determined the breadth of the current catalogue. It indexes BBC-generated material from 1966. Older film material held by the BBC's Film and Videotape Library is gradually being incorporated into the Sports Library system. The Library also incorporates the Radio Sports Archive.

69 BBC WALES FILM AND VIDEOTAPE LIBRARY

Broadcasting House, Llandaff, Cardiff CF5 2YQ
Email: liz.veasey@bbc.co.uk
Web: http://www.bbc.co.uk/wales
☎ 029 2032 2198 **Fax**: 029 2032 2873
Contact: Liz Veasey, Sales and Marketing Manager
Access: Mon-Fri 09.30–17.30. Staff are available to assist. Access for disabled. The Library endeavours to deal with all enquiries but priority is given to BBC personnel

The Library holds all BBC Wales material post-transmission. In addition to complete programmes a general stock shot collection has been built up on both film and videotape. The subject area covered is of a very general nature with obvious emphasis on Welsh events and personalities; programme title and transmission date are held on an on-line computer system. In addition there are news and sports libraries which catalogue the BBC Wales output in those areas.

70 BBC WRITTEN ARCHIVES CENTRE

Peppard Road, Caversham Park, Reading, Berkshire RG4 8TZ
Email: heritage@bbc.co.uk
Web: http://www.bbc.co.uk/heritage/research/wac_home.shtml
☎ 0118 948 6281 **Fax**: 0118 946 1145
Contact: Jacqueline Kavanagh, Written Archivist
Access: Wed-Fri 09.45–17.00 by appointment only

Holds the BBC's permanent written records from 1922 to c.1980. They include the BBC's correspondence with prominent organisations and individuals – politicians, writers, musicians, entertainers and sportsmen, as well as files on and all other aspects of the Corporation's work. Holdings include BBC publications, radio and television scripts, news bulletins, daily programme-as-broadcast logs of output and indexes for national programmes. Topics include moral standards, popular taste, broadcasting overseas, social issues, wartime propaganda etc., including information on BBC overseas services, regions, audiences and press reaction, facts, dates, signature tunes and firsts.

71 BE-ME VIDEO ARCHIVE

Light House Media Centre, Chubb Buildings, Fryer Street,
Wolverhampton WV1 1HT
Email: Raj.c@light-house.co.uk
Web: http://www.be-me.org
Contact: Raj Chaha

BE-ME (Black and Ethnic Minority Experience) was established in 1999 to record the experiences of African-Caribbean and Asian people who came to Wolverhampton after World War II. Over 400 audio/video interviews were recorded and with the assistance of the New Opportunities Fund. A subset of these interviews is now available over the internet. The website also contains on-line learning packages created in conjunction with local schools and universities. These packages are available to the public and demonstrate BE-ME's resolve to create models of good practice in education. The original video and audio tapes are now safely preserved in Wolverhampton City Council's Archive (qv).

72 BERKSHIRE RECORD OFFICE

9 Coley Avenue, Reading RG1 6AF
Email: arch@reading.gov.uk
Web: http://www.berkshirerecordoffice.org.uk
☎ 0118 901 5132 **Fax**: 0118 901 5131
Contact: Peter Durrant, County Archivist
Access: Tue and Wed 09.00–17.00 Thu 09.00–21.00 Fri 09.00–16.30. Access
for disabled. Advance appointment must be made to view this material as
the office does not have the necessary equipment to hand

County Record Office holding a few films acquired incidentally to the main
deposits of written records: (a) Royal Borough of Windsor and
Maidenhead, Windsor Borough Freedom Ceremonies: HRH PRINCE OF
WALES (ITN 1970); BRIGADE OF GUARDS (Pathé 1968); Civic Trust Windsor
Project 1969 (Pathé). (b) A DAY IN THE LIFE OF RADIO 210 (1977, 17 mins).
(c) Festival of Britain activities in Newbury (1951) – original now in Wessex
Film & Sound Archive (qv). Berkshire Record Office has video copy.

73 BERNIE GRANT COLLECTION

Middlesex University, Cat Hill, Barnet EN4 8HT
Email: j.vaknin@mdx.ac.uk Web: http://www.berniegrantarchive.com
☎ 020 8411 6686
Contact: Judy Vaknin, Middlesex University Archivist
Access: Mon-Tue 0.900–17.00 and Wed 13.00–17.00

Collection of original documentation and publications relating to Bernie
Grant's personal life and public role, largely dating from 1963 until he died
on 8 April 2000. The collection includes: photographs and audio and video
recordings (e.g. interviews/speeches, television and radio appearances),
subdivided into audio and video recordings of his civic and political activities.
Notably, audio recordings of his meetings, interviews and speeches dealing
with a variety of local, national and international concerns. Also includes
extensive video coverage of Bernie Grant at the House of Commons, Labour
Party conferences, and as founder of the African Reparations Movement.

Photo courtesy of Sharon Grant

Bernie Grant with Nelson Mandela

74 BEWDLEY MUSEUM

Load Street, Bewdley, Worcestershire DY12 2AE
Email: bewdley.museum@wyreforestdc.gov.uk
Web: http://bewdleymuseum.tripod.com/index.html
☎ 01299 403573 **Fax**: 01299 405306
Access: Fri 13.00 to 16.30 (25 March to 30 September), 11.00 to 16.00
(October)

Bewdley Museum's library focuses on the history of Bewdley,
Kidderminster, Stourport and outlying regions within the Wyre Forest
District, together with materials on trades and crafts associated with this
area. There are also photographic and oral history archives. Bewdley
Museum has a research library open to anyone interested in finding out
more about the history and families of the Wyre Forest area.

75 BIRMINGHAM BLACK ORAL HISTORY PROJECT

University of Birmingham Information Services, Special Collections
Department, Edgbaston, Birmingham B15 2TT
Email: special-collections@bham.ac.uk
☎ 0121 414 5838 **Fax**: 0121 471 4691
Access: All bona fide researchers. All papers held at the Orchard Learning
Resources Centre will be viewed at the Birmingham University
Information Services, Special Collections Department. Please contact the
University Archivist for further information

Listening cassettes and transcripts of interviews, of elderly black
immigrants to Birmingham, with video and photographs of interviewees.

76 BIRMINGHAM CITY ARCHIVES

Central Library, Seventh Floor, Chamberlain Square, Birmingham, B3 3HQ
Email: archives@birmingham.gov.uk
☎ 0121 303 4217 **Fax**: 0121 212 9397
Contact: Sian Roberts, Senior Archivist
Access: 10.00–17.00 Tue, Wed, Fri, Sat; 10.00–20.00 Thu. Closed Mon. It is
necessary to phone in advance if you want to listen to a recording. All
users of the City Archives are required to produce official proof of name
address and signature in order to obtain a County Archive Research
Network ticket

There are substantial collections of oral history and folk music revival
related sound recordings, nearly all master copies only. Highlights include
the Charles Parker Archive (BBC radio producer, writer, actor, etc.); CD
copies of about 1,200 recordings of folk music and song, traditional and
revival singers, and classes held by Ewan MacColl and Peggy Seeger on
song, performance, etc. with the Critics group, c.1965–1972. Banner
Theatre Company Archive (permission needed). Philip Donnellan Archive
(film material in need of conservation and currently unavailable). Oral
history tapes deposited by Professor Carl Chinn, local historian (MS 1902,
permission needed).

77 BIRMINGHAM LIBRARY SERVICES

Central Library, Chamberlain Square, Birmingham B3 3HQ
Email: arts.library@birmingham.gov.uk
Web: http://www.birmingham.gov.uk/artslibrary
☎ 0121 303 4511 or Arts Languages and Literature 0121 303 4227
Contact: Niki Rathbone
Access: Free access to all members of the public. Proof of identity
required for some items; some items served under supervision

The collection includes *Radio Times* and *TV Times, The Listener, Sight & Sound*, and the trade directory *Kinematograph Yearbook*. There is a small collection of classic films on video and DVD and some videos relating to arts and crafts. Also in the Birmingham Shakespeare Library are the complete BBC TELEVISION SHAKESPEARE series on video, an extensive collection of BBC radio scripts and some ITV, BBC TV and film scripts. There are also some Shakespeare film and television production photographs. The local studies service area holds extensive collections of film and video relating to local history and the music library has extensive loan collections of music, ballet and opera on video.

78 BLACK DIAMOND FILMS

Bedford Chambers, The Piazza, Covent Garden, London WC2E 8HA
Email: jim@blackdiamond.co.uk
Web: http://www.blackdiamond.co.uk
☎ 020 7240 4071 **Fax**: 020 7836 6339
Contact: Jim Odoire

Specialises in extreme sports footage, including: canoeing, climbing, kiteboarding, motocross, skateboarding, skiing, snowboarding, surfing.

79 BLACK WATCH ARCHIVES

RHQ The Black Watch, Balhousie Castle, Hay Street, Perth, PH1 5HR
Email: archives@theblackwatch.co.uk
Web: http://www.theblackwatch.co.uk/archives/index.html
☎ 01738–621281 ext 8530 **Fax**: 01738–643245
Contact: S.J. Lindsay, Regimental Secretary
Access: By arrangement only

The collection consists of copies of films given to the regiment over the years. Only one appears to have been specially commissioned. The remainder are straightforward reporting of events. There are seventeen films or bits of film. All films concern life in the Black Watch, mostly ceremonial parades but some training and barrack life.

80 BODLEIAN JAPANESE LIBRARY

University of Oxford, 27 Winchester Road, Oxford OX2 6NA
Email: ikt@bodley.ox.ac.uk
Web: http://www.bodley.ox.ac.uk/dept/oriental/bjl.htm
Contact: Izumi Tytler, Bodleian Japanese Librarian
Access: Accredited readers of the Bodleian Library only

A collection of over 160 videotapes, consisting of educational materials on Japan (for anthropologists), Japanese films, television drama, theatre, documentary films.

81 BODLEIAN LIBRARY OF COMMONWEALTH & AFRICAN STUDIES AT RHODES HOUSE

South Parks Road, Oxford, Oxon OX1 3RG
Email:lucy.mccann@bodley.ox.ac.uk
Web: http://www.bodley.ox.ac.uk/dept/rhodes
☎ 01865 270908 **Fax**: 01865 270912
Contact: Lucy McCann, Archivist
Access: Bodleian Library reader's ticket required

The library, which opened in Rhodes House in 1929, specialises in the history and current affairs – political, economic and social – of the Commonwealth and sub-Saharan Africa. In addition to some 200,000 books in these subjects and long runs of Commonwealth government publications, the library holds over 4,000 manuscript collections including the papers of the Anti-Slavery Society, the United Society for the Propagation of the Gospel, the Anti-Apartheid Movement, Sir Roy Welensky and many people who served in the Colonial Service or as teachers, doctors, soldiers and engineers in the territories covered. Some film and sound holdings.

82 BORDER TELEVISION NEWS AND ARCHIVE LIBRARY

Border Television plc, Television Centre, Harraby Industrial Estate, Carlisle, Cumbria CA1 3NT
Email: dutyoffice@itv.com
Web: http://www.itvregions.com/border
☎ 01228 525101 **Fax**: 01228 541384
Contact: Tony Steer, Film Research Manager
Access: Limited

Border Television serves all but the extreme south of Cumbria, the Isle of Man, Dumfries and Galloway, and Scottish Borders. Holdings include news and current affairs, sport, documentary, light entertainment, music, children's programmes, travel and local interest material.

83 BORDER TELEVISION NEWSFILM COLLECTION, CUMBRIA RECORD OFFICE

Cumbria Archive Service, Cumbria Record Office, The Castle, Carlisle, Cumbria CA3 8UR
Email: carlisle.record.office@cumbriacc.gov.uk
Web: http://www.cumbria.gov.uk/archives
☎ 01228 607285 **Fax**: 01228 607299
Contact: David M. Bowcock, Assistant County Archivist
Access: Mon-Fri 09.00–17.00. Access for disabled. The material is accessible to bona fide researchers

Collection deposited by Border Television between 21 May 1969 and 7 December 1971, and held on permanent loan.

84   BOSTON COLLEGE

Learning Resource Centre, 45 Market Place, Boston, Lincolnshire PE21 6NF
Email: enquiry@boston.ac.uk
Web: http://www.boston.ac.uk
☎ 01205 362031 **Fax**: 01205 362031
Contact: David Cunniffe, Learning Resource Centre Manager

For over thirty years, Boston College has been providing high quality further education and training to local students over the age of sixteen years. During the last ten years, it has expanded this provision to reach students from over twenty countries around the world, and to provide courses up to HND and degree levels. There are extensive library facilities on the main Boston campuses with access to books, multimedia, computers, Internet and journals. Also, laptops, videos and DVDs are available to rent on a nightly basis.

85   BOURNEMOUTH UNIVERSITY

Library and Learning Centre, Talbot Campus, Fern Barrow, Poole,
Dorset BH12 5BB
Email: mholland@bournemouth.ac.uk
Web: http://www.bournemouth.ac.uk/library
☎ 01202 595460 **Fax**: 01202 595475
Contact: Matt Holland, Subject Librarian
Access: Prior permission is required, limited to library opening hours

The archive comprises collections of journals, reports, series and annuals connected with British broadcasting and broadcasting organisations. Interest in broadcasting history within Bournemouth University stems from the Centre for Broadcasting History Research. The archive is in the very early stages of development, comprising programme journals and an extensive range of texts, journals and other material in the area of broadcasting and media research located in the Library and Learning Centre, Talbot Campus.

86   BPVL – BP VIDEO LIBRARY

c/o Metro, 53 Great Suffolk Street, London SE1 0DB
Email: bpvl@bp.com
Web: http://www.bpvideolibrary.com/contact.asp
☎ 020 7928 2097 **Fax**: 020 7928 2101
Access: Mon-Fri, 09.30–17.00, by arrangement. Staff are available to assist

Originally a collection of oil company archives from the early twentieth century, the library has since expanded to include historic and current activities of BP's operations worldwide in oil exploration, production and chemicals. It also includes general footage of the locality and population in areas where BP operates, and a wide selection of events BP has contributed to, such as motor racing and bike racing and land-speed record attempts. It also holds material of companies now owned by BP such as Super National, National Benzole, Arco, Amoco, Gulf and Sohio. The library offers a record of the last century through one of Britain's largest industrial companies.

87 BRIAN TRENNERY'S ARCHIVE

47 Leyborne Avenue, Ealing, London W13 9RA
Email: btren@globalnet.co.uk
☎ 020 8840 2411. Mobile: 07977 142758
Contact: Brian Trenerry
Access: Limited, 09.00–18.00

The basis of the collection is the 16mm Kodachrome film shot by the late Ivo Peters. Filmed between 1959 and 1977, the footage provides a wide coverage of steam-powered railways in Britain. Covers steam-hauled express and freight trains and railways in dockyards, quarries and mines. There is also footage relating to the railways of Britain pre-World War II and modern footage featuring diesel traction. In addition there is a collection of films featuring various aspects of the British way of life during the 1930s and 1950s. Other footage covers the Caribbean, Cuba and Palestine in the pre World War II era, as well as film of ocean going liners pre- and post-World War II.

88 BRIGHTON MUSEUM AND ART GALLERY

Royal Pavilion Gardens, Brighton, East Sussex BN1 1EE
Email: visitor.services@brighton-hove.gov.uk
Web: http://www.brighton.virtualmuseum.info
☎ 01273 290900
Access: Tue 10.00–19.00 Wed-Sat 10.00–17.00, Sun 14.00–17.00, closed Mon, except public holidays 10.00–17.00, closed 24–27 December

4 May 2002 saw the reopening of Brighton Museum and Art Gallery, transformed by a £10 million redevelopment, with a complete redisplay of its rich and diverse collections. Holdings include recordings made for its large oral history collection for the Exploring Brighton and Images of Brighton Local History Galleries, as well as video and film material and equipment relating to the film and cinema industries.

89 BRISTOL RECORD OFFICE

'B' Bond Warehouse, Smeaton Road, Bristol BS1 6XN
Email: bro@bristol-city.gov.uk
Web: http://tinyurl.co.uk/pdqh
☎ 0117 922 4224 **Fax**: 0117 922 4236
Contact: John Williams, City Archivist
Access: Mon-Thu 09.30–16.45, strictly by arrangement only. Staff are available to a limited degree. Access for disabled

The collection of films consists of items acquired by, commissioned by or presented to the city, primarily relating to various activities such as the Port and the former Health Department, and special occasions in Bristol. Over 300 films dating from between 1902 and 1980, mostly of Bristol and the surrounding area. A number of civic ceremonies, royal visits, wartime bomb damage and public works. The collection is added to at irregular intervals.

90 BRITISH AGRICULTURAL ARCHIVE FILM UNIT

Springs Farm, Edingley, Newark, Nottinghamshire NG22 8DB
☎ 01623–882223
Contact: A. Richard Watts, Archivist
Access: By arrangement. Access to all bona fide potential users, students, researchers, etc

The private collection was inaugurated in 1981, as the increase in the use of video created the demise of 16mm film. The object of the archive was to trace, salvage and preserve all gauges of film, amateur and professional, relating to the development of agriculture and allied industries, assembling it into a specialist reference library for the industry. The oldest film dates back to 1908. The main period covered is the 1930s to the 1960s, with others up to the present day. Now also holds the Milk Marketing Board Film Library and a substantial proportion (some 400 films) of the Massey Ferguson Tractors Ltd collection.

91 BRITISH ANTARCTIC SURVEY

High Cross, Madingley Road, Cambridge CB3 0ET
Email: basarchives@bas.ac.uk
Web: http://www.antarctica.ac.uk
☎ 01223 221400 **Fax**: 01223 362616
Contact: Joanna Rae, Archivist
Access: Consultation of finding aids and viewing access are by appointment only. Access to material less than thirty years old may be restricted

BAS began in 1943 with Operation Tabarin, a British wartime expedition in the Antarctic and was re-named the British Antarctic Survey in 1962. Since 1944 many official and semi-official films about the work of the Survey have been made, often using professional cine photographers. Staff serving in the Antarctic also made amateur films, a number of which have been donated or loaned to the Archives. Since 1990 BAS has been more systematic in keeping a visual record of its activities and infrastructure. Professional staff from the Photographic and Film Unit update footage regularly for use in educational and publicity material.

92 BRITISH ARTISTS' FILM AND VIDEO STUDY COLLECTION

Room 203, Central St Martins College of Art and Design, Southampton Row, London WC1B 4AP
Email: info@studycollection.org.uk
Web: http://www.studycollection.co.uk
☎ 020 7514 8159
Contact: David Curtis, Senior Research Fellow

Established in 2000, the British Artists' Film and Video Study Collection is a research project led by Senior Research Fellow David Curtis concentrating on the history of artists' film and video in Britain. The collection welcomes post-graduate researchers, curators, programmers, artists, anyone interested in the academic study of British Artists' Film and Video. The collection is a unique resource; it consists of an extensive range of reference materials including video copies of artists' works, still images, historical posters and publicity materials, paper documentation and a publications library. Researchers are welcome to make an appointment to visit and browse the collection.

93 BRITISH BOARD OF FILM CLASSIFICATION COLLECTION (BBFC)

3 Soho Square, London W1D 3HD
Email: contact_the_bbfc@bbfc.co.uk
Web: http://www.bbfc.co.uk
☎ 020 7440 15780 **Fax**: 020 7287 0141
Contact: David Cooke, Director
Access: Full access details on website

Media regulation. Classification of film, video and some interactive works. Holdings include all video works and some interactive works classified by the British Board of Film Classification. These are not available to view although some material has been donated to the National Film and Television Archive (qv).

94 BRITISH DEFENCE FILM LIBRARY

Chalfont Grove, Narcot Lane, Chalfont St Peter, Buckinghamshire SL9 8TN
Email: robert.dungate@ssvc.com
Web: http://www.ssvc.com
☎ 01494 878278 **Fax**: 01494 878007
Contact: Robert Dungate, Librarian
Access: Mon-Fri, 09.00–17.00, by arrangement only. Access for disabled

The Services Sound & Vision Corporation (SSVC) has long been associated with the armed forces, providing radio and television broadcasting for military personnel around the world. The company has also produced hundreds of training films commissioned by the Ministry of Defence for the Royal Navy, Army, and RAF. It is these programmes along with others, spanning nearly forty years, that are now available to broadcasters and programme makers. With unequalled access to the military and covering various subjects, it is one of the official suppliers of Ministry of Defence footage, providing unique contemporary material. The library continues to expand as new material is constantly being added.

95 BRITISH DENTAL ASSOCIATION

64 Wimpole Street, London W1G 8YS
Email: r.farbey@bda.org
Web: http://www.bda.org
☎ 020 7563 4193
Contact: Roger Farbey, Head of Library Services
Access: BDA members only. Access to outside researchers by appointment, with special permission in writing

Our current holdings are 350 (dental) videos (VHS PAL).

96 BRITISH FILM INSTITUTE: ARCHIVE FOOTAGE SALES

British Film Institute, 21 Stephen Street, London W1T ILN
Email: http://www.bfi.org.uk/help/contact
Web: http://www.bfi.org.uk/nftva/afs
☎ 020 7957 4842 **Fax**: 020 7436 4014
Contact: Sarah Wilde, Footage sales officer
Access: Mon to Fri, 9.30–17.45

Archival Footage Sales is the gateway for programme and filmmakers to the *bfi* National Film and Television Archive (qv), the world's leading collection of moving image materials. For over sixty years, the *bfi* NFTVA has collected the full range of the UK's moving image heritage, an unrivalled wealth of black and white and colour, silent and sound, documentary and fiction, professional and amateur footage. The collection chronicles all aspects of life and times since the invention of film. New collections of material are constantly being acquired thus ensuring that Archival Footage Sales continues to be the most diverse source of footage for film and television programme makers.

97 BRITISH FILM INSTITUTE: BFI NATIONAL LIBRARY

British Film Institute, 21 Stephen Street, London W1T ILN
Email: david.sharp@bfi.org.uk
Web: http://www.bfi.org.uk
☎ 020 7957 4806 **Fax**: 020 7436 2338
Contact: David Sharp, Head of Library
Access: Mon and Fri, 10.30–17.30; Tue and Thu, 10.30–20.00; Wed, 13.00–20.00

The *bfi* National Library has the world's largest collection of information on film and television. The main priority is to provide comprehensive coverage of British film and television, but the collection is international in scope. It collects books, pamphlets, periodicals and other printed materials, as well as published resources on microfilm and electronic media. The purpose is to provide a major resource to meet information, research and study needs relating to all aspects of the moving image (film, television, regardless of delivery method, video, video games, interactive multimedia, virtual reality), as culture and as industry, as social indicator and influence.

98 BRITISH FILM INSTITUTE: SPECIAL COLLECTIONS

21 Stephen Street, London W1T 1LN
Email: janet.moat@bfi.org.uk
Web: http://www.bfi.org.uk/nationallibrary/visiting/special.html
☎ 020 7957 4772 **Fax**: 020 7436 2338
Contact: Janet Moat, Special Collections Manager
Access: Only two study places available, appointment system operated; advance notice needed

bfi Special Collections includes approximately 20,000 unpublished scripts, a similar number of press (campaign) books, donations of personal and company papers from the film and television industries, and extensive sequences of ephemera such as cinema programmes (London, the regions and abroad), souvenir brochures, autographed letters and general promotional material. The collections focus mainly on British film and television production, ranging from the 1890s to the present. There is a random collection of sound recordings, a mixture of interviews, radio promotions and some soundtracks. Finally, some complete film music scores, a large amount of sheet music and a separate sequence of music cue sheets.

99 BRITISH FILM INSTITUTE: STILLS, POSTERS & DESIGNS

First Floor, 21 Stephen Street, London W1P 2LN
Email: http://www.bfi.org.uk/nftva/stills/contact.html
Web: http://www.bfi.org.uk
☎ 020 7957 4797 **Fax**: 020 7323 9260
Access: Tue-Thu, 10.30–16.30

About seven million black and white original photographs, colour transparencies, posters, set and costume designs, illustrating the history of world cinema from c.1895 to the present day, and including a comprehensive collection of television stills (approx one million). The stills are catalogued by original film/television title, also personality files, film studios, pre-cinema, cinema buildings, awards, equipment, etc. Special emphasis throughout on British cinema and television.

100 BRITISH GEOLOGICAL SURVEY LIBRARY

Kingsley Dunham Centre, Keyworth, Nottingham NG12 5GG
Email: libuser@bgs.ac.uk
Web: http://www.bgs.ac.uk
☎ 0115 936 3205 **Fax**: 0115 936 3200
Contact: Graham McKenna
Access: Material held in the Archives is subject to the provisions of the Public Records Act

BGS Library holds a geoscience information resource of worldwide significance. Developed over 150 years, it contains the extensive holdings of the former Geological Survey and Museum as well as those of the Overseas Geological Surveys and its predecessors. The archives contain material of historical and national interest. There are 200,000 maps and atlases of the UK and overseas. The photographic collection which dates back into the last century includes both BGS and deposited collections.

101 BRITISH LIBRARY SOUND ARCHIVE

96 Euston Road, London, London NW1 2DB
Email: sound-archive@bl.uk
Web: http://www.bl.uk/soundarchive
☎ 020 7412 7676 **Fax**: 020 7412 7441
Contact: Crispin Jewitt, Director
Access: Mon 10.00–20.00; Tue-Thu 09.30–20.00; Fri-Sat 09.30–17.00

The British Library Sound Archive holds the national collection of sound recordings and collects video and DVD recordings in selected areas and aims to receive copies of all sound recordings commercially published in the UK. Recordings of interviews, performances and events are made or commissioned by Sound Archive staff, and unpublished recordings made by others are acquired. The Archive provides access to the holdings of the BBC Sound Archive. Among holdings of independent radio material are the IBA radio archive and the Capitol Radio archive. Video recordings are collected in specific areas such as pop music, and limited off-air television recording is carried out.

102 BRITISH MEDICAL ASSOCIATION LIBRARY

BMA House, Tavistock Square, London WC1H 9JP
Email: frobertson@bma.org.uk
Web: http://www.bma.org.uk
☎ 020 7383 6690 **Fax**: 020 7388 2544
Contact: Fiona Robertson, Film & Video Librarian
Note: The BMA prefers not to have a detailed entry at present as, owing to major departmental re-organisation, it is not currently providing footage and research services.

103 BRITISH MOTOR INDUSTRY HERITAGE TRUST FILM & VIDEO ARCHIVE

Heritage Motor Centre, Banbury Road, Gaydon, Warwick CV35 0BJ
Email: hmcarch@heritage-motor-centre.co.uk
Web: http://www.heritage-motor-centre.co.uk
☎ 01926 641188 **Fax**: 01926 641555
Contact: Gillian Bardsley, Archivist
Access: Limited, by appointment. Access for researchers

The film archive of the British Motor Industry Heritage Trust has been assembled from the film collections of the many motor companies and factories which combined to form British Leyland in 1968. These include Rover, Morris, Austin, Triumph, Standard, MG, Riley, Wolseley, and Vanden Plas.

104 BRITISH MOVIETONEWS FILM LIBRARY

Head Office, Denham Media Park, North Orbital Road, Denham UB9 5HQ
Email: library@mtone.co.uk
Web: http://www.movietone.com
☎ 01895–833071 **Fax**: 01895–834893
Contact: Barbara Heavens, Senior Librarian
Access: 09.00–17.30. Staff are available to assist

British Movietonews is one of the great 35mm newsreel collections of the world, covering the period from 1929–1979. The library also has the Henderson Collection with film material from 1895 to World War I and the Pinewood Feature Film Stock Shot Library. Also the TV-AM News Library, rushes of news stories from the period 1983 to 1990.

105 BRITISH MUSEUM – ETHNOGRAPHY DEPARTMENT, CENTRE FOR ANTHROPOLOGY

Burlington Gardens, London W1X 2EX
Email: ethnography@thebritishmuseum.ac.uk
Web: http://www.thebritishmuseum.ac.uk/ethno/ethhome.html
☎ 020 7323 8065 **Fax**: 020 7323 8013
Contact: Staff, Audio-Visual Unit

Over 100 different film and video programmes are held. Most of the films have been purchased since 1970, primarily for use in public shows at the museum, but others are kept mainly for reference. Subjects relevant to cultural anthropology and some archaeology are included.

ITN Source/British Pathe

Jayne Mansfield at Cannes Film Festival (1958)

106 BRITISH PATHE

c/o ITN Source, 200 Gray's Inn Road, London WC1 X 8XZ
Email: sales@itnsource.com
Web: http://www.britishpathe.com
☎ 020 7430 4480 **Fax**: 020 7430 4453

British Pathe footage sales are now managed by ITN Source (qv). PATHE'S ANIMATED GAZETTE: started regular bi-weekly publication in London in June 1910. PATHE SUPER SOUND GAZETTE, and PATHE GAZETTE continued until the end of 1945. PATHE NEWS: this was the new title given to the Pathe newsreel from newsreel number 1, 1946. In 1960 PATHE NEWS produced its first reels in colour. The last release of the newsreel was no. 70–17, 26 February 1970. PATHE PICTORIAL: from March 1918 until 27 March 1969. EVE'S FILM REVIEW: this news magazine for women began in 1921 and continued until 1933. PATHETONE WEEKLY (1930 to 1941).

107   BRITISH RECORD INDUSTRY TRUST SCHOOL

60 The Crescent, Croydon CR0 2HN
Email: vfairbra@brit.croydon.sch.uk
Web: http://www.brit.croydon.sch.uk
☎ 020 8665 5242 **Fax**: 020 8665 8676
Contact: Valerie Fairbrass, Librarian

The collection is part of the Performing Arts Library used by students at KS4 and KS5, in particular those studying for BTEC qualifications.

108 BRITISH RED CROSS MUSEUM AND ARCHIVES

44 Moorfields, London EC2Y 9AL
Email: HPugh@redcross.org.uk
Web: http://www.redcross.org.uk
☎ 020 7877 7058
Contact: Helen Pugh, Archives Assistant
Access: Research hours are between 10.00–13.00 and 14.00–16.00,
Monday to Friday

The archives record the history and activities of the British Red Cross Society
from its foundation in 1870 as the British National Society for Aid to the
Sick and Wounded in War. Photographs: an extensive photograph
collection covers work at home and overseas. See a selection in the WWI
Gallery and the WWII Gallery. Film and sound: a small audio-visual
collection covers British Red Cross activities mainly from the second half of
the twentieth century.

109 BRITISH SKY BROADCASTING SPORTS ARCHIVE

British Sky Broadcasting Ltd, Unit One, Grant Way, Isleworth,
Middlesex TW7 5QD
Email: libsales@bskyb.com
Web: http://www.sky.com/skynewslibsales
☎ 020 7705 2956 **Fax**: 020 7705 2963
Contact: Iain Cameron

Sales from BSKYB's sports library. The Sky Sports archive holds all Sky Sports
News material – cut stories and rushes. See separate entry under Sky.

110 BRITISH SOCIETY OF SCIENTIFIC GLASSBLOWERS VIDEO LIBRARY

Kaimes Farm, Dumbarton Road, Stirling FK8 3AB
Email: graham.reed13@ntlworld.com
Web: http://www.bssg.co.uk
☎ 01786 473305 **Fax**: 01786 446995
Contact: Graham Reed
Access: By arrangement only

Started in 1983 by transferring some old (1950) cine film on to video. By
1992, there were over 130 titles in the library.

111 BRITISH VIDEO HISTORY TRUST

c/o BUFVC, 77 Wells Street, London W1T 3QJ
Email: ask@bufvc.ac.uk
Web: http://www.bufvc.ac.uk
☎ 020 7393 1500 **Fax**: 020 7393 1555
Contact: Geoff O'Brien, Assistant Director
Access: Mon-Fri 10.00–17.30, by arrangement only

The Trust was established to encourage the collection on videotape of first-
hand testimony and scenes of everyday life in Britain. It was set up by the
British Broadcasting Corporation and the British Universities Film & Video
Council. High quality video equipment (donated by Sony Broadcast, W.
Vinten Ltd and Rank Strand Electric) is lent to groups which have submitted
suitable projects for recording. The aim is to enable applicants to gather
video recordings of broadcast quality and adequate documentation to
allow the widest possible use of the material in future years.

112 BRITTEN-PEARS LIBRARY

The Red House, Golf Lane, Aldeburgh, Suffolk IP15 5PZ
Email: j.tydeman@brittenpears.org
Web: http://www.brittenpears.co.uk
☎ 01728 451703 **Fax**: 01728 453076
Contact: Judith Tydeman, Archivist
Access: Mon-Fri, 10.00–13.00 and 14.15–17.15 by prior appointment only

The Britten-Pears Library was originally assembled by Benjamin Britten (1913–1976) and Peter Pears (1910–1986) as a working collection of manuscripts, books, music, and sound and video recordings reflecting their interest and careers. Adjacent to The Red House, where Britten and Pears came to live in 1957, the Library is housed in former farm buildings first adapted in 1963 and greatly expanded in 1993. The collections continue to grow, serving the educational and informational needs of users, school groups and other visitors from all over the world.

113 BROADLAND 102

St George's Plain, 47–39 Colegate, Norwich NR3 1DB
Email: steve.martin@creation.com
Web: http://www.broadland102.co.uk
☎ 01603 630621 **Fax**: 01603 671175
Contact: Steve Martin, Programme Controller

Heavily music-based radio station. Holds logging tapes to meet legal requirement. Keeps interviews with music celebrities.

114 BRUNEL UNIVERSITY

Uxbridge, Uxbridge, Middlesex UB8 3PH
Email: penny.lyndon@brunel.ac.uk
Web: http://www.brunel.ac.uk/life/study/library
☎ 01895 274000, ext 2787 **Fax**: 01895 203263
Contact: Penny Lyndon, Special Collections Librarian
Access: Check website for current access

Brunel Library provides printed and electronic resources to support teaching and research within the university. Specialist library staff work with each academic school to ensure that appropriate resources are provided for all areas of teaching and research.

115 BRUNSWICK FORMULA ONE FILM AND VIDEO ARCHIVE

26 Macroom Road, Maida Vale, London W9 3HY
Email: diannefalls@brunswickfilms.com
Web: http://www.brunswickfilms.com/index.html
☎ 020 8960 0066 **Fax**: 020 8960 4997
Contact: Dianne Falls

The Brunswick Films Formula One Film and Video Archive is the most comprehensive collection of 1970s Formula One coverage available. It features eleven years of the most exciting period in Formula One history. From the great Tyrrell vs. Lotus battles of the early years including two Jackie Stewart championships, Niki Lauda's fiery exit on the Nordschleife in 1976 and James Hunt's title of the same year, the Tyrrell six wheeler and Ferrari's last pre-Schumacher world title, to Alan Jones claiming his and Frank Williams' first title at the end of 1980. There are over 450 hours of film, much of which has never been seen before.

116 BT ARCHIVES FILM GALLERY

Third Floor, Holborn Telephone Exchange, 268–270 High Holborn, London WC1V 7EE
Email: lucy.e.jones@bt.com
Web: http://www.btplc.com/Thegroup/BTsHistory/BTgrouparchives/index.htm
☎ 020 7440 4220 **Fax**: 020 7242 1967
Contact: Lucy Jones, Group Archivist
Access: The public search room is open Tuesday and Thursday, 10.00–16.00 all year round except for public holidays and on occasions when scheduled events may be occurring

BT Group Archives preserves the historical information of British Telecommunications plc and its predecessors from the early part of the nineteenth century up to the present day. BT Archives undertakes the company's statutory responsibilities to preserve and make available public records to members of the public after thirty years. BT Group Archives also acts as the corporate memory for the BT Group of companies; vital historical information is preserved and made available where appropriate to aid BT's performance, raise the company profile and support BT as one of the world's leading providers of telecommunications services.

117 BUFVC OFF-AIR RECORDING BACK-UP SERVICE

British Universities Film & Video Council, 77 Wells Street, London W1T 3QJ
Email: geoff@bufvc.ac.uk
Web: http://www.bufvc.ac.uk
☎ 020 7393 1500 Direct: 020 7393 1503 **Fax**: 020 7393 1555
Contact: Geoff O'Brien, Assistant Director
Access: Available only to educational institutions which hold an ERA licence and are members of the BUFVC

Since June 1998 the BUFVC has retained off-air recordings from the five British terrestrial television channels. BBC3 and BBC4 are now also recorded. This material accumulates at a rate of around 44,000 hours of transmitted material each year. Staff from any educational institution which has BUFVC membership and which holds an ERA licence can call upon access to this library. It should be noted that at the present time the BUFVC does not supply copies of missed recordings transmitted by the Open University.

BUFVC

Digital VHS tapes stored by the BUFVC Off-air Recording Back-up Service

118 BULLETIN VIDEO LIBRARY

Bulletin International, 121–141 Westbourne Terrace, Paddington,
London W2 6JR
Email: chris.foulerton@uk.bulletin.com
Web: http://www.bulletin.com
☎ 020 7479 0450 **Fax**: 020 7479 0490
Contact: Chris Foulerton, Production Assistant
Access: By arrangement. Staff are available to assist

Bulletin International is a production/PR company making all kinds of promotional material for many different companies, organisations, charities and governmental agencies. Since 1989 a large collection of general and specific images has been built up which Bulletin makes available to producers and broadcasters at competitive rates.

119 BUZZ 97.1

Media House, Claughton Road, Birkenhead CH41 6EY
Email: clive.douthwaite@musicradio.com
Web: http://www.wirralsbuzz.co.uk
☎ 0151 650 1700 **Fax**: 0151 647 5427
Contact: Clive Douthwaite, Sales/Commercial Director

The radio station holds forty-two days' output to meet legal requirement.

120 CADBURY FILM COLLECTION

Bournville, PO Box 12, Birmingham B30 2LU
Web: http://www.cadbury.co.uk
☎ 0121 458 2000 ext 3518 **Fax**: 0121 451 4333
Contact: Sarah Foden, Library and Archives
Access: Limited to loans to major organisations with their own viewing facilities, not to members of the public

Cadbury were trading in cocoa on the Gold Coast by 1907 and as early as 1913 began using film for promotional purposes.

121 CADMIUM

Church House, Castle Frome, Ledbury, Herefordshire HR8 1HQ
Email: sales@cadmium.co.uk
Web: http://www.cadmium.co.uk
☎ 01531 641 100 **Fax**: 01531 641 101

Footage is a new addition to the royalty free collection. The idea behind royalty free footage is to provide film clips that can be used instantly without of any further clearances; the cover topics like beauty, business, children, people, time lapse, medical and scenics. The Cadmium footage collection is growing fast, with close to 700 titles currently available from Artbeats, Digital Vision, Eyewire, FilmDisc and Think Stock. Although most titles now come in both NTSC and PAL formats, it is always a good idea to check that it comes in the format you need.

122 CALDERDALE COLLEGES CORPORATION

Percival Whitley Centre, Francis Street, Halifax HX1 3UZ
Email: andyw@calderdale.ac.uk
Web: http://www.calderdale-colleges.com
☎ 01422 357357 ext 9028
Contact: Andy Wright, Assistant Librarian
Access: Mon-Thu, 08.45–21.45. Fri, 08.45–16.00 for college students

The videos cover all areas of the curriculum. The book collection covers media studies and the visual arts. Around 2,000 VHS video cassettes held containing 8,000 programmes, plus 300 audiocassettes.

123 CALYX TV

41 Churchward Avenue, Rodbourne Cheney, Swindon, Wiltshire SN2 1NJ
Email: richard@calyxpix.com
Web: http://homepage.ntlworld.com/calyxpix
☎ 01793 520131 / 07836 205196,
Contact: Richard Wintle, cameraman / news editor
Access: By appointment

A collection of footage of the British royal family and some foreign royals at play and off-guard, or at official events. Foreign royals include members of the Greek royal family. The collection is continually being updated and expanded, and includes footage of friends and celebrities associated with the Royal Family. The library also contains footage of emergency services in action at crashes, fire and other incidents, as well as traffic chaos. Also wartime (since 1999) activity at RAF Fairford showing B52s, B1bs, U2 spy planes and support activities.

124 CAMBRIDGE AND COUNTY FOLK MUSEUM

2/3 Castle Street, Cambridge, Cambridgeshire CB3 0AQ
Email: cameron@folkmuseum.org.uk
Web: http://www.folkmuseum.org.uk
☎ 01223 355159,
Contact: Cameron Hawke-Smith, Curator
Access: April to September (Monday to Saturday): 10.30–17.00; Sunday: 14.00–17.00 October to March (Tuesday to Saturday): 10.30–17.00; Sunday: 14.00–17.00

The Cambridge and County Folk Museum has been open to the public for over sixty years. The collections include three-dimensional objects; documents and books (primary and secondary sources); iconographic sources (pictures, paintings and maps); and photographs, film and electronic archives and tape-recordings.

125 CAMBRIDGE COUNTY RECORD OFFICE

County Record Office, Shire Hall, Castle Hill, Cambridge CB3 0AP
Email: county.records.cambridge@cambridgeshire.gov.uk
Web: http://www.cambridgeshire.gov.uk/leisure/archives
☎ 01223 717281 **Fax**: 01223–718823
Contact: E. A. Stazicker, County Archivist
Access: By arrangement only. Staff are available to assist. Access for disabled. As the equipment to use the film must be brought from elsewhere, an appointment is essential

The Record Office was established in stages between 1930 and 1958 and acts as an archive for the records of the County Council and a place of deposit for records of other local authorities, societies, businesses, private persons etc. for the county. Film is occasionally received as part of these records.

126 CAMBRIDGE SOUTH ASIAN ARCHIVE

Centre of South Asian Studies, University of Cambridge, Cambridge CB2 1SD
Email: webmaster@s-asian.cam.ac.uk
Web: http://www.s-asian.cam.ac.uk
☎ 01223 338094 **Fax**: 01223 316913
Contact: Kevin Greenbank, Archivist
Access: Mon-Fri, 09.30–13.00 and 14.00–17.30. The Centre does close during certain times of the year, so checking by telephone ahead of a visit is advised. A term of access contract must be completed by commercial users

The film collection was started in the early 1970s. It comprises principally amateur cinefilm taken by Britons in India and South Asia from the early 1920s to the mid-1950s. Thirty-three collections totalling just over forty hours of footage depict all aspects of life in colonial South Asia. The collection has been transferred onto DVD for viewing purposes and DigiBeta for use by researchers and broadcasters. The collection contains excellent footage of railways, army, engineering and civil service work as well as extensive scenes from South Asian life for both British and Asian inhabitants. A detailed shot list of the films is available on a searchable database via the Centre's website

127 CAMERON LIFE FILM ARCHIVE

5 Carew Place, Winch-Wen, Swansea SA1 7DX
Email: emeryejr@hotmail.com
☎ 01202 744331
Contact: Nicholas Emery, Archivist
Access: By prior appointment

The film collection is a subsidiary of the Cameron Life Photographic Archive and contains material relating predominantly to the Solent area and the Isle of Wight from the early 1950s until the mid 1960s.

128 CAMERON MACKINTOSH ARCHIVE

1 Bedford Square, London WC1B 3RA
Email: rosy@camack.co.uk
☎ 020 7637 8866 **Fax**: 020 7436 2683
Contact: Rosy Runciman
Access: Mon-Thu 10.00–18.00. By appointment only

Cameron Mackintosh Limited is a theatre production company that has been presenting shows internationally since 1967. The Cameron Mackintosh Archive was established on an official basis in March 1995 with the primary remit of collating, cataloguing and making accessible material relating to all these shows. This material includes press cuttings, programmes, posters, photographs, recordings, correspondence, business records and all associated ephemera. The archive is an acknowledged theatrical information resource receiving up to 400 enquiries per year from within the company and from outside bodies.

129 CANAL+ IMAGE UK

Pinewood Studios, Pinewood Road, Iver, Buckinghamshire SL0 0NH
☎ 01753 631111 **Fax**: 01753 655813
Contact: John Herron, Library Manager
Access: By arrangement only. Immediate requests by telephone, letter and fax, or if necessary, by personal visit

Canal + controls the rights to the television series and feature films from British International Pictures, Welwyn Films, Associated British Picture Corporation, Anglo-Amalgamated, Ealing Films, British Lion, EMI, Thorn-EMI and Lumiere Pictures. Also available is stock shot footage from the 1920s to the present day.

130 CANTERBURY CATHEDRAL ARCHIVES

The Precincts, Canterbury, Kent CT1 2EH
Email: archives@canterbury-cathedral.org
Web: http://www.canterbury-cathedral.org/archives.html
☎ 01227 865287 **Fax**: 01227 865222
Contact: Keith O'Sullivan O'Sullivan, Cathedral Librarian
Access: Mon-Thu, 09.00–17.00; Sat: Open 1st and 3rd of each month from 09.00–13.00

Canterbury Cathedral Archives now forms part of the Kent Archives Service. Collections include records of the cathedral, Canterbury diocese, parishes in the Canterbury archdeaconry, Canterbury City Council and its predecessors, and other organisations, businesses, administrations and individuals in the Canterbury area. *Note*: The archives of the Archbishops of Canterbury are held at Lambeth Palace Library. Includes video recordings of the enthronement of Rowan Williams as well as talks and visits by Archbishop George Carey. Also included are audio recordings on 2-inch and $\frac{1}{2}$-inch of ceremonies and events in the Cathedral since the 1970s and slides going back to the 1930s.

131 CAPITAL GOLD (1152)

9 Brindley Place, 4 Oozells Square, Birmingham, West Midlands B1 2DJ
Email: info@capitalgold.co.uk
Web: http://www.capitalgold.com
☎ 0121 245 5000 **Fax**: 0121 245 5245
Contact: Christine Dowling
Access: No public access

The radio station holds three months' output to meet legal requirement. Other programmes have gone to the British Library Sound Archive (qv), including early programmes from the start of Capital FM. The Capital Group's central library is based in London. A music library is maintained.

132 CAPITAL GOLD (1170 & 1557)

Radio House, Whittle Avenue, Segensworth West, Fareham, Hants PO15 5SH
Email: info@capitalgold.co.uk
Web: http://www.capitalgold.com
☎ 01489 589911 **Fax**: 01489 589453
Contact: Mark Sadler, Programme Controller
Access: No public access

The radio station holds three months' output to meet legal requirement. Other Capital Group programmes have gone to the British Library Sound Archive (qv), including early programmes from the start of Capital FM. The Capital Group's central library is based in London. A music library is maintained.

133 CAPITAL GOLD (1242 & 603)

Radio House, John Wilson Business Park, Whitstable, Kent CT5 3QX
Email: info@capitalgold.co.uk
Web: http://www.capitalgold.com
☎ 01227 772004 **Fax**: 01227 774450
Contact: Luis Clark
Access: No public access

Covers the Kent region. The radio station holds three months' output to meet legal requirement. Other Capital Group programmes have gone to the British Library Sound Archive (qv), including early programmes from the start of Capital FM. The Capital Group's central library is based in London. A music library is maintained.

134 CAPITAL GOLD (1305 & 1359)

Atlantic Wharf, Cardiff Bay, Cardiff, Wales CF10 4DJ
Email: david.rees@RedDragonfm.com
Web: http://www.capitalgold.com
☎ 029 2066 2066 **Fax**: 029 2037 3011
Contact: David Rees, Programme Director
Access: No public access

The radio station holds three months' output to meet legal requirement. Various local audio news and local interest programmes are kept indefinitely on digital recording system. The Capital Group's central library is based in London.

135 CAPITAL GOLD (1323 & 945)

Radio House, PO Box 2000, Brighton, East Sussex BN41 2SS
Email: info@capitalgold.co.uk
Web: http://www.capitalgold.com
☎ 01273 430111 **Fax**: 01273 430098
Contact: Gina Chapman-Lunn
Access: No public access

Based in Brighton. Holds three months' output to meet legal requirement. Other Capital Group programmes have gone to the British Library Sound Archive (qv), including early programmes from the start of Capital FM. A music library is maintained.

136 CAPITAL GOLD (1548)

30 Leicester Square, London WC2H 7LA
Email: info@capitalradio.co.uk
Web: http://www.capitalgold.com
☎ 020 7766 6000 **Fax**: 020 7766 6100
Contact: Andy Turner, Programme Controller
Access: No public access

Now part of the GCap Media Group. The radio station holds three months' output to meet legal requirement. Other programmes have gone to the British Library Sound Archive (qv), including early programmes from the start of Capital FM.

137 CAPITAL RADIO PLC

30 Leicester Square, London WC2H 7LA
Email: info@capitalradio.co.uk
Web: http://www.gcapmedia.com
☎ 020 7766 6000 **Fax**: 020 7766 6100
Contact: Richard Park, Group Director of Programmes
Access: No public access

Stations owned by Capital Radio plc hold three months' output to meet legal requirement. Other programmes have gone to the British Library Sound Archive (qv), including early programmes from the start of Capital FM. The Capital Group's central library is based in London. A music library is maintained.

138 CARLTON TELEVISION

Footage sales c/o ITN Source, 200 Gray's Inn Road, London WC1X 8XZ
Email: sales@itnsource.com
Web: http://www.itnsource.com
☎ 020 7389 8664 **Fax**: 020 7430 4453
Contact: Liz Cooper
Access: via ITN Source

Carlton has now merged with Granada (qv). Its library (footage sales controlled via ITN Source, qv) houses one of the country's largest collections, incorporating Midlands regional news from 1956 to the present day; Central Television's programmes from 1982 and Carlton's programming from 1993.

139 CASTROL FILM ARCHIVE

c/o Duke International Sales, Champion House, Douglas,
Isle of Man IM99 1DD
Email: info@dukesales.com
Web: http://www.dukesales.com/about.htm
☎ 01624 640020
Contact: Jon Quayle, Archivist & Market Information Manager
Access: Mon-Fri 09.00–17.00, by arrangement only. Staff are available to
assist. Access for disabled

BN Sales now handled by Duke Sales (qv). Since 1950 Castrol has
commissioned two motor sport films annually. Until the 1980s 16mm prints
of the films were available to motorcar/cycle clubs for film shows
(nowadays, clubs can borrow VHS copies). The Archive collection consists
mainly of 16mm prints (not masters), most of which have been transferred
onto video format.

140 THE CCTV ARCHIVE

14 Ardilaun Road, London N5 2QR
Email: info@cctvarchive.com
Web: http://www.cctvarchive.com
☎ 07850 926 637 **Fax**: 01795 530 771

Collection of closed circuit television footage including material from the
police.

141 CENTRAL COLLEGE OF COMMERCE

Robertson Trust Resource Centre, Central Business Learning Zone, 190
Cathedral Street, Glasgow G4 0ND
Email: kirsteen@central-glasgow.ac.uk Web:
http://www.centralcollege.ac.uk
☎ 0141 552 3941, ext 4001 **Fax**: 0141 552 7179
Contact: Kirsteen Dowie
Access: Limited to library opening hours

A small collection of videos held on various subjects, including
management, information technology/computing, secretarial studies,
human resource management, and art and design. The collection is used by
staff for teaching purposes and by students for general information.

142 CFM – CARLISLE

PO Box 964, Carlisle, Cumbria CA1 3NG
Email: david.bain@cfmradio.com
Web: http://www.cfmradio.com
☎ 01228 818964 **Fax**: 01228 819444
Contact: David Bain, Programme Manager/Controller

Radio station holding output to meet legal requirement.

143 CHAMPION 103 FM

Llys-y-Dderwen, Parc Menai, Bangor, Wales LL57 4BN
Email: sarah.smithard@musicradio.com
Web: http://champion103.musicradio.com
☎ 01248 671888 **Fax**: 01248 671971
Contact: Sarah Smithard, Managing Director

The radio station holds forty-two days' output only to meet legal requirement.

144 CHANNEL 4 CLIP SALES

ITN Source, 124 Horseferry Road, London SW1P 2TX
Email: clipsales@channel4.co.uk
Web: http://www.itnsource.com
☎ 020 7306 8490 **Fax**: 020 7306 8366
Contact: Paul McAllister, Research Manager
Access: The Clip Library deals only with broadcast enquiries

The library holds Channel 4's commissioned output since it began broadcasting in November 1982. Some material is originated on film but transferred onto tape and therefore available only on tape. Clip sales are now handled by ITN Source (qv).

ITN Source

Still from TRAINSPOTTING (1995)

145 CHANNEL TELEVISION

The Television Centre, La Pouquelaye, St Helier, Jersey JE2 3ZD
Email: broadcast@channeltv.co.uk
Web: http://www.channeltv.co.uk
☎ 01534 816816 **Fax**: 01534 816689
Contact: Alan Watts

Channel Television holds all broadcast items from October 1962. In addition to broadcast news and feature items, rushes of some specific events have been retained. These include: boy falls into gorilla pit at Jersey Zoo and is protected by animal; passenger ferry hits rocks off Jersey, footage of passengers escaping into life rafts; the Newall murder enquiry; rare footage of the Liberation of the Islands from German Occupation in 1945 (restricted access); early black and white footage of Island life, including motor racing and aircraft landing on the beach (restricted access); restricted access to moving footage of David and Frederick Barclay; aerial shots of all Channel Islands etc.

146 CHANNEL TUNNEL LIBRARY

Hard Hat Archive, C/O Tandem TV & Film Ltd, 10 Bargrove Avenue, Boxmoor, Hemel Hempstead, Hertfordshire HP1 1QP
Email: info@tandemtv.com
Web: http://www.tandemtv.com
☎ 01442 61576 **Fax**: 01442 219250
Contact: Terry Page, Director
Access: 10.00–17.00, by arrangement only

The Library consists of footage of the construction and current operation of the Tunnel from when it was first started in 1986 to its opening in 1994 by Her Majesty Queen Elizabeth and President Mitterand of France. Footage is available of all aspects of construction from tunnelling to aerial footage of terminals and was shot principally in France and the UK, but there is also footage of equipment manufacture in Canada, Italy, Belgium and Germany.

147 CHESTER COLLEGE (now UNIVERSITY OF CHESTER)

Parkgate Road, Chester CH1 4BJ
Email: c.stockton@chester.ac.uk
Web: http://www.chester.ac.uk/lr
☎ 01244 375 444 **Fax**: 01244 392 811
Contact: Christine Stockton, Director

There are 200,000 items in the College Library. Collection of videos includes off-air recordings and bought-in videos and feature films to support courses, e.g. Drama, Art, Languages, European Cinema.

148 CHILTERN FM (97.6)

Chiltern Road, Dunstable, Beds LU6 1HQ
Email: francis.flanagan@musicradio.com
Web: http://www.chilternfm.co.uk
☎ 01582 676200 **Fax**: 01582 676201
Contact: Francis Flanagan, Sales/Commercial Director

Keeps three months' holdings of all output (full twenty-four hours).

149 CHOICE FM

291–299 Borough High Street, London SE1 1JG
Email: ivor.etienne@choicefm.com
Web: http://www.choicefm.net
☎ 020 7378 3969 **Fax**: 020 7378 3391
Contact: Ivor Etienne, Programme Controller

Holds output to meet legal requirement plus paper file. All news items are kept for one year. Maintains a large private black music library.

150 CHRYSTAL RADIO

Sheffield Children's NHS Trust, Western Bank, Sheffield S10 2TH
Email: info@chrystalradio.co.uk
Web: http://www.destinyhost.co.uk/chrystal
☎ 0114 2717396
Contact: Brett Hadley, Station Manager

Launched in July 1984 and based in the Sheffield Children's NHS Trust Hospital, Chrystal serves patients and staff with music and talk, seven days a week. Broadcasting hours have increased over the years, and now total over fifty hours a week of live radio. Every person that works for Chrystal is an unpaid volunteer. In 1991 Chrystal ventured into the world of providing a sustained television service for the patients and staff, which went live at weekends with original programmed presented and made inside the hospital.

151 CITY BEAT 96.7

Lamont Buildings, Stranmillis Embankment, Belfast,
Northern Ireland BT9 5FN
Email: music@citybeat.co.uk
Web: http://www.citybeat.co.uk
☎ 028 9020 5967 **Fax**: 028 9020 0023
Contact: John Roxborough, Station Director

Radio station. Holds forty-two days' output only to meet legal requirement.

152 CLASSIC GOLD DIGITAL

Alpha Business Park, 6–12 White House Road, Ipswich IP1 5LT
Email: admin@classicgolddigital.com
Web: http://www.classicgolddigital.com
☎ 01473 461000 **Fax**: 01473 741200
Contact: Mark Pryke

Radio station. Holds forty-two days' radio output only.

153 CLASSIC GOLD MARCHER 1260

The Studios, Mold Road, Wrexham, Wales LL11 4AF
Email: admin@classicgolddigital.com
Web: http://www.classicgolddigital.com/index.php
☎ 01978 751818 **Fax**: 01978 759701
Contact: Terry Underhill, Programme Director

Formerly known as Marcher Gold. The radio station holds forty-two days' output only to meet legal requirement.

154 CLASSIC HOME CINEMA

51 Cambridge Street, Cleethorpes, N.E. Lincs DN35 8HD
Email: chcinema@aol.com
Web: http://valueservices.org/classichomecinema
☎ 0870 744 6798 **Fax**: 01472 291934
Contact: Phil Sheard, Manager and Owner

Holds home movies of 1920s – 16mm amateur footage of Lincolnshire, holiday resorts, families, fishing, the sea, seaside, boats, vehicles, wartime, railways, aircraft, mining. There is also a collection of 35mm vintage cinema and television ads, vintage newsreels and trailers to pre-1950s nostalgic films. Holds negatives of B-westerns and 1950s sci-fi films for which limited rights are held.

155 CLIPS AND FOOTAGE

Studio 112, Spitfire Studios, 63–71 Collier Street, London N1 9BE
Email: info@clipsandfootage.com
Web: http://www.clipsandfootage.com
☎ 020 7287 7287 **Fax**: 020 7439 4886
Contact: Alison Mercer
Access: By appointment. Free viewing and VHS tapes for visitors. online searchable catalogue and demo reel

Clips and Footage is a film library containing thousands of hours of archive and modern colour imagery. Collections include aviation from early days of flight; transport footage; Americana from the turn of the century up to the 1960s. WW2 home front, education, drug abuse, propaganda films and crazes such as the hula hoop. Contemporary footage includes world locations and time-lapse cityscapes, landscapes. Clips and Footage holds the largest feature film trailer archive in the UK. There is also a terrific B-movie archive and a sci-fi library. The News Collection: material on world events and historical personalities such as Eva Peron, Gandhi, Khrushchev banging the desk and much more.

156 CLIVE GARNER VINTAGE RECORDS & FILMS

39 Mosslands Drive, Wallasey, Merseyside CH45 8PE
Email: radio.merseyside@bbc.co.uk
☎ 0151 638 4711 **Fax**: 0151 638 4711
Contact: Clive Garner, Owner
Access: By prior arrangement only

Film collection started in 1960s as an adjunct to a large collection of 78 r.p.m. gramophone records (over 40,000). Films cover same period as the records from the late 1920s to the early 1950s. Emphasis is on films that would form part of 'full supporting programme' at a cinema during the 'golden years' (1929 to 1949). Included are trailers, special cinema advertising shorts and other similar material, organ interlude films, cinema 'Day Titles', ice cream trailers, interest/documentary films, etc. (all 16mm). Also over 4,000 cinema organ song slides. The archive now also includes audio recordings from pre-war commercial radio and wartime broadcasts from Berlin in English.

157 CNN IMAGESOURCE

Turner House, 16 Great Marlborough Street, London W1F 7HS
Email: cnn.imagesourceuk@turner.com
Web: http://www.cnnimagesource.com/CNIS/index.html
☎ 020 7693 1540 **Fax**: 020 7693 1541
Access: Transcripts and tapes for personal/institutional viewing are available for most CNN programs and stories from FDCH at 1.800.CNN.NEWS (outside the U.S. call + 1 301 883 2178)

A broad selection of video is available from CNN ImageSource – ranging from actual news events to generic b-roll of 'people, places and things'. Friendly and efficient assistance is our hallmark, with highly-trained staff ready to meet your video needs and production deadlines. Full-level cataloguing and sophisticated retrieval software allow us to quickly locate exactly what you need, and we can provide you with still images as well as video on any format required.

158 COAST 96.3

PO Box 963, Bangor, Wales LL57 4ZR
Email: clive.douthwaite@musicradio.com
Web: http://coastfm.musicradio.com
☎ 01248 673401 **Fax**: 01248 673409
Contact: Clive Douthwaite, Sales/Commercial Director

Formerly known as Coast FM. The radio station holds forty-two days' output only to meet legal requirement.

159 COI FOOTAGE FILE

Film Images (London) Ltd, 2 The Quadrant, 135 Salusbury Road,
London NW6 6RJ
Email: research@film-images.com
Web: http://www.film-images.com
☎ 020 7624 3388 **Fax**: 020 7624 3377
Contact: Tony Dykes, Senior Researcher
Access: Appointments necessary. Access for disabled. Research can be
carried out on behalf of customers

COI Footage File (Central Office of Information) is a unique visual record of
Britain's culture, heritage, way of life and aspirations covering the last sixty
years. The collection begins with John Grierson's documentary masterpiece
DRIFTERS. It moves on to include a wealth of material shot by the Crown
Film Unit during the war and today encompasses an outstanding selection
of Government-commissioned material that is constantly being updated.
Footage File is a kaleidoscope of imagery – social, historical, geographical,
scientific and political including many subjects ranging from landscapes to
laser surgery, churches to Churchill, forestry to forensic science.

Film Images

Still from LIVING TOMORROW, Issue 159 (1975)

160 COLLEGE OF ST MARK AND ST JOHN

Derriford Road, Plymouth PL6 8BH
Email: vreardon@marjon.ac.uk
Web: http://www.marjon.ac.uk
☎ 01752 636 700 ext 4297
Contact: Valerie Reardon, Subject Group Leader, Media Studies
Access: Prior permission by letter preferred

The main video collection supports the taught modules on Media Studies, and to a lesser extent English Literature and History. The video collection comprises a large number of feature films from the USA, the UK and a collection of foreign language films. Many of these have an historical significance. Also there is a collection of documentaries, some of which are used as teaching aids and others which are studied as media artefacts. The collection includes a large number of popular television programmes, from game shows to soap operas to drama, as well as some corporate work. At present the College is building its archive of films and television programmes directed by women.

161 COLSTAR INTERNATIONAL TELEVISION

78 York Street, London W1H 1DP
Email: stevegoddard@colstar.tv
Web: http://www.colstar.tv
Contact: Steve Goddard, Director, International Licensing and co-productions

Colstar International specialises in content management, licensing, new-author publishing and merchandising. We represent innovative output from writers, directors, producers as well as our own films. Our drama and animation catalogues include classic period series BOX OF DELIGHTS and BAKER STREET BOYS, compelling features A QUIET DAY, SIGNS OF LIFE; HDTV features CONFLICT OF INTERESTS etc. Many of the shorts in our catalogues have won major international awards. In 2001 Colstar acquired Documedia Films and in 2004, Picture Parade. Our documentary catalogues present films and series on the arts, world sciences, history and politics, sport and travel, wildlife and exploration.

162 COMPUTERISED TIME-LAPSE LIBRARY

27 Birstall Road, London, London N15 5EN
Email: info@time-lapse.co.uk
Web: http://www.time-lapse.co.uk
☎ 020 8802 8791 **Fax**: 020 8211 82 86
Contact: Maxim Ford

Time-lapse shots of nature, landscapes and places around the world. Cityscapes, flowers, sunsets and dawns, the midnight sun. Some with camera moves.

163 CONCORD VIDEO & FILM COUNCIL

Rosehill Centre, 22 Hines Road, Ipswich IP3 9BG
Email: sales@concordvideo.co.uk
Web: http://www.concordvideo.co.uk
☎ 01473 726012 **Fax**: 01473 274531
Contact: Lydia Vulliamy, Member, Council of Management
Access: Mon, Tue, Thu, Fri only, 09.00–17.00. Staff are sometimes available
to assist

Originally started as 16mm film collection of material on the anti-nuclear
weapon activities in Britain and elsewhere in the 1960s. The collection
widened to include sociology, arts and general education with specialist
collections on anthropology and social work, art and medicine (Graves
Medical A/V Library). Concord Video & Film Council specialises in sale and
hire of educational videos on a variety of social and moral issues. It has
interesting videos on addictions of many types including alcohol addiction,
drug addiction and smoking.

164 CONTEMPORARY DOCUMENTARY ARCHIVE

School of Media, Music & Performance, University of Salford, Salford,
Greater Manchester M5 4WT
Email: I.Calloway@salford.ac.uk
Web: http://www.smmp.salford.ac.uk/research/media/cda/index.html
☎ 0161 295 6138 **Fax**: 0161 295 4704
Contact: Ian Calloway, Archivist
Access: Prior permission is needed to access the Archive. Opening hours
are Tuesday (10.00–13.00); Thursday & Friday (10.00–14.00)

Since 1997, the Contemporary Documentary Archive (CDA) based at the
School of Music, Media and Performance, University of Salford has been
building a vast archive of documentary programmes broadcast in Britain.
The focus of the Archive has been surveillance, crime, the police and reality
TV. The Archive holds thousands of hours of major documentaries and
continues to add to its collection. Examples of our holdings include
CRIMEWATCH UK, POLICE CAMERA ACTION, CUTTING EDGE, BIG BROTHER,
NEIGHBOURS FROM HELL and many others. The CDA also has a significant
amount of press cuttings which supplement these recordings which are
also available for loan by staff and post graduate students.

165 CONTEMPORARY FILMS

24 Southwood Lawn Road, London N6 5SF
Email: eric@contemporaryfilms.freeserve.co.uk
Web: http://www.contemporaryfilms.com
☎ 020 8340 5715 **Fax**: 020 8348 1238
Contact: Eric Liknaitzky, Archive Controller
Access: During office hours Mon-Fri 09.30–12.30 and 14.00–17.00

Contemporary Films was established in 1951. The collection was initially
politically-orientated (much on Chinese and Soviet Communism) but over
the decades it has expanded to include many diverse subjects. It also has
material on Cuba, Nazi Germany and South Africa under Apartheid, rare
footage from India, and the social and political scene in Britain. The archive
also covers the Spanish Civil War, the 1950s McCarthy witch hunts, the civil
rights movement of the 1960s, hippie culture, feminism, gender politics,
and anti-nuclear campaigns etc. Footage is also offered from classic films
like Renoir's LA REGLE DU JEU and Bunuel's collaboration with Salvador
Dali, UN CHIEN ANDALOU.

166 COOL FM

PO Box 974, Belfast, Northern Ireland BT1 1RT
Email: music@coolfm.co.uk
Web: http://www.coolfm.co.uk
☎ 028 9181 7181 **Fax**: 028 9181 4974
Contact: David Sloane, Managing Director
Access: Office hours

Radio station. Holds a selection of radio programmes, spanning twenty-five years, of interest to the Northern Ireland audience.

167 CORBIS MOTION

111 Salusbury Road, London NW6 6RG
Email: uk@corbismotion.com
Web: http://www.corbismotion.com

Corbis Motion offers the most comprehensive selection of high-quality moving images in the footage industry. Every day, advertisers, feature film producers, and corporate communications professionals turn to our 30,000+ hours of both archival and contemporary film for footage that will bring added impact to their projects. Contemporary – including categories such as people, lifestyles, business and technology, nature and wildlife, travel, time lapse, CGI and sports. Archival – vintage footage of the famous and not-so-famous. Our collection includes imagery from such high-profile providers as Paramount Pictures, ESPN, Hearst Entertainment, Oxford Scientific Films, and US soccer.

168 THE CORNISH AUDIO VISUAL ARCHIVE (CAVA)

Institute of Cornish Studies, University of Exeter in Cornwall, Tremough Campus, Penryn, Cornwall TR10 9EZ
Email: g.h.tregidga@exeter.ac.uk
Web: http://www.cava-studies.org
☎ 01326 371 888
Contact: Garry Tregidga, Director

The Cornish Audio Visual Archive (CAVA) was created in 2000 for the study and documentation of the oral and visual culture of Cornwall. It advocates an innovative and interdisciplinary approach towards interpreting the events of the past and present that harnesses the multimedia power of oral history, cultural memory, film representations, photographic studies, ethnomusicology, socio-linguistics and landscape narrative. Its major project, Cornish Braids, was a two-year fieldwork programme principally funded by the Heritage Lottery Fund and to create a multigenerational profile of community life in the twentieth century through oral history.

169 CORNISH FILM AND VIDEO ARCHIVE

c/o Cornish Studies Library, Cornwall Centre, Alma Place, Redruth,
Cornwall TR15 2AT
Email: cornishstudies.library@cornwall.gov.uk
Web: http://www.cornwall.gov.uk/library/Ccentrehome.htm
☎ 01209 216760 **Fax**: 01209–210283
Contact: Terry Knight, Principal Librarian/Cornish Studies
Access: Open 10.00–18.00 Mon-Fri; 10.00–16.00 Sat. Prior notice of
requirements is helpful

The Cornish Film and Video Archive was started by volunteer enthusiasts.
The Cornish Studies Library film and video collection was created as part of
the Library's stock. The two are run as one now. The Cornish Film and Video
Archive surveyed extant Cornish film and video (report 1990), but
collection awaits necessary staffing and funding. Service comprises access
for research only, but collecting continues.

170 COSTAIN GROUP FILM & PHOTO LIBRARY

Hard Hat Archive, Tandem TV & Film Ltd, 10 Bargrove Avenue, Boxmoor,
Hemel Hempstead, Hertfordshire HP1 1QP
Email: info@tandemtv.com
Web: http://www.tandemtv.com
☎ 01442 61576 **Fax**: 01442 219250
Contact: Terry Page, Director
Access: 10.00–17.00, by arrangement only

The Library started life as a film unit in the 1920s, when Costain was
primarily engaged in house building. As the Group's operations have
expanded and diversified, so the Library's stock of films and videos has
grown. Footage, shot mainly on film around the world, covers the Group's
operations in mining, civil and process engineering and construction.

171 COVENTRY ARCHIVES

John Sinclair House, Canal Basin, Coventry CV1 4LY
Email: archives@coventry.gov.uk
Web: http://tinyurl.co.uk/3e7q
☎ 024 76785164 **Fax**: 024 7683 2421
Contact: Liz Doull, City Archivist
Access: Mon-Fri 9.30–16.45. As Coventry Archives is in temporary
accommodation, all material must be ordered in advance

The archive was created by Coventry City Council. Acquisitions were made
from 1948 to 1996. It holds several films of local interest, including civic
films made by the corporation, one on the consecration of Coventry
Cathedral, and some miscellaneous material, including films on the city's
reconstruction following wartime bombing, and films on the motor
industry. Also held are videos for city council policy, training and induction.
In early 2007 the City Archives will move into purpose built accommodation
as part of the Coventry History Centre.

172 COVENTRY CITY CENTRAL LIBRARY

Smithford Way, Coventry CV1 1FY
Email: Central.library@coventry.gov.uk
Web: http://tinyurl.co.uk/u2fu
☎ 024 7683 2314 **Fax**: 024 7683 2440
Contact: Rachel Speake, Librarian

Holdings include: A wide variety of music on CD and tape and DVDs for loan for a small charge; language sets for learning a second language.

173 CREATAS

Dynamic Graphics (UK) Ltd., Unit 5, Finch Drive, Springwood Industrial Estate, Braintree, Essex CM7 2SF
Email: sales@creatas.co.uk
Web: http://www.creatas.com
☎ 01376 333780 **Fax**: 01376 528522

Creatas.co.uk is your source for downloadable stock photography, illustration and footage. The extensive collection features thousands of sophisticated, eye-catching, royalty free images available for order online. The site offers in-depth search, an easy-to-manage lightbox system, secure purchasing and reliable downloads. Formerly known as Creative Solutions. Our long-time brands are still here: Thinkstock, Triangle Images, Image 100 and Digital Vision. Creatas.co.uk, based in England, draws on the extensive experience of its parent company, Dynamic Graphics, a stock image supplier since 1981.

174 CREATIVE ARTS TELEVISION

Web: http://www.footage.org.uk
Email: info@catarchive.com
Contact: Stephan Chodorov

Creative Arts Television manages several collections of filmed and videotaped arts footage from 1950 to date. For years we have been servicing BBC, PBS, CBS, arte, ZDF, etc. and independent filmmakers worldwide. We have coverage of all the arts in the last half of the twentieth century. People, performance, conversation, demonstration, interview, insight. We have hundreds of hours covering dance, theatre, cinema, music, fine arts, literature, poetry, photography, architecture, sculpture, painting, cartooning and animation, ethnic arts and popular culture. We also have some science material and some remarkable conversations between eminent men and women.

175 CULTURAL FANTASISTS – MUSIC ARCHIVE

Lower Drumbuie, Drumnadrochait, Invernesshire, IV63 6XP
Email: archive@culturalfantasists.co.uk
Web: http://www.culturalfantasists.co.uk
☎ 01456 450155 **Fax**: 01456 450528
Contact: Jennie Macfie
Access: By arrangement. Free accommodation for researchers. Staff available to assist

Established in 1991, Cultural Fantasists began with a library of about a hundred film clips produced in the early seventies. Since then it has steadily expanded and now includes films and videos by Don Letts, Chris Boger, Peter Whitehead, Tony Palmer, Brian Gibson, Mike Mansfield, Derek Jarman, Ken O'Neil, Jack O'Connell, Brian Simmons, Piers Bedford, Jack Hazan and David Mingay, Lindsey Clennell, Nick Abson, Brian Grant, Russell Mulcahy, Julien Temple and many others, covering a period from the 1930s to the 1990s. Archive videotape of early 1980s fashion series is also held.

Cultural Fantasists

The Ramones

176 DARTINGTON HALL TRUST ARCHIVE AND COLLECTION

High Cross House, Dartington Hall, Totnes, Devon, TQ9 6ED
Email: a.palmer@dartingtonhall.org.uk
Web: http://www.dartingtonarchive.org.uk
☎ 01803 864114 **Fax**: 01803 867057
Contact: Angie St John Palmer, General Manager
Access: Tue, Wed, Thu by appointment – 9.30–12.30; 14.00–17.00 on above days

Holds correspondence, documents, programmes, brochures, photographs, tape/video recordings relating to the Trust and enterprises in the arts, education and commercial. By 1934 teachers and students at Dartington Hall School began making short documentary and classroom films. By 1939 they had produced twenty factual films. When war broke out, Dartington was selected to house the Ministry of Information film library for South West England. They distributed thousands of factual films regionally during the war. The South West Film and Television Archive (qv) in Plymouth preserves surviving films. A growing collection of reference copies on videotape are maintained at the Trust Archive.

177 DAVID FINCH DISTRIBUTION

PO Box 264, Walton-on-Thames KT12 3YR
Email: dfa@cwcom.net
☎ 01932 882733 **Fax**: 01932 882108
Contact: David Finch, Director
Access: By appointment

A library representing a number of producers. Emphasis on 'reality' with police chases, surveillance camera footage, celebrities, fishing and war.

178 DAVID KENTEN FILM COLLECTION

29 Fishergate, Norwich, Norfolk NR3 1SE
☎ 01603 624255 **Fax**: 01603 624255
Contact: David Kenten, Owner
Access available by arrangement. Prospective users should apply in writing prior to making an appointment

A private hobby that has grown over thirty-five years into a vast cross-section of subjects, and is still growing as material can be found.

179 DECAPOD.TV

Email: inquiries@decapod.tv
Web: http://www.decapod.tv

Decapod.tv is a television production unit which specialises in marine wildlife. Since we began operation in the autumn of 2002, we have founded Ireland's first marine archive of digital footage. This archive is now available on-line to broadcasters and independent production companies. We have over 500 clips of around seventy-five different species and habitats with fighting, mating, feeding and scavenging. One of the aims is to present it to the widest audience through an interactive educational package, a multimedia DVD-ROM as well as to produce a series on Ireland's seas.

180 DENBIGHSHIRE RECORD OFFICE

46 Clwyd Street, Ruthin LL15 1HP
Email: archives@denbighshire.gov.uk
Web: http://www.denbighshire.gov.uk
☎ 01824 708250 **Fax**: 01824 708258
Contact: R. K. Matthias, County Archivist
Access: Limited. Mon-Thu 09.00–16.45 Fri 09.00–16.15. Staff are available to assist. Access to the video collection only. It is not possible to view original film

Denbighshire Record Office, formerly part of the Clwyd Record Office, has been collecting films and videos of local history significance since the 1980s. Holdings cover several areas of the former (pre-1974) county of Denbighshire, particularly Colwyn Bay, Denbigh, Ruthin and Wrexham – the earliest film dates from 1919. Subjects include a visit of the Prince of Wales to Colwyn Bay, 1928, Conway Bridge centenary celebrations, 1927, and a royal visit to Ruthin, 1984. The Record Office has received video tapes of films, mostly relating to Rhyl. These are part of a deposit received from Philip Lloyd of Mold, formerly the Clwyd Museums Education Officer.

181 DEPARTMENT FOR CULTURE, MEDIA AND SPORT

Information Centre, 2–4 Cockspur Street, London SW1Y 5DH
Email: enquiries@culture.gov.uk
Web: http://www.culture.gov.uk/default.htm
☎ 020 7211 6200 **Fax**: 020 7211 6032
Contact: Abigail Humber, Information Centre Manager
Access: By appointment only if material not available elsewhere

Established in July 1997. Responsible for arts, broadcasting, the press, museums and galleries, libraries, sport and recreation, historic buildings and more. Audio-visual holdings include a small collection covering DCMS subjects.

182 DIAMOND TIME

2nd Floor, Foframe House, 35–37 Brent Street, Hendon, London NW4 2EF
Email: lee.taylor@diamondtime.co.uk
Web: http://www.diamondtime.net
☎ 020 8203 3303 **Fax**: 020 8203 3222
Contact: Lee Taylor, Head of Programmes
Access: No access

A comprehensive collection of music on video from the 1970s to the present with historic additions going back to the 1930s.

183 DIGITAL VISION (GETTY IMAGES)

101 Bayham Street, London NW1 0AG
Email: motion.sales@gettyimages.com
Web: http://www.gettyimages.com
☎ 0800 279 9255

Now controlled by Getty Images (qv) and part of its 'Royalty Free' collections. Founded in 1995, Digital Vision has rapidly expanded to a worldwide presence in the royalty-free creative content market. Headquartered near Tower Bridge, London, Digital Vision also has an office in Manhattan, New York and sells directly in France, Germany, Holland and Spain through an International Sales Centre based in London. Additionally, the design elements are distributed by over 100 partners in seventy countries around the world. Digital Vision specialise in providing exciting royalty free stock photography, illustrations, and stock motion footage. Additionally, it provides a stock music library.

184 DIXONS CITY ACADEMY

Ripley Street, Bradford, West Yorkshire BD5 7RR
Email: lynn@dixonsctc.org.uk
Web: http://www.dixonsca.com
☎ 01274 776 777 **Fax**: 01274 391 928
Contact: Lynn Barrett, Information Sources Manager

This very small collection is for use within the college's curriculum. The hundreds of videos can be borrowed overnight by students only.

185 DON BOYD PAPERS

University of Exeter Bill Douglas Centre, The Old Library, Prince of Wales Road, Exeter EX4 4SB
Email: M.L.Allen@exeter.ac.uk
Web: http://www.library.ex.ac.uk/special/guides/bdc/bdc_002.html#extent
☎ 01392 264321 **Fax**: 01392 263871
Contact: Michelle Allen, Curator
Access: An online catalogue is browsable at
http://www.bill.douglas.org/eve. Further information about research
access is available on the website

Don Boyd (1948-) is a film director, producer and writer. The collection incorporates a wide range of personal and business papers. For the films initiated between 1968 and 2000 (including those never completed), the collection houses screenplay drafts and script notes, budget documents, correspondence, production schedules, publicity material and press cuttings. For each of the companies he has founded or co-founded (Boyd's Co., Kendon Films, Berwick St. Studios, Anglo-International Films, Lexington Films) there are accounts files, correspondence, invoices and other documents pertaining to various business procedures. There is also a significant amount of personal correspondence.

186 DONCASTER COLLEGE

Church View, Doncaster, Yorks DN1 1RF
Email: rodney.challis@don.ac.uk
Web: http://www.don.ac.uk
☎ 01302 553826 **Fax**: 01302 553700
Contact: Rodney Challis, Lecturer
Access: Reference only unless registered staff/student of the college.
External membership available

Very small collection relating to moving image and radio.

187 DORSET FILM AND SOUND ARCHIVE

Dorset History Centre, Bridport Road, Dorchester, Dorset DT1 1RP
Email: archives@dorsetcc.gov.uk
Web: http://www.dorsetforyou.com/index.jsp?articleid=2843
☎ 01305–250550 **Fax**: 01305–257184
Contact: Hugh Jacques, County Archivist
Access: Mon-Fri 09.00–17.00 Sat 09.30–12.30. Access for disabled. Access to video holdings only, by appointment. Searches can by made by staff

Although film and photographs have been collected by the county for some time, this film collection could properly be said to date from 1991, when the Record Office moved to its present site incorporating specially designed storage facilities.

188 DOWNTOWN RADIO

Newtownards, Co Down BT23 4ES
Email: programmes@downtown.co.uk
Web: http://www.downtown.co.uk
☎ 028 9181 5555 **Fax**: 028 9181 8913
Contact: David Sloane, Programme Controller
Access: Office hours

Holds a selection of radio programmes, spanning twenty-five years, of interest to the Northern Ireland audience.

189 DREAM 100 FM

Northgate House, St Peter's Street, Colchester, Essex CO1 1HT
Email: info@dream100.com
Web: http://www.dream100.com
☎ 01206 764466 **Fax**: 01206 715102
Contact: Gary Ball, Programme Controller

Radio station. Holds output to meet legal requirement.

190 DUKE SALES

Champion House, Douglas, Isle of Man IM99 1DD
Email: info@dukesales.com
Web: http://www.dukesales.com
☎ 01624 640020 **Fax**: 01624 640001
Contact: Jon Quayle, Director International Sales

Duke Marketing was founded by Peter Duke and started publishing special-interest videos in 1981. Duke have a substantial range of archive and historic material, fascinating fly-on-the-wall documentaries, exclusive behind-the-scenes insights, official end-of-season sports reviews and increasingly popular, personal profiles of sports personalities, plus the highly successful weekly television shows AUTO MUNDIAL, MOTORSPORT MUNDIAL MAX POWER and BIKE SPORT.

191 DUKE VIDEO POWERSPORT

PO Box 46, Champion House, Douglas, Isle of Man IM99 1DD
Email: intsls@dukevideo.com
Web: http://www.dukevideo.com
☎ 01624 640022 **Fax**: 01624 640001
Contact: Jon Quayle, International Sales Director
Access: 09.00–17.30, by arrangement. Access for disabled

The collection comprises 1,200 titles relating to powersport.

192 DUNCAN OF JORDANSTONE COLLEGE LIBRARY

Duncan of Jordanstone College, University of Dundee, 13 Perth Road, Dundee DD1 4HT
Email: library@dundee.ac.uk
Web: http://www.dundee.ac.uk/library
☎ 01382 345252 **Fax**: 01382 229283
Contact: Marie Simmons, College Librarian
Access: AV for staff and students only. No outside access. Mon-Thu, 09.00–20.30. Fri, 09.00–1700, Sat, 12.00–17.00. Reduced hours in vacations

Books and videos support the teaching of the School of Television and Imaging, and also support other courses which run film studies options. Areas of strength include animation, video art, cinema films and special effects.

193 DURHAM UNIVERSITY LIBRARY: BASIL BUNTING POETRY ARCHIVE

Palace Green Section, Palace Green, Durham DH1 3RN
Email: pg.library@durham.ac.uk
Web: http://aesica.dur.ac.uk/delores/asc/other.asp
☎ 0191 374 3001 **Fax**: 0191 374 3002
Contact: E. Rainey
Access: Open to all bona fide researchers, Mon-Fri, 0900–1700. Searchers are required to give prior notice of visits

The University Library's Basil Bunting Poetry Archive is an extensive collection of published works by and relating to the poet Basil Bunting (1900–1985), with manuscripts and papers, photographs, films and sound recordings. Bunting's poetry is deeply rooted in the landscape, history, language and culture of his native Northumbria, where he spent his youth, and to which he returned for the last three decades of his life. He believed that sound was integral to poetic form, and that poetry must be heard. The collection's films are chiefly copies on video of television programmes relating to Bunting, while the recordings include poetry readings and interviews made for television and radio.

194 DURHAM UNIVERSITY LIBRARY: SUDAN ARCHIVE

Palace Green Section, Palace Green, Durham, Co. Durham DH1 3RN
Email: s.m.hingley@durham.ac.uk
Web: http://aesica.dur.ac.uk/delores/asc/other.asp
☎ 0191 334 2972 **Fax**: 0191 334 2942
Contact: Sheila Hingley, Head of Heritage Collections
Access: Open to all bona-fide researchers, Mon to Fri, 09.00–17.00. Searchers are required to give prior notice of visits

The University Library's Sudan Archive includes 136 cinefilms, most of which are the work of amateurs. They record the lives of district commissioners, doctors and other officials in various regions of the Sudan, and provide a visual record of Sudanese tribal life in the North and South, and buildings of Khartoum, Omdurman and other major centres in the provinces from the late 1920s to the 1960s. Recent accessions have included publicity films produced by the Sudan Government in the 1950s, just before and after independence. The collection provides valuable material for the study of the social and cultural history, anthropology and ethnography of the area.

195 EAST ANGLIAN FILM ARCHIVE

The Archive Centre, Martineau Lane, Norwich NR1 2DQ
Email: eafa@uea.ac.uk
Web: http://www.uea.ac.uk/eafa
☎ 01603 592664 **Fax**: 01603 458553
Contact: Jane Alvey
Access: Mon–Fri 09.00–17.00 or by arrangement. Staff are available to assist. Access for disabled

The Archive was established in 1976 to locate and preserve films and videos showing life and work in Norfolk, Suffolk, Essex and Cambridgeshire, and to provide a service of access and presentation where copyright allows. The collection spans the years from 1896 to the present day and is continuing to grow rapidly. It aims to reflect all aspects of the region its people, society, economy, geography, history and the work of its film and video makers, both amateur and professional. EAFA is also preserving unique and growing collections of regional television output and it now houses the original film collection of the Hertfordshire Film Archive.

Liz Sutton collection of home movies/EAFA

Liz Sutton holding a camera in one of her family's films

196 EAST MIDLANDS ORAL HISTORY ARCHIVE (EMOHA)

Centre for Urban History, University of Leicester, Leicester LE1 7RH
Email: emoha@le.ac.uk
Web: http://www.le.ac.uk/emoha
☎ 0116 252 5065 / 5066 **Fax**: 0116 252 5769
Contact: Colin Hyde

The East Midlands Oral History Archive was originally funded by the Heritage Lottery Fund to establish the first large-scale archive of oral history recordings for Leicestershire and Rutland. This includes the collections of the former Leicester Oral History Archive, the Mantle archive from North West Leicestershire, the Community History archive of Leicester City Libraries, and the sound archive of BBC Radio Leicester, along with smaller collections donated by local organisations or individuals. The recordings are deposited in the Record Office for Leicestershire, Leicester and Rutland, and are currently being catalogued to make them more accessible.

197 EASTLEIGH COLLEGE

Chestnut Avenue, Eastleigh, Hants SO50 5FS
Email: mpsheedy@eastleigh.ac.uk
Web: http://www.eastleigh.ac.uk
☎ 023 8091 1026 **Fax**: 023 8032 2133
Contact: Mike Sheedy, Central Learning Resources Manager

The Learning Centre facilities are available to all students. Information can be accessed via books, videos, CD-ROMs and the Internet, student intranet and the Virtual Learning Environment (VLE). Facilities include scanners, colour laser printer, video playback equipment, lamination and binding machines, as well as a card-operated photocopier. Our fully equipped photographic and media studio boasts the following equipment: five full size VHS cameras; four digital video cameras; ten digital still cameras; ten 35mm SLRs; fourteen photographic enlargers; three digital edit suites; three flatbed scanners; nine PCs with industrial standards software; one colour printer.

198 EBS TRUST

36–38 Mortimer Street, London W1N 7RB
Email: maillist@shotlist.co.uk
Web: http://www.shotlist.co.uk
☎ 020 7765 5023 **Fax**: 020 7580 6246
Contact: Jim Stevenson, Chief Executive
Access: Mon-Fri, 09.00–18.00

EBS is The Educational Broadcasting Services Trust, a charitable trust company set up by the BBC in 1987, but now both legally and financially independent. MINET (The Moving Images Network) is a consortium of twenty-one universities and FE colleges, with academic and technical steering groups. It is a growing bank of over 160 titles of high quality programmes in the subject areas of Biology, Business Studies, Chemistry, Engineering, Information Systems, Practical Maths, Psychology, and Lectures (Irish Literature and Quantum Physics) – and the Skillbank (FE) Collection comprising series on construction, basic engineering, catering, caring and office management.

199 EDEN PROJECT VIDEO ARCHIVE

Eden Project, Bodelva, St Austell, Cornwall PL24 2SG
Email: anna@meneer.fsnet.co.uk
Web: http://www.edenproject.com/4436.htm
☎ 01726 811968 **Fax**: 01726 811909
Contact: Anna Meneer, Archive Producer

The Eden Project video archive consists of over 2,000 hours of footage filmed throughout the building of the project. It records the rollercoaster ride that was 'the making of Eden' with privileged access to everyone from the boardroom to the clay pit. This unique record is available to broadcasters and filmmakers for inclusion in their programmes.

200 EDINBURGH COLLEGE OF ART LIBRARY

Lauriston Place, Edinburgh EH3 9DF
Email: w.smith@eca.ac.uk
Web: http://tinyurl.co.uk/sc6o
☎ 0131 221 6033 **Fax**: 0131 221 6033
Contact: Wilson Smith, Principal Librarian
Access: Library opening hours

Book, journal and video collection contains material in support of teaching, research and studio work in the College's School of Visual Communication. A small collection of photocopied original film scripts is held.

201 EDINBURGH UNIVERSITY DATA LIBRARY/EDINA

Main Library Building, George Square, Edinburgh EH8 9LJ
Email: a.bevan@ed.ac.uk
Web: http://www.emol.ac.uk
☎ 0131 650 3346 **Fax**: 0131 650 3308
Contact: Andrew Bevan, Helpdesk Manager
Access: Via secure academic network and/or username/password

Film and Sound Online (formerly Education Media Online) is a collection of hundreds of hours film and video, hosted by EDINA and cleared and digitised through the BUFVC/JISC Managing Agent and Advisory Service (MAAS). The films are of high quality, fully downloadable, either in full or as segments, and can be used freely in learning, teaching and research. Collections include: Amber Films Documentaries; Biochemical Society; Digital Himalaya; Educational and Television Films Ltd (ETV); Imperial War Museum; IWF Knowledge and Media GmbH; Logic Lane; Open University Worldwide; Royal Mail Film Classics; St George's Hospital Medical School Collection; Sheffield University Learning Media Unit Collection.

202 EDITIONS AUDOVISUEL BEULAH

66 Rochester Way, Crowborough, East Sussex TN6 2DU
Email: beulah@enterprise.net
Web: http://www.eavb.co.uk/library
☎ 01892 652413 **Fax**: 01892 652413
Contact: Barry Coward, Proprietor

Film and video stock shots available through Film Images (qv). Stills can be sourced from us. Stills/Film/Video – our motion picture stock shot and 35mm negative and transparency collection covers: agriculture of the 40s and 50s; aircraft from bi-planes to jets, mainly in the 1970s; buses, trolleybuses and coaches of the 1950s and 1960s; docks in the ports of Bristol, Dover, Gloucester, Hull, London and Southampton; musicians; natural history, British butterflies; people at work and play; places mainly in Britain from the 1950s onwards; railways in Britain and France; shipping; sports and games; waterways; Audio Library – effects from Africa (mainly West Africa and Ethiopia) 1960s and 1970s.

203 EDUCATIONAL & TELEVISION FILMS (ETV)

c/o British Film Institute, Archive Footage Sales, 21 Stephen Street,
London W1T 1LN
Email: http://www.bfi.org.uk/help/contact.php?eid=5
Web: http://www.bfi.org.uk/nftva/afs/etv
☎ 020 7957 4842 **Fax**: 020 7436 4014
Contact: Sarah Wilde

Established in 1950, ETV has amassed a wide and varied range of documentary archive material from the ex-Socialist world, with particular emphasis on the ex-Soviet Union, the former Eastern Block countries and China. Material is also held from Vietnam, Cuba, Chile, Afghanistan and the other Arab Nations. ETV also houses material from the British labour movement and the Spanish Civil War. *Note: The ETV collection is now housed at the bfi National Film and Television Archive (qv) and all queries should be addressed to their archive footage sales department.*

204 ELMBRIDGE FILM HERITAGE CENTRE

c/o Elmbridge Museum, Church Street, Weybridge KT13 8DX
Email: ebcmuseum@elmbridge.gov.uk
Web: http://elmbridgemuseum.org.uk
☎ 01932 843573 **Fax**: 01932 846552
Contact: Jason Finch, Temporary Assistant Manager
Access: By arrangement

The Elmbridge Film Heritage Centre was established in 1996. It exists to promote and develop the moving image heritage of Elmbridge. It is building a collection of moving images made in Elmbridge and related to the work of R.C. Sherriff for use in Elmbridge Museum and the borough. The Centre was created by the South East Film & Video Archive (qv) with valuable support from the R.C. Sherriff Rosebriars Trust.

205 ELSBURY IMAGES

61 Thingwall Park, Fishponds, Bristol BS16 2AL
Email: david@elsbury61.freeserve.co.uk
☎ 0117 965 5952,
Contact: David Elsbury
Access: By prior arrangement. Usually 10.00–16.00 weekdays

From an initial collection of lantern slides, this archive now contains photographs, film strips, and film footage documenting the last 100 years. Moving images of cities and town, particularly in the south and south west of Britain, are held as well as family occasions and celebrations from the late 1920s onwards. Coverage includes amateur sport, naval reviews, holidays, works outings, school life and pets; travel in UK and Europe from the 1920s to the 1960s inter-war cruises and travels in the USA, Australia and New Zealand in the 1950s and 60s. Also contains a collection of instructional 16mm films and 35mm filmstrips from a former educational film library.

Elsbury Images

Britsol estate children await excursion bus (1933)

206 EMAP RADIO

Castle Quay, Castlefield, Manchester M15 4PR
Email: karen.yates@emap.com
Web: http://www.emap.com
☎ 0161 288 5000
Contact: Karen Yates

Radio licencee group. Its acquisitions are: 96.3 Aire FM, 96.9 Viking FM, Hallam FM, Key 103, Kiss 100 FM, Magic 105.4 FM, Magic 828, Magic 999, Magic 1152. Magic 1152 MW, Magic 1161 AM, Magic 1170, Magic 1548, Magic AM, Metro FM, Radio City 96.7, Rock FM, and TFM. Digital radio stations also include: the Hits, Smash! Hits Radio, Kerrang!, Q, Mojo, heat and The Box. All its stations hold forty-two days' output only to meet legal requirement. The Magic stations share large private music collections.

207 EMI MUSIC ARCHIVES

Dawley Road, Hayes UB3 1HH
Email: jackie.bishop@emimusic.com
Web: http://www.emigroup.com
☎ 020 8848 2000 **Fax**: 020 8848 2018
Contact: Jackie Bishop, Archivist
Access: Tue-Thu 9.00–16.30

The EMI Music Archive is home to one of the world's largest and most diverse music collections, dating back to the late 1890s. It houses $\frac{1}{2}$ million master audio and video tapes, seven million music-related paper documents, 80,000 metal master stampers, a collection of 78s and LPs and thousands of artist photos. The Archive also houses many artefacts related to the company's history. Paperwork relating to majority of artists who have recorded for EMI, including general correspondence, press cuttings, recording sheets, contracts; files also on specific subjects such as development of television and recording, manufacture of gramophones, including service manuals.

208 ENVIRONMENTAL INVESTIGATION AGENCY

62/63 Upper Street, London N1 0NY
Email: ukinfo@eia-international.org
Web: http://www.eia-international.org
☎ 020 7354 7960 **Fax**: 020 7354 7961

The Environmental Investigation Agency (EIA) is an international campaigning organisation committed to investigating and exposing environmental crime. EIA has one of the world's largest collections of video and photo material devoted to the illegal trade in wildlife products and other environmentally damaging commodities. The collection is databased and is available on a professional basis to journalists, publishers and programme-makers. EIA's broadcast quality video news releases are available for a limited period to news broadcasters. Compressed online versions of a selection of our video broadcasts can be found in the online multimedia area.

209 ESPRESSO TV ARCHIVE

9 York Villas, Brighton BN1 3TS
Email: archive@espressotv.co.uk
Web: http://www.espressotv.com/archives.htm
☎ 0208 960 5525 **Fax**: 0208 960 4054
Contact: Simon Wilding

Espresso TV Archive is a clip sales/footage service to the television, corporate and commercials industries. Libraries – Aviation & Space: footage dating back to the beginning of the 1900s. Celebrities/movies: American movie artists and singers, television shows. Extreme sports: quality extreme footage from exotic locations. General footage: from art and aviation to waterfalls and volcanoes. Military history: contains over 200 hours of military history footage. Travel, arts and location: over 5,000 hours of travel-orientated archive. Underwater and marine: nearly 500 hours of underwater cinematography shot on 16mm and Super 16mm by the renowned Canadian filmmaker John Stoneman.

210 ESSEX FM

Radio House, Clifftown Road, Southend-on-sea, Essex SS1 1SX
Email: studios@essexradio.co.uk
Web: http://www.essexfm.co.uk
☎ 01702 333711 **Fax**: 01702 345224
Contact: Jeff O'Brien, Programme Director

Radio station. News programming only kept to meet legal requirement.
Maintains large private music collection.

211 ESSEX SOUND AND VIDEO ARCHIVE

Essex Record Office, Wharf Road, Chelmsford, Essex CM2 6YT
Email: ero.enquiry@essexcc.gov.uk
Web: http://www.essexcc.gov.uk/ero
☎ 01245 244644 **Fax**: 01245 244655
Contact: Martin Astell

The Archive is a collection of sound and video recordings covering many
aspects of local history and culture in Essex. It has been designed to ensure
that our county's past is preserved in words, sounds and images and is
safeguarded for the future and made accessible. The archive holds
significant collections of oral history recordings relating to Essex; selected
items from BBC Essex radio; selections from local hospital television and
talking newspapers; videos of local interest, including many from the East
Anglian Film Archive (qv); dialect recordings; and recordings of music
performed by local musicians, including a major collection of folk music
and folk dance drawn from Essex sources.

212 FALKIRK COLLEGE
(now known as FORTH VALLEY COLLEGE)

Grangemouth Road, Falkirk FK2 9AD
Email: info@falkirkcollege.ac.uk Web: http://www.falkirkcollege.ac.uk
☎ 01324 403000
Contact: Allan Robertson
Access: College staff and students only

Forth Valley College was created on 1 August 2005 out of a merger of
Clackmannan and Falkirk Colleges. The collection comprises course related
materials. 50% of video holdings are off-air recordings.

213 FERNHURST SOCIETY ORAL HISTORY GROUP ARCHIVES

c/o The Fernhurst Society, Fernhurst, Surrey GU27 3JF
Email: fernhurst.society@btopenworld.com
Web: http://www.fernhurst.society.btinternet.co.uk/oralhistory.html
Contact: Christine Maynard, Archive Director
Access: Limited opening hours

This small group is undertaking taped interviews of villagers in Fernhurst
Parish. So far over fifty interviews have been made on cassette. The original
recordings are archived in the West Sussex Record Office. Copies of each
recording on cassette, on audio CD, and as MP3 files on CD-ROM, are
lodged in the Fernhurst Archives. The aim of the project is to develop a
picture of how everyday life in the village has changed over the last 100 or
so years, with particular emphasis on the period 1920–1980. The project is
based on interviews with long-time residents of Fernhurst. Ultimately it is
hoped that we will have some seventy to eighty completed interviews.

214 FETLAR INTERPRETIVE CENTRE FILM AND VIDEO ARCHIVE

Beach of Houbie, Fetlar, Shetland ZE2 9DJ
Email: info@fetlar.com
Web: http://www.fetlar.com/archives.htm
☎ 01957 733206
Contact: Jane Coutts

Fetlar Interpretive Centre's extensive film and video archive starts with film taken at Brough Lodge in the 1930s and ends with some of the most recent events in the island, but material is added to the archive all the time to provide an ongoing record of island life. Some of the video material has been edited into manageable, documentary-type presentations which are available for public viewing at the Centre. Popular clips include the Brough Lodge film, Houbie Mondays when the flit-boat was unloaded with the week's goods in the 1950s and 60s, and video of snowy owls. The Interpretive Centre also holds around 3,000 photographs or copies of photographs and oral history recordings.

215 FILM IMAGES (LONDON)

2 The Quadrant, 135 Salusbury Road, London NW6 6RJ
Email: research@film-images.com
Web: http://www.film-images.com
☎ 020 7624 3388 **Fax**: 020 7624 3377
Contact: Tony Dykes, Senior Researcher
Access: Appointments necessary. Access for disabled. Research can be carried out on behalf of customers

Established in 1990, Film Images now manages film collections from both America and Europe. It represents the material on behalf of collectors, distributing them to Film Images' International network of offices. Holds thousands of hours of historical footage from Europe, the USA and Africa: all formats from 16mm/35mm OCN to DigiBeta. Early cinema, actuality, newsreels, educational and instructional films, industrial films, features, commercials, music performance, cartoons, comedies and amateur films. Important collections are: COI Footage File (qv), Film Archives (USA), Historic Films (USA), Lobster Films (France), and the Overseas Film and TV Centre (Africa).

216 FILM LONDON

20 Euston Square, Regent's Place, London NW1 3JH
Email: daniela.kirchner@filmlondon.org.uk
Web: http://www.filmlondon.org.uk
☎ 020 7387 8787 **Fax**: 020 7387 8788
Contact: Daniela Kirchner, Information Manager
Access: Library open Mon-Fri, 09.00–18.00

Formed in March 2003, Film London is the strategic agency for the film and media sector in London, absorbing the roles of the London Film Commission and the London Film and Video Development Agency. It invests in film production, exhibition and education and in the economic and industry development initiatives across the capital. The agency leads the drive to enhance London's status as a world-class film location. The datastore holds records of over 12,000 locations, 15,000 crew and 8,000 facility companies and local services, and a further 20,000 useful contacts. The locations area covers mainly Greater London but also includes the Home Counties and other parts of the UK.

217 FILM RESEARCH & PRODUCTION SERVICES

PO Box 28045, London SE27 9WZ
Email: frps@aol.com
Web: http://www.filmresearch.co.uk
☎ 01228 712 937 **Fax**: 01228 712 938
Contact: James Webb, Researcher
Access: 09.30–17.30. Staff are available to assist. Company biased towards commercial rather than academic enquiries, but all requests welcome

Film Research provides both contemporary and archive moving footage and stills sourced from all genres including: news, sport, wildlife, feature films and television programmes. Footage is supplied for use in all media production formats, including: commercials, feature films, corporate films, pop promos, documentaries and television series. Film Research specialises in cinema and television commercials, both in the UK and abroad. Offers a comprehensive selection of viewing tapes with immediate access, including some master material. We have viewing facilities for 35mm and 16mm film; Betacam SP; low band three-quarter inch U-matic; NTSC, Secam and PAL VHS.

218 FILMFINDERS

c/o Moving Image Communications, Maidstone Studios, Vinters Park, Maidstone, Kent ME14 5NZ
Email: mail@milibrary.com
Web: http://www.milibrary.com/2003site/pages/filmfinders.html
☎ 01622 684 569 **Fax**: 01622 687 444
Access: 10.00–17.00, by arrangement only

Vintage (1900 to about 1934) feature, interest, documentary material covering most aspects of silent cinema and introduction of sound. *Note: Collection now controlled by Moving Image Communications (qv).*

219 FILTON COLLEGE

Filton Avenue, Bristol BS34 7AT
Email: info@filton.ac.uk
Web: http://www.filton.ac.uk
☎ 0117 931 2121 **Fax**: 0117 931 2233
Contact: Adam Ranson, Media Lecturer
Access: College hours

The brand new vocational campus offers the following performing arts facilities: theatre with 250 seats; recording studio; music laboratory; dance studios; base studio for all the creative arts students according to their subject; specialist studio for fashion and textiles; specialist studio for printmaking; Apple Macintosh Suite for graphic design and 3D design; ceramics facility; two fully equipped black and white dark rooms; audio-visual projection units; video cameras; 5x4 and various medium format cameras; four Apple Mac suites.

220 FIRE SERVICE COLLEGE

Moreton-in-Marsh, Glos GL56 0RH
Email: library@fireservicecollege.ac.uk
Web: http://www.fireservicecollege.ac.uk
☎ 01608 650831
Contact: Marion Barnes, Acquisitions & Cataloguing Librarian, Library
Access: Closed access. Apply in writing

The collection covers fire, fire disasters and firefighter training.

221 FIRST GARDEN CITY HERITAGE MUSEUM

296 Norton Way South, Letchworth Garden City, Hertfordshire SG6 1SU
Email: fgchm@Letchworth.com
Web: http://tinyurl.co.uk/lqu3
☎ 01462 482710 **Fax**: 01462 486056
Contact: Elizabeth Cummings, Assistant Curator
Access: By arrangement only. Access for disabled

Local archive film has been collected since the 1950s.

222 FLASHBACK LIBRARY

Flashback Television Ltd, 9–11 Bowling Green Lane, London EC1 0BG
Email: mailbox@flashbacktv.co.uk Web:
http://www.flashbacktelevision.com
☎ 020 7490 8996 **Fax**: 020 7490 5610
Contact: Stuart Heaney, Film Archivist
Access: By arrangement. Staff are available to assist

Independent production company Flashback Television has been in continuous production since 1982. Over these years it has retained rights to much of the material shot, which has now been catalogued. The library contains: landscapes, townscapes and scenics throughout Great Britain and Ireland, ranging from Spitalfields Market (before its refurbishment) to beautiful scenics of Glencoe and the Isle of Skye. Historically important locations, from Dunottar Castle to the First World War graves at Tyncote and the Somme. Material of contemporary political importance including Orange Marches through Belfast, the comings and goings at Downing Street (1990), and Diana's funeral.

223 FLINTSHIRE RECORD OFFICE

The Old Rectory, Hawarden, Flintshire, Wales CH5 3NR
Web: http://www.flintshire.gov.uk
☎ 01244 532414 **Fax**: 01224 538344
Contact: Rowland Williams, County Archivist
Access: Researchers are advised to enquire before visiting. Mon-Thu 09.00–16.45; Friday 09.00–16.15

The county of Flintshire was formed in April 1996 out of the former county of Clwyd and comprises the central area of the historic county of Flintshire. The Flintshire Record Office was established in 1951 and moved to the Old Rectory, Hawarden, an eighteenth-century, Grade II-listed building set within its own grounds, in 1956. The record office seeks to preserve our county's unique archival heritage by collecting, listing, storing and making available to the public historic records of all kinds.

224 FM 102 THE BEAR

The Guard House Studios, Banbury Road, Stratford-upon-Avon, Warwickshire CV37 7HX
Email: steve@thebear.co.uk
Web: http://www.thebear.co.uk
☎ 01789 262636 **Fax**: 01789 263102
Contact: Steve Hyden, Head of Programming

Radio station. Holds output to meet legal requirement.

225 FM 103 HORIZON

Broadcast centre, Crown Hill, Milton Keynes, Bucks MK8 0AD
Email: trevor.marshall@musicradio.com
Web: http://103.musicradio.com
☎ 01908 269111 **Fax**: 01908 564063
Contact: Trevor Marshall, Programme Controller
Access: Happy to point researchers in the right direction if looking at the Milton Keynes area

Radio station. Holds forty-two days' output to meet legal requirement.

226 FOOTAGE FARM

22 Newman Street, London W1T 1PH
Email: English@Footagefarm.co.uk
Web: http://www.footagefarm.co.uk
☎ 020 7631 3773 **Fax**: 020 7631 3774
Contact: Orly Yadin, Managing Director
Access: Office hours are 09.00–18.00

Footage Farm was established in 2001 to provide video master tapes of public domain material. This means that you no longer have to worry about licences or counting seconds and frames. The broad subjects include: the two World Wars (both battle scenes and home front including colour material of WWII), Vietnam, Korea, Spanish Civil War, the Middle East conflicts etc. Particular emphasis on world political events and personalities. These are from the Universal newsreels (1929–1967), MARCH OF TIME outtakes (c.1934–1951) and others. Over 300 films from the Library of Congress Paper Prints, the only extant copies of many short items recorded between c.1895–1915.

227 FOOTAGEDIRECT.COM

Email: filmarchive@mailcity.com
Web: http://www.footagedirect.com/index.html
☎ 020 8748 9600 **Fax**: 020 8748 9607
Contact: Sue Draper

The editors and producers at footagedirect have been involved in making network programmes, commercials and corporate videos for many years. The range of subjects and events the archive covers is very comprehensive. It is seen regularly in productions on major networks around the world, from the BBC and Discovery Channel, to PBS and NHK. We are now offering royalty free archives as a major new service for programme makers.

228 FORTH ONE 97.3

Forth House, Forth Street, Edinburgh EH1 3LF
Email: info@forthone.com
Web: http://www.forthone.com
☎ 0131 556 9255 **Fax**: 0131 558 3277
Contact: Luke McCullough, Programme Director

Radio station which began transmission on 22 January 1975 as Radio Forth 194. In 1990 the FM and AM bands were separated out as FORTH FM and Max AM and in 2000 they were rebranded as FORTHONE 97.3 and 1548 FORTH2. Holds forty-two days' output to meet legal requirement (note: quality not suitable for re-broadcasting). Various news and local interest programmes are kept for both stations.

229 FRANK SMITH 'GRIMSBY FILM PRESERVATION SOCIETY'

28 Barry Avenue, Grimsby, North East Lincolnshire DN34 5LS
☎ 01472–878623
Contact: Frank Smith
Access: By arrangement

An extensive collection of 16mm film, obtained from second-hand dealers, or from the families of the person who shot the films, dating from 1903 onwards. Most of the films have been reprinted in the form of documentaries with magnetic sound tracks and music etc. In some cases the music was composed especially. There is also 16mm material from the Hull area. Negatives from much of the material are also available. Some of the collection has been used by Anglia Television, the BBC, Channel Four, Yorkshire Television and Sky Television.

230 FRED GOODLAND FILM & VIDEO ARCHIVES

Fred Goodland Film and Video Services, 81 Farmilo Road, Leyton, London E17 8JN
☎ 020 8539 4412 (24 hours) **Fax**: 020 8539 4412
Contact: Fred Goodland MBKS
Access: All research enquiries are welcomed but there are no facilities for visitors

These ever expanding, privately owned, archives of film, video and sound recordings are the result of over fifty years of enthusiast collecting and personal restoration work. Mr Goodland joined the film industry as a laboratory technician in 1959. Many years were spent preparing 35mm nitrate negatives and master positives for preservation onto safety stocks. Following years working as a picture and sound editor of film and video documentaries, he now utilises modern restoration facilities in maintaining image and sound materials held in his own collections. Fast access to most material is available on VHS with BITC. Subsequent transfers to professional broadcast formats are personally supervised.

231   FRED GOODLAND SOUND ARCHIVES

Fred Goodland Film and Video Services, 81 Farmilo Road, Leyton, London E17 8JN
☎ 020 8539 4412 (24hours) **Fax**: 020 8539 4412
Contact: Fred Goodland MBKS
Access: There is no visitor access

The sound collection began back in the 1940s and consists of many kinds of recorded material (1900–2005). There are over 10,000 discs and tapes including almost 5,000 original 78s in fine condition. Thousands of examples of twentieth century music include popular tunes, jazz, light orchestral, classical and documentary material. USA 33 1/3 rpm radio transcription discs include popular vocalists, dance music, comedy stars and dramatic programmes.

Fred Goodland Film and Video Archives

Over 100 years of pictures and sound

232 FUTURE HISTORIES – BLACK PERFORMANCE AND CARNIVAL ARCHIVE

Middlesex University, Cat Hill, Barnet EN4 8HT
Email: j.vaknin@mdx.ac.uk
Web: http://www.futurehistories.org.uk
☎ 020 7281 3709
Contact: Judy Vaknin, Middlesex University Archivist

The archive material dates from 1979 to 2000. It consists of the records of the Black Theatre Co-operative, which became the Nitro Theatre Company in 1999. Records include: administrative paperwork of the organisation, such as correspondence, financial documents and minutes of meetings; records related to the production activities of the organisation (theatre, television, choirs, and youth theatre); records related to the development of relationships with external organisations, such as Independent Theatre Council, Theatrical Management Association, and the Arts Council of England, etc. 85% of the collection is paper-based, the rest photographs, and video and audio recordings.

233 G.B. ASSOCIATES

7 Marion Grove, Woodford Green, Essex IG8 9TA
Email: filmview@dial.pipex.com
☎ 020 8504 6340 **Fax**: 020 8505 1850
Contact: Malcolm Billingsley, Administrator
Access: The collection is available to all researchers

Three private archives are the basis of this collection. For the convenience of researchers it is administered from one central point. The collections are still being added to, so there is no cut-off point. Research and viewing fees are payable depending on the amount of material involved. Material may be viewed on VHS cassettes.

234 GALAXY 102.2

1 The Square, 111 Broad Street, Birmingham B15 1AS
Email: martyn.healy@galaxy1022.co.uk
Web: http://www.galaxybirmingham.co.uk
☎ 0121 695 0000 **Fax**: 0121 696 1007
Contact: Martyn Healy, Managing Director
Access: Mon-Fri 08.00–17.30

Music-based radio station. Holds output to meet legal requirement. Other than this keeps no programming unless individual radio DJs want copies of particular shows.

235 GEMINI FM

Hawthorn House, Exeter Business Park, Exeter, Devon EX1 3QS
Email: gavin.marshall@musicradio.com
Web: http://geminifm.musicradio.com
☎ 01392 444444 **Fax**: 01392 444433
Contact: Gavin Marshall, Programme Controller

Music-based radio station. Holds output to meet legal requirement. Also keeps interviews with celebrities.

236 GLASGOW CALEDONIAN UNIVERSITY

Cowcaddens Road, Glasgow G4 0BA
Email: mmi@gcal.ac.uk
Web: http://www.learningservices.gcal.ac.uk/library/resources/av.html
☎ 0141 273 1136 **Fax**: 0141 331 3005
Contact: Marion Miller, Resources Manager
Access: Videos cannot be borrowed by students but can be viewed in the library

The LRC holdings include: videocassettes, slides, microfiches, microfilms and audio tapes.

237 GLASGOW SCHOOL OF ART LIBRARY

167 Renfrew Street, Glasgow G3 6RQ
Email: g.rawson@gsa.ac.uk
Web: http://www.gsa.ac.uk/library
☎ 0141 353 4708
Contact: George Rawson, Subject librarian
Access: viewing and listening facilities (VHS, DVD)

The collection covers art, design and architecture.

238 GLASGOW UNIVERSITY MEDIA GROUP TELEVISION NEWS ARCHIVE

c/o Professor John Eldridge, Department of Sociology, University of Glasgow, Glasgow G12 8RT
Email: g.philo@socsci.gla.ac.uk
Web: http://www.gla.ac.uk/Acad/Sociology/units/media.htm
☎ 0141 339 8855 ext 4684 **Fax**: 0141 330 4925
Contact: Greg Philo
Access: Researchers wishing to make use of the material can apply to Professor Eldridge at the above address

The collection is a product of the research work undertaken by the above Media Group and constitutes the industrial and economic news from all channels for the period January-June 1975. There are also some specimen examples of whole news bulletins from this period. Later research projects on a number of themes have led to the collection of news and current affairs on a range of topics. The collection is ongoing.

239 GLOBAL SCENES

4 St John's Road, Tunbridge Wells TN4 9NP
Email: gordonbutt@mistral.co.uk
Web: http://www.globalscenes.co.uk
☎ 01892 544043 **Fax**: 01892 544043
Contact: B.R. Ware, Proprietor

Global Scenes maintains and loans out promotional travel videos on behalf of twenty tourist boards, covering Europe, the USA and the Far East. The collection is being constantly updated. The company also represents embassies which supply video material for educational purposes. Pollock Collection, covering Kenya, India, Pakistan, Sri Lanka, and other far eastern countries, held along with transparencies.

240 GLYNDEBOURNE FESTIVAL OPERA

Glyndebourne, Lewes, East Sussex BN8 5UU
Email: julia.aries@glyndebourne.com
Web: http://www.glyndebourne.com
☎ 01273 812321 **Fax**: 01273 812783
Contact: Julia Aries, Archivist
Access: By arrangement only, 10.00–16.00 Monday to Friday. Staff are available to assist

The Glyndebourne Archive was established in November 1987. It aims to provide a complete historical record of Glyndebourne Festival Opera, and Glyndebourne Touring Opera, from their beginnings in 1934 and 1968 respectively, up to the present day, for the purposes of research or private study. Now re-housed in newly renovated premises, the Archive contains a large collection of programme books, press cuttings, posters, printed ephemera, audio and video recordings, books and articles, all of which are available for consultation, and there is access to the majority of correspondence files. The collection consists of commercially released videos of Glyndebourne operas from 1972 to date.

241 GMTV LIBRARY SALES

The London Television Centre, Upper Ground, London SE1 9TT
Email: librarysales@gmtv.co.uk
Web: http://www.gm.tv/index.cfm?articleid=1542
☎ 020 7827 7363 / 7366 **Fax**: 020 7827 7043
Contact: Sandra Bamborough, Library Sales Manager
Access: Mon-Fri 09.00–18.00 excluding bank holidays

GMTV is the UK's leading television breakfast show, going out live every weekday morning. GMTV Library Sales has a growing archive of footage from 1993 to the present day, ranging across a broad variety of subjects, including; celebrity/showbiz news, events and interviews, hard news, travel and scenics material, human interest stories, political issues, animal quirkies, bloopers, the royal family, lifestyle items, stock footage of everyday life images and much more.

242 GOLDSMITHS' COMPANY

The Worshipful Company of Goldsmiths, Goldsmiths' Hall, Foster Lane, London EC2V 6BN
Email: the.library@thegoldsmiths.co.uk
Web: http://www.thegoldsmiths.co.uk/thelibrary/films.htm
☎ 020 7606 7010 **Fax**: 020 7606 1511
Contact: Jane Bradley, Librarian
Access: Limited. Material available for loan to institutions and groups but not individuals

Collection of 16mm film and video material of aspects of silversmithing and jewellery trade including assaying and hallmarking for loan to interested groups including institutions, colleges, manufacturers and retailers, etc.

243 GRAMPIAN TELEVISION

Queen's Cross, Aberdeen AB15 4XJ
Email: lyndsay.scatterty@smg.plc.uk
Web: http://www.grampiantv.co.uk
☎ 01224 846551 **Fax**: 01224 846877
Contact: Lyndsay Scatterty, Head of Public Relations
Access: By appointment only

Grampian Television holds a library containing complete programmes, news stories and production rushes. The programmes date back to the 1960s and cover a wide range of documentary, entertainment and sports topics. Production rushes include material shot and edited for Grampian's programmes. News stories are specifically those occurring in the North and North East of Scotland, dating back to the 1960s.

244 GRANADA INTERNATIONAL MEDIA SALES (incorporating CARLTON INTERNATIONAL MEDIA)

48 Leicester Square, London WC2H 7FB
Email: liz.cooper@granadamedia.com
Web: http://www.int.granadamedia.com/sf/international/index.asp
☎ 020 7389 8664,
Contact: Liz Cooper, Sales Executive – Extracts & Non-Theatric

Carlton and Granada have merged and what was Carlton International Media is now controlled through Granada International Sales. Carlton International Media was the largest owner of British made films in the world with a catalogue of over 18,000 hours of programming through the Carlton Film Collection and the Carlton International Programme Catalogue. The collection comprises over 1,700 films from the Rank, Rohauer, Romulus, Korda and ITC libraries.

245 GRANADA MEDIA CLIP SALES – GRANADA TELEVISION

c/o ITN Source, 200 Gray's Inn Road, London WC1X 8XZ
Email: sales@itnsource.com
Web: http://www.itnsource.com
☎ 020 7430 4480 **Fax**: 020 7430 4453
Contact: Kathey Battrick, Research Manager
Access: By arrangement, if there is material available to view. Access for disabled

Material dates back to Granada's first transmission in May 1956. Specialities: anthropology, music (an eclectic collection), political and social documentaries concerning the UK and international affairs, varied arts collection, north west of England material and prestigious drama productions.

ITN Source/Granada

Jean Alexander as Hilda Ogden in CORONATION STREET

246 GRANADA MEDIA CLIP SALES – LONDON WEEKEND TELEVISION

c/o ITN Source, 200 Gray's Inn Road, London WC1X 8XZ
Email: sales@itnsource.com
Web: http://www.itnsource.com
☎ 020 7430 4480 **Fax**: 020 7430 4453
Contact: Kathey Battrick, Research Manager
Access: By arrangement. Access for disabled. Lifts are available

The library contains all of LWT's productions for local and network UK transmission since 1968: drama; entertainment; comedy; game shows; pop music; classical music; opera; ballet; chat shows; magazine shows; documentaries; politics; current affairs; arts. Local programmes cover a rich social history of London including transport, housing, police, news, politics, history and wildlife.

247 GRANADA MEDIA CLIP SALES – TYNE TEES TELEVISION/CHANNEL 3 NORTH EAST

c/o ITN Source, 200 Gray's Inn Road, London WC1X 8XZ
Email: sales@itnsource.com
Web: http://www.itnsource.com
☎ 020 7430 4480 **Fax**: 020 7430 4453
Contact: Kathey Battrick, Research Manager
Access: Enquiries for any particular item can be made to the library

Tyne Tees Television is the ITV contractor for the north east of England. Its collection includes 16mm film of local news from 1960–80 (black and white and colour), hi-band U-matic news tapes from 1980–1992 with current news output on Beta-SP. Local sport, especially football is also well represented. There is also a collection of local documentary (current affairs, farming, arts, etc.), features and drama programmes available from various sources (film, 1-inch, 2-inch and Beta-SP). Some non-TTTV material, both amateur and newsreel footage from c.1912–1960s is held in the company's Flashback Library on Beta and VHS.

248 GRANADA MEDIA CLIP SALES – YORKSHIRE TELEVISION

c/o ITN Source, 200 Gray's Inn Road WC1X 8XZ
Email: sales@itnsource.com
Web: http://www.itnsource.com
Contact: Kathey Battrick, Research Manager
Access: By arrangement only. Staff are available to assist. Access for disabled

Yorkshire Television started broadcasting programmes in the Yorkshire, Humberside, North Lincolnshire and North Derbyshire area in July 1968. The library contains all transmitted programmes and regional news items produced since its inception. The complete holdings amount to over 60,000 film cans and tape spools which increase according to the number of programmes YTV transmits each year. Production departments cover all subject areas (documentaries, drama, education, light entertainment, science, sport, etc.) including FIRST TUESDAY, WHICKER'S WORLD, JIMMY'S, DARLING BUDS OF MAY, HOW WE USED TO LIVE, EMMERDALE, NEW STATESMAN, HEARTBEAT, RISING DAMP, 3D and TOUCH OF FROST.

249 GREENPARK IMAGES

Greenpark Productions Ltd, Illand, Launceston, Cornwall PL15 7LS
Email: info@greenparkimages.co.uk
Web: http://www.greenparkimages.co.uk
☎ 01566 782107 **Fax**: 01566 782127
Contact: Leonore Morphet, Production Assistant
Access: By arrangement only

Greenpark Productions, founded in 1938, has kept much of the shorts, documentary and sponsored footage which it shot between the 1930s and the present. Some silent black and white advertising films date back to the 1920s.

250 GWR FM – SWINDON & WEST WILTSHIRE

1st Floor, Chiseldon House, Stonehill Green, Westlea, Swindon, Wiltshire SN5 7HB
Email: paul.kaye@musicradio.com
Web: http://www.wiltshiresgwrfm.co.uk
☎ 01793 842600 **Fax**: 01793 942602
Contact: Paul Kaye, Programme Controller

Radio station. Holds forty-two days' radio output only to meet legal requirement.

251 GWYNEDD ARCHIVES AND MUSEUMS SERVICE

County Offices, Caernarfon, Gwynedd LL55 1SH
Email: archives.caernarfon@gwynedd.gov.uk
Web: http://tinyurl.co.uk/uw4n
☎ 01286 679095 **Fax**: 01286 679637
Contact: Ann Rhydderch, Principal Archivist and Heritage Officer
Access: Through the National Screen and Sound Archive of Wales (qv)

The collection includes films of railway interest – Penrhyn Railway and Nantlle Tramway, Bangor-Afonwen Railway – film shot on Bardsey Island, c.1948 and a small stock of commercial videos of local or professional interest.

252 HALAS AND BATCHELOR COLLECTION

Southerham House, Southerham, Lewes, East Sussex BN8 6JN
Email: vivien@haba.demon.co.uk
Web: http://www.halasandbatchelor.com
☎ 01273 488 322 **Fax**: 01273 483 060
Contact: Vivien Halas, Director
Access: Halas & Batchelor Collection (for rights issues); the Animation Research Centre, British Film Institute, Imperial War Museum (all qv)

The archive was completed in September 1996 to document the contribution Halas and Batchelor have made to the development of animation in England and Europe. Most of the collection is on permanent loan to the Animation Research Centre (ARC) at the Surrey Institute of Art & Design in Farnham (qv). The collection consists of film, tapes and production materials such as scripts, storyboards and related materials.

The animals read the commandments – cel from ANIMAL FARM (1954)

The Halas & Batchelor Collection Limited

253   HALLAM FM

Radio House, 900 Herries Road, Sheffield S6 1RH
Email: amy.ward@hallamfm.co.uk
Web: http://www.hallamfm.co.uk
☎ 0114 285 3333 **Fax**: 0114 285 3159
Contact: Anthony Gay, Programme Director

Radio station. Holds output to meet legal requirement. All documents regarding radio are kept for five years for financial purposes. News articles are kept for one year.

254   HAMMERSMITH & FULHAM ARCHIVES AND LOCAL HISTORY CENTRE

The Lilla Huset, 191 Talgarth Road, London W6 8BJ
Email: archives@lbhf.gov.uk
Web: http://tinyurl.co.uk/t0jm
☎ 020 8741 5159 **Fax**: 020 8741 4882
Contact: Jane Kimber, Borough Archivist
Access: There are no facilities for viewing films at present. Enquirers should contact the Borough Archivist

The collection is very small and comprises a miscellaneous group of films transferred to the Archives Department from other departments within the council.

255   HARD HAT ARCHIVE

Tandem TV & Film Ltd, Charleston House, 13 High Street, Hemel Hempstead HP1 3AA
Email: hardhat@tandemtv.com
Web: http://www.tandemtv.com
☎ 01442 261576 **Fax**: 01442 219250
Contact: Terry Page,

Hard Hat is the archive branch of Tandem TV & Film Ltd, who are specialist producers to: a) the construction and civil engineering industries; b) charitable organisations working in the developing world. Archives include the Channel Tunnel construction, rolling stock development and current Eurotunnel operations. Crown jewels include time-lapse sequences, aerials, undersea breakthroughs and a moody sunset over the French Eurotunnel tolls. We also hold Costain's construction archive, which goes back to the 1920s and various other marine and costal defence footage.

256 HARVEYS OF BRISTOL

Bristol Record Office, 'B' Bond Warehouse, Smeaton Road, Bristol BS1 6XN
Email: bro@bristol-city.gov.uk
Web: http://www.bristol-city.gov.uk/recordoffice
☎ 0117 922 4224 **Fax**: 0117 922 4236
Contact: John Williams, City Archivist
Access: Tue-Fri, 09.30–16.30 pm, plus: 09.30–19.00 first two Thursdays of
the month and 10.00–16.00 first two Saturdays of the month

Administrative, estate, financial, historical, and personal records of Harveys
including subsidiary companies such as Cockburn Smithes and Co Ltd,
William Perry Wine Merchants Ltd, Stewart and Son of Dundees Ltd and
European companies. The collection contains over two dozen films (16mm)
and video items, including a Spanish sherry promotion video featuring
Orson Welles as well as other advertising materials made for the company.

257 HASTINGS MUSEUM

Johns Place, Bohemia Road, Hastings, East Sussex TN34 1ET
Email: museum@hastings.gov.uk
Web: http://www.hastingsmuseum.org
☎ 01424 781155 **Fax**: 01424 781165
Contact: Teresa Kreutzer-Hodson, Curator
Access: Enquiries to Hastings Museum or South East Film and Video
Archive (qv)

The material has been acquired by donation over the last twenty years. It
includes publicity films passed on by the tourism department and from the
Borough Engineer, 1940s-1970s. There is some footage by Harry Furniss
(1854–1925) and a collection of amateur film from St Nicholas children's
home, also the RAC rally 1956. The video collection includes an amateur
survey of the town centre prior to development, a commissioned feature
on Grey Owl and recorded talks by a local historian. Most of the film of the
collection has now been deposited with the South East Film & Video
Archive (qv) at the University of Brighton.

258 HAWLEY COLLECTION AT
THE UNIVERSITY OF SHEFFIELD

University of Sheffield, ARCUS, The Research School of Archaeology and
Archaeological Science, Westcourt, 2 Mappin Street, Sheffield S1 4DT
Email: hawley.tools@sheffield.ac.uk
Web: http://www.sheffield.ac.uk/hawley
☎ 0114 222 7100 **Fax**: 0114 222 7001
Contact: Joan Unwin, Research Associate

The collection is owned by a charitable trust and stored at the University in
a refurbished building. Its film and video material consists of: a) material shot
by Ken Hawley and other amateurs; b) promotional and publicity materials
made by manufacturers; and c) specially commissioned films recording work
practices, including hours of interviews, filmed by the university television
team. A wide range of subjects is covered by the material, e.g. cutlery making
and tool-making, razor forging, scissors forging, manufacture of silver
spoons, sickle making, thatching and pewter spinning. The collection houses
trade catalogues, artefacts and graphical material relating to the films.

259 HEART 106

City Link, Nottingham NG2 4NG
Email: info@heart106.com
Web: http://www.Heart106.com
☎ 0115 9106 100 **Fax**: 0115 9106 107
Contact: Anna Riggs, Programme Controller

A full-service talk and music station with twenty-four hour news for the East Midlands region. Music policy is 'Adult Contemporary'. Previously known as Century 106. Radio station holding legal requirement plus special news items and programmes which are kept for in-house use, e.g. in compiling end of year review.

260 HILLCROFT COLLEGE

South Bank, Surbiton KT6 6DF
Email: hkent@hillcroft.ac.uk Web: http://www.hillcroft.ac.uk
☎ 020 8399 2688 **Fax**: 020 8390 9171
Contact: Hannah Kent, Learning Resources Manager
Access: Prior permission required

Hillcroft College is the national residential college for women. General collection suited to adult education (women) curriculum.

261 HILLINGDON HERITAGE SERVICE

Central Library, High Street, Uxbridge UB8 1HD
Email: ccotton@hillingdongrid.org
Web: http://www.hillingdon.gov.uk/central/tourism/hlhs.php#arc
☎ 01895 250702 **Fax**: 01895 239794
Contact: Carolynne Cotton, Local Heritage Coordinator
Access: By appointment. Access for disabled

Films made for local councils in Hillingdon area since 1950s. Some earlier material donated by members of the public on local events since 1935.

Heart 106

262 HISPANIC AND LUSO BRAZILIAN COUNCIL

Canning House Library, 2 Belgrave Square, London SW1X 8PJ
Email: ibarranco@canninghouse.com Web: http://www.canninghouse.com
☎ 020 7235 2303 **Fax**: 020 7235 3587
Contact: Irene Barranco, Librarian
Access: Entry is free

Canning House represents a unique combination of business, educational and cultural interests which share a belief in the growing importance of the Spanish and Portuguese speaking world, acting as a forum for politicians, business people, academics and artists with the common aim of promoting links between the UK, Spain, Portugal and Latin America. The video collection includes 250 titles on Latin America, Spain and Portugal.

263 HISTORY OF ADVERTISING TRUST ARCHIVE

HAT House, 12 Raveningham Centre, Raveningham, Norwich,
Norfolk NR14 6NU
Email: archive@hatads.demon.co.uk
Web: http://www.hatads.org.uk
☎ 01508 548623 **Fax**: 01508–548478
Contact: Margaret Rose, General Manager & Head of Research
Access: By appointment only, Mon-Fri 09.00–17.00. Closed 25 December – 2 January. Staff are available to assist

Founded in 1976 as an archive and educational research organisation. With material dating from 1800 to last month's commercials, the collection contains some two million items: advertising product (print, television, radio); market research; media and public relations; historical archives of advertisers, advertising organisations and agencies. Information and image service; academic and other researchers by appointment. It also holds advertising statistics, market research and trends, industry journals and a large library of over 4,000 books. HAT Archive contains over 10,000 UK television commercials dating back to the first advertisements broadcast in 1955.

264 HOME 1079-FM

The Old Stableblock, Brewery Drive, Lockwood Park, Huddersfield,
West Yorkshire HD1 3UR
Email: studio@home1079.com
Web: http://www.home1079.com
☎ 01484 321 107 **Fax**: 01484 311 107
Contact: John Harding, Programme Controller

107.9 Home FM is part of the The Local Radio Company, which owns twenty-seven stations within the UK. We broadcast twenty-four hours a day from our studios in Huddersfield. We hold sixty days' radio output to meet legal requirement. We have recently begun archiving news items, local interest programmes and interviews.

265 HORNIMAN MUSEUM

100 London Road, Forest Hill, South London SE23 3PQ
Email: enquiry@horniman.ac.uk
Web: http://www.horniman.ac.uk
☎ 020 8699 1872 **Fax**: 020 8291 5506
Contact: Collections Manager
Access: Open daily 10.30–17.30

The museum holds in total some 350,000 objects and related items. The holdings include video footage and stills collections. The museum opened in 1901 and was dedicated with the surrounding land as a free gift to the people of London by Frederick Horniman for ever for their recreation instruction and enjoyment. The original collections comprised natural history specimens, cultural artefacts and musical instruments. Over the last 100 years the museum has added significantly to the original bequest with Horniman's original collections comprising only 10% of current ethnography and musical instrument holdings.

266 HOT UNDER THE COLLAR

PO Box 141, Tatsfield, Westerham TN16 2XA
Email: pam@hutc.co.uk
Web: http://www.hutc.co.uk/footage-archive.htm
☎ 01959 575779
Contact: Pam Harris

A collection of library pictures and unusual clips, covering an array of sports, a vast range of British and 'eccentric' footage as well as wildlife/nature and stock shots from around the world.

267 HOUSE OF LORDS RECORD OFFICE (THE PARLIAMENTARY ARCHIVES)

House of Lords, London SW1A 0PW
Email: hlro@parliament.uk
Web: http://www.parliament.uk
☎ 020 7219 3074 **Fax**: 020 7219 2570
Access: Initial enquiries about all aspects of access (including charges, copyright and viewing) should be made to the Clerk of the Records

Audio-visual material consists mainly of: (i) film and videotape of the House of Lords Closed Circuit TV Experiment, 1968. A small amount of material connected with the public televising of both Houses is held, but enquiries about material from the Chambers should be directed to the Head of the Parliamentary Recording Unit (tel: 020 7219 5512); (ii) films and videocassettes from the Central Office of Information, broadcasters and others, of material connected with Parliament. The earliest dates from the late 1940s; (iii) films and videocassettes in deposits received by the Record Office; (iv) films and videocassettes of events on the Parliamentary Estate.

268 HOVE MUSEUM AND ART GALLERY

19 New Church Road, Hove, East Sussex BN3 4AB
Email: Suzanne.Plumb@brighton-hove.gov.uk
Web: http://www.hove.virtualmuseum.info
☎ 01273 292831 **Fax**: 01273 292827
Contact: Suzie Plumb, Curator of Toys, Film and Media
Access: Mon-Fri, 1000–1700, by prior appointment

In 1997 Hove Museum and Art Gallery purchased the portion of the Barnes Collection relating to the South East. This collection reflects the important role the region played in the birth of the film industry. Local film pioneers George Albert Smith, James Williamson, William Friese-Greene, Esme Collings, Alfred Darling and Charles Urban were individually responsible for technical, artistic and commercial practices which underpin today's film industry. The collection is made up of early apparatus, photographs, programmes, rare publications and other ephemera relating to these pioneers.

269 HTV WALES (ITV WALES)

The Television Centre, Culverhouse Cross, Cardiff CF5 6XJ
Email: angela.jones@itvwales.com
Web: http://www.itvregions.com/wales
☎ 029 2059 0177 ext 731 **Fax**: 020 2059 7183
Contact: Angela Jones, Librarian
Access: Research is undertaken by library staff only

The library holds all transmitted material from Wales and the West ITV franchise area from 1958 to the present day.

270 HULL CITY ARCHIVES

79 Lowgate, Kingston Upon Hull HU1 1HN
Email: city.archives@hullcc.gov.uk
Web: http://www.hullcc.gov.uk/libraries
☎ 01482–615102 **Fax**: 01482–613051
Contact: Carol Tanner, Senior Archivist
Access: By appointment, Mon-Thu 09.00–12.15 and 13.30–16.45. Closed Wednesday afternoon and Friday. Access for disabled

Films acquired by donation or made by, or for, Council departments.

271 HUNTLEY FILM ARCHIVES

191 Wardour Street, London W1F 8ZE
Email: films@huntleyarchives.com
Web: http://www.huntleyarchives.com
☎ 020 7287 8000 **Fax**: 020 7287 8001
Contact: Amanda Huntley, Archivist
Access: By appointment. Access for disabled. Ramp access

Founded by John Huntley in the mid-1940s, the collection is centred on a catalogue of documentary films. The emphasis has always been on maintaining a film-based archive, mainly 35mm and 16mm, although the Archive holds large numbers of Standard and Super 8mm films as well as 9.5mm. The footage can also be supplied to researchers and commercial users on their chosen tape or disc format. Viewing copies are available on VHS. The collections are increasing by about 1,000 titles per month. The bulk of the holdings are loosely, social history: the life of the ordinary person world-wide – work, domestic lives, transport, food, living conditions, leisure, education, traditions and religion.

272 I.A. RECORDINGS VIDEO ARCHIVE

PO Box 476, Telford, Shropshire TF7 4RB
Email: info@iarecordings.org
Web: http://www.iarecordings.org
Contact: Kelvin Lake, Director
Access: No facilities for visitors, so copies of material are sent to researchers for a nominal fee

Original material recorded by the self-funded, voluntary organisation I.A. Recordings. From 1982 onwards it covers British industrial activity past and present, e.g. remains of old industries and intensive recording of existing industries, many of which were threatened and have since closed. The work is funded by the sale of compilations and productions based on the archive material. I.A. Recordings maintain an extensive web site at www.iarecordings.org with general information about industrial archaeology and details of archive recordings including an A-Z subject index.

273 IMAGE BANK LONDON (GETTY IMAGES)

101 Bayham Street, London NW1 0AG
Email: sales@gettyimages.co.uk
Web: http://www.gettyimages.com
☎ 0800 376 7977 **Fax**: 020 7391 9123
Access: By arrangement

The Image Bank is a leader in rights-protected film, offering more than 10,000 hours of creatively shot, conceptually driven footage. The collection offers instant access to the work of more than 200 cinematographers, including Academy Award winners and some of the industry's hottest commercial directors. Image Bank Film provides 35mm footage covering landscapes, contemporary lifestyles, industry, wildlife, and sports. Time-lapse sequences are also included. *Note: Image Bank is now controlled by Getty Images (qv).*

274 IMAGE DIGGERS VIDEO

Image Diggers, 618b Finchley Road, London NW11 7RR
Email: ziph@macunlimited.net
Web: http://imagediggers.netfirms.com
☎ 020 8455 4564 **Fax**: 020 8455 4564
Contact: Neil Hornick, Director
Access: No access for disabled. Collection is stored on second floor and there is no lift

An on-going collection of VHS tapes, mostly recorded off-air since 1986 for personal/academic use. They are available for research and academic purposes only and also include a substantial collection of stills material (photographs, 35mm slides, postcards, magazine cuttings, etc.), plus sheet music, ephemera, books, magazines and newspaper clippings. The range of videos covers cinema, theatre, literature, television; with numerous full-length movies and television plays, anthologies of clips from musicals, and animation shorts. There is also an audiocassette collection, covering drama, radio features, popular music (from all countries and periods, and personal performances and interviews).

275 IMAGES OF EMPIRE

British Empire and Commonwealth Museum, Clock Tower Yard, Temple Meads Bristol BS1 6QH
Email: anna.motrescu@empiremuseum.co.uk
Web: http://www.empiremuseum.co.uk
☎ 0117 925 4980, Ext 217 or 0117 929 3851 **Fax**: 0117 9254983
Contact: Anna Motrescu, Film Research Consultant
Access: By arrangement only

The moving image collection consists of 16mm, 9.5mm, and standard and super 8mm cinefilm and currently contains over 1,000 titles, comprising over 450 hours of footage dating from the early 1920s onwards. They reflect the life of indigenous people, colonial settlers and government officials. Amateur filmmakers in Africa and India shot the majority of the films. They include footage of industrial and commercial activities, agriculture and forestry, momentous political events and conflicts, sporting and ceremonial occasions, holiday and travel footage, and family footage; government produced information and travel films, commercial documentary and news film, and television material.

276 IMAGES OF WAR

31a Regents Park Road, Camden, London NW1 7TL
Email: derek@dircon.co.uk
Web: http://www.warfootage.com
☎ 0207 267 9198 **Fax**: 0207 8852
Contact: Derek Blades, Director
Access: None

The War Archive is a collection of original footage from both the First and Second World Wars and the preceding periods. The archive consists of over 200 hours of footage from Great Britain, Germany, Russia, the USA and Japan, and covers all aspects of these important periods in recent history. To compliment the 1900–1945 library, the new archive covers the Korean War, the War in Vietnam, the invasion of Grenada, The first Gulf War, and the conflict with Libya plus numerous bushfire wars.

277 IMPERIAL WAR MUSEUM DEPARTMENT OF DOCUMENTS

Imperial War Museum, Lambeth Road, London SE1 6HZ
Email: docs@iwm.org.uk
Web: http://collections.iwm.org.uk/server.php?show=nav.00g002
☎ 020 7416 5220 **Fax**: 020 7416 5374
Contact: R.W.A. Suddaby, Keeper
Access: Prior appointment requested

The Department's holdings in relation to film include the papers of Lord Bernstein, the Film Adviser to the Ministry of Information during the Second World War, which consist of official correspondence and reports containing much detail on the production and distribution of films made under their aegis, and the public reaction to them. Also held are a small number of film and television scripts, a few collections of papers of individuals who served with the Film Units of the armed forces, and within the holdings occasional references can also be found in personal diaries and letters to film-going since 1914.

278 IMPERIAL WAR MUSEUM DEPARTMENT OF EXHIBITS AND FIREARMS

Imperial War Museum, Lambeth Road, London SE1 6HZ
Email: exfire@iwm.org.uk
Web: http://www.iwm.org.uk
☎ 020 7416 5270 **Fax**: 020 7416 5374
Contact: David Penn, Keeper

The Department of Exhibits and Firearms collections cover three-dimensional objects, including artillery, vehicles and small craft, uniforms, medals and insignia, weapons, flags, communications equipment, models, medical equipment, cameras, toys, currency and ephemera.

Imperial War Museum

Second Lieutenant Bertram Brooks-Carrington, British official cameraman, with a Moy and Bastie camera and a German anti-tank rifle, September 1917 (IWM neg. Q111226)

279 IMPERIAL WAR MUSEUM FILM AND VIDEO ARCHIVE

Lambeth Road, London SE1 6HZ
Email: PSargent@iwm.org.uk
Web: www.iwmcollections.org.uk
☎ 020 7416 5291/5292 **Fax**: 020 7416 5299
Contact: Paul Sargent, Deputy Keeper
Access: As a public archive it is open to anyone with a bone fide interest.
Opening hours: Mon-Fri 10.00–17.00, by appointment only. There is a lift
for researchers with disabilities

The Imperial War Museum's Film and Video Archive represents a wide and
diverse range of material from overt propaganda, documentaries, unedited
combat film, instructional films, dramatisations and technological and
public information films to travelogues, newsreels and amateur films shot
by both civilians and service personnel. There are also large collections of
film shot by both civilian organisations during the Second World War, such
as the London Fire Brigade, British Transport Films (encompassing the then
privately owned railways) and the Ford Motor Company. Two substantial
collections from NATO and the UN in the former Yugoslavia are also held.

280 IMPERIAL WAR MUSEUM SOUND ARCHIVE

Imperial War Museum, Lambeth Road, London SE1 6HZ
Email: sound@iwm.org.uk
Web: http://collections.iwm.org.uk/server/show/nav.00g007
☎ 020 7416 5360 **Fax**: 020 7416 5379
Contact: Margaret Brooks, Keeper
Access: Mon-Fri, 10.00–17.00

The Sound Archive was established in 1972 as the national centre for audio
recordings relating to twentieth century conflict involving Britain and the
Commonwealth. It was a pioneer of oral history and these personal
reminiscences dominate the collection, now over 83 million feet (33,200
hours) and growing at the rate of about 3.5 million feet per annum.
Historic recordings include considerable wartime BBC material, examples of
the German High Command's communiqués, ENSA and ORBS light
entertainment from the 1940s, daily recordings of the Nuremberg war
crimes trials, poetry readings, NATO briefings, relevant recent radio
programmes and a very wide range of sound effects.

281 INDEPENDENT TELEVISION COMMISSION LIBRARY

c/o bfi National Library, 21 Stephen Street, London W1T 1LN
Email: http://www.bfi.org.uk/help/contact.php
Web: http://www.bfi.org.uk/nationallibrary/index.html
☎ 020 7255 1444 (switchboard) **Fax**: 020 7436 2338
Access: Reading room hours: Mon (10.30–17.30), Tue/Thu (10.30–20.00),
Wed (13.00–20.00), Fri (10.30–17.30)

The strength of the library is in the special television industry collections, such
as the archives, audience reports collection, ITV/Channel 4 programme and
company publicity, as well as the more traditional stock of books, journals,
official publications, annual reports and press cuttings. The ITC archive
collections are important and increasingly well used. The ITC operates the
thirty-year rule for public records. Some records may be made available
earlier, depending on the nature of the records and purpose of research.
*Note: since the closure of the ITC and its absorption within OFCOM, the ITC
library has become part of the collection of the bfi National Library (qv).*

282 INDEX STOCK SHOTS

33 Greenwood Place, Kentish Town, London NW5 ILD
Email: info@indexstockshots.com
Web: http://www.indexstockshots.com
Contact: Philip Hinds, Manager
Access: Available to professionals working in all areas of film, television and associated production

Index Stock Shots is primarily a source of 35mm colour film footage, a proportion of which continues to be shot specially for library use. The company also maintains an archival collection dating back to the early 1900s. The contemporary collection includes: aerials, aviation, cities, landmarks, lifestyle, time-lapse, wildlife. The historical archive features: aircraft, industry, motor racing, Third World, travel.

283 INGENIOUS TV

13 Clayton Grove, Bracknell, Berks RG12 2PT
Email: mail@ingenioustv.co.uk
Web: http://www.ingenioustv.co.uk
☎ 01344 483748

Holds a wide range of stock footage, including images of cities, countryside, motorsports, underwater, wildlife and more but our speciality is the weather. We have many hours of weather related footage, from rain to tornadoes. The company constantly adding more top quality footage, much of which is 16:9 and High Definition. The extensive and expanding library of severe weather events contains dramatic images of thunderstorms, tornadoes, hurricanes, lightning, hail storms, supercells, blizzards and many other severe weather events. Most has been filmed using PAL broadcast equipment. Camera crews are in the field all year round bringing in a constant flow of spectacular pictures.

284 INSTITUTE OF AMATEUR CINEMATOGRAPHERS – IAC LIBRARY

24c West Street, Epsom KT18 7RJ
Email: info@theiac.org.uk
Web: http://www.fvi.org.uk/central/filmlibrary.htm
☎ 01372–739672 **Fax**: 01372–739672
Contact: Janet Smith, Administrative Secretary
Access: No access

Largest collection of amateur films dating back to 1932. Films are only available for hire. The Library includes major award winning titles from the IAC International Competition, the Ten Best Competition, the BAVA Competition, Film Making, North v South, Guernsey Lily and other competitions. It is growing every year. Entertaining and informative programmes of films and videos may be hired by individuals or clubs in the UK, and the library is also a valuable source of information for students. Of the hundreds of cine films in the library many have already been transferred to tape. Cine films can still be hired by arrangement, subject to their condition.

285 INSTITUTE OF COMMUNICATION STUDIES

University of Leeds, Roger Stevens Building, Level 5, Leeds LS2 9JT
Email: p.m.taylor@leeds.ac.uk
Web: http://ics.leeds.ac.uk
☎ 0113 233 5829 **Fax**: 0113 233 5820
Contact: Philip M. Taylor, Director
Access: By prior permission, Mon-Fri, 09.00–17.00

The ICS audio-visual holdings comprise individual film and television collections of staff and three principal archives: the Gulf War Archive dating from January 1991 to March 1991 – twenty-four hour coverage of all UK terrestrial coverage, plus CNN, Sky, TR1, GRD, RAI, Moscow; the ESRC Electoral Archive – television coverage of all UK general elections (embracing the periods from when they were called to when they were completed) from 1971; the Kosovo War Archive dating from March to May 1999 – coverage by BBC World, RAI, TFI and GRD twenty-four hour coverage.

286 INSTITUTE OF CONTEMPORARY HISTORY & WIENER LIBRARY

4 Devonshire Street, London W1N 2BH
Email: kat@wienerlibrary.co.uk
Web: http://www.wienerlibrary.co.uk
☎ 020 7636 7247 **Fax**: 020 7436 6428
Contact: Katharina Hübschmann, Senior Librarian
Access: Mon-Fri 10.00–17.30. By letter of introduction (readers needing to use the Library for any length of time should become members)

Private library. One of the leading research centres on European history since World War I, with special reference to the era of totalitarianism and to Jewish affairs. Founded by Dr Alfred Wiener in Amsterdam in 1933, it holds material that is not available elsewhere. Books, periodicals, press archives, documents, pamphlets, leaflets, brochures and videos. Much of the material can be consulted on microfilm. The video collection – Oskar Joseph Video Collection – began in approximately 1989.

287 INSTITUTION OF CIVIL ENGINEERS

1 Great George Street, London SW1P 3AA
Email: claire.delgal@ice.org.uk
Web: http://www.ice.org.uk
☎ 020 7665 2258 **Fax**: 020 7976 7610
Contact: Claire Delgal, Assistant Librarian
Access: Prior permission required

The ICE library is the biggest resource in civil engineering in the world. It has a massive collection of books, periodicals, videos and historic photographs. Many of its books can be borrowed by members. Copies of papers can be supplied from the 10,000 journals and conference held at ICE. Audio-visual holdings include approximately 470 videos (all films have been transferred on to video) and 8,000 slides. The library also has photographs, sound recordings and 35mm slides. Much of this is unique material or requires special storage conditions, and is therefore accessible via the archives.

288 INSTITUTION OF ELECTRICAL ENGINEERS

Savoy Place, London WC2R 0BL
Email: archives@iee.org
Web: http://www.iee.org/theiee/research/archives
☎ 020 7344 8407 **Fax**: 020 7497 3557
Contact: Anne Locker, Senior Archivist
Access: By prior appointment only

The archives of the Institution of Electrical Engineers contain films of scientists who were awarded the Faraday Medal or an honorary fellowship by the Institution, talking about their work. There are also occasional film and video items in other collections, relating to various technological developments such as radar and transatlantic cables. These, however, are not numerous.

289 INSTITUTO CERVANTES

326–330 Deansgate, Manchester M3 4FN
Email: bibman@cervantes.es
Web: http://manchester.cervantes.es
☎ 0161 661 4210 **Fax**: 0161 661 4203
Contact: Jose Maria Fernandez, Librarian
Access: Mon-Thu, 1200–1945. Fri, 11.00–15.30

The library of the Instituto Cervantes in Manchester is a resource centre specialising in the Spanish language and the culture of the Spanish-speaking world. Its collection includes approximately 500 Spanish and Latin-American films on video and about 100 videos of Spanish television drama.

290 INTERNATIONAL PARALYMPIC COMMITTEE VIDEO TAPE ARCHIVE

Input Media, The Production Centre, 191a Askew Road, London W12 9AX
Email: dw@input-video.co.uk
Web: http://www.inputmedia.tv
☎ 020 8740 5222 **Fax**: 020 8746 0811
Contact: David Wood, Managing Director

The International Paralympic Committee (IPC) has appointed London-based television production and facility company, The Input Video Group, to market and manage its expanding video tape archive. The archive contains paralympic footage from a number of events dating back to Barcelona 1992 and more recently Nagano 1998, Sydney 2000 and Salt Lake City 2002. Input Video will market material for both broadcast and commercial use as well as handling requests from associations and their members affiliated to the IPC.

291 INVICTA FM

Radio House, John Wilson Business Park, Whitstable, Kent CT5 3QX
Email: info@invictaradio.co.uk
Web: http://www.invictafm.com
☎ 01227 772004 **Fax**: 01227 771560
Contact: Craig Boddy, Programme Director

Invicta FM became part of GCap Media PLC on 9 May 2005. Holds forty-two days' output to meet legal requirement.

292 IRONBRIDGE GORGE MUSEUM TRUST FILM AND VIDEO COLLECTION

The Ironbridge Gorge Museum Trust, The Wharfage, Ironbridge, Telford, Shropshire TF8 7AW
Email: library@ironbridge.org.uk
Web: http://www.ironbridge.org.uk
☎ 01952–432141 **Fax**: 01952–432237
Contact: John Powell, Librarian
Access: Mon-Fri 09.00–17.00, by appointment only. Staff are available to assist. Access for disabled – ramps and toilet

The museum has built up an extensive research library, which is based in the Long Warehouse, adjacent to the Coalbrookdale Museum of Iron. Collections include material on the history of the iron industry, bridge building, civil engineering, brick and tile manufacture, coal mining, the pottery and porcelain industries, railways, canals, the social history of the East Shropshire Coalfield etc. Special collections include the Elton Collection, strong on images of industry. Some archive material is also held relating to the Darby family and local firms such as the Coalbrookdale Company, the Lilleshall Company, the Horsehay Company and Maw & Co.

293 ISKRA TELEVISION

Iskra Centre, 26–28 Wendell Road, London W12 9RT
Email: sales@iskratv.com
Web: http://www.iskratv.com
☎ 020 8749 7711 **Fax**: 020 8740 7774
Contact: Andrew Sparke, Managing Director

Based in London and with contacts in the Russia and CIS, across Europe, America and in Australia and the Pacific Rim, ISKRA TV has proved a unique resource for programme makers worldwide. Across boundaries of state, politics, cost and even taste, this youthful international resource serves programme makers in nearly every market. With its base firmly rooted in clips and programme extracts, ISKRA now represents some of the most amazing and daring programming and has recently undertaken representation of formats – some of the most challenging and remarkable formats in the market today.

294 ISLE OF WIGHT RADIO

Dodnor Park, Newport, Isle of Wight PO30 5XE
Email: mail@iwradio.co.uk
Web: http://www.iwradio.co.uk
☎ 01983 822557 **Fax**: 01983 822109
Contact: Tom Stroud, Programme Controller

Radio station. Holds forty-two days' output to meet legal requirement. Keeps an archive of news items for one year for own use. Chat shows are recorded at presenters' discretion.

295 ISLES OF SCILLY MUSEUM AUDIO VISUAL ARCHIVE

IOS Museum, Church Street, St. Mary's, Isles of Scilly
Email: info@iosmuseum.org
Web: http://www.iosmuseum.org
☎ 01720 422 337
Contact: Amandas Martin

In order to preserve some link with the rich Scillonian past, the Museum has a comprehensive collection of oral history videos and has attempted to record day-to-day life. These are the memories of ordinary folk whom we have encouraged to look back at life as they remember it. Over time the local community interest has grown and islanders have come forward with photographs and film from their own archives. Areas covered include wrecks, diving, shipbuilding, occupations, creatures, birds, lighthouses and communication; farming and the flower industry, flora and fauna; wars, transport and family life. The information amassed is stored on audio cassettes and video tapes.

296 ITN SOURCE

Independent Television News Ltd, 200 Gray's Inn Road, London WC1X 8XZ
Email: sales@itnsource.com
Web: http://www.itnsource.com
☎ 020 7430 4480 **Fax**: 020 7430 4453
Contact: Matthew Keene
Access: By arrangement. Access for disabled

Worldwide news events from 1955 to the present day and a wealth of associated feature footage, rushes and clip reels. News information service, cuttings and reference. Also exclusive representation of British Pathe, the SURCAT Survival catalogue, Channel 4 clip sales (including Film Four productions) as well as Granada Media (all qv). Represents the entire newsreel archive (from 1896) of the Reuters Television Library (qv). Other collections include: Airtime Television News, Tinseltown Entertainment, Sam Silver Films, Open Media and the Images of War archive. *Note: previously known as ITN Archive.*

297 ITV ANGLIA

[Footage inquiries via ITN Source] Anglia Television Ltd, Anglia House, Norwich NR1 3JG
Email: sales@itnsource.com
Web: http://www.itvregions.com/anglia
☎ 020 7430 4480 **Fax**: 020 7430 4453
Contact: Matthew Keene
Access: By arrangement. Access for disabled

All material is of Anglia TV news stories, features and documentaries. Selected black and white film retained between 1959 and 1969. Thereafter all transmitted material retained. The source of news material is mainly Anglia TV Region (East Anglia). Documentaries and features of wider interest. Over 7,500 transmitted film items are taken in each year. News, current affairs, magazine items, local interest, farming and local crafts. Multi-subject features and documentaries. See also ITN Source.

298 ITV MERIDIAN

Unit 1–3 Brookway, Hambridge Lane, Newbury, Berkshire RG14 5UZ
Email: library.newbury@granadamedia.com
Web: http://www.itvregions.com/meridian
☎ 01635 522322 **Fax**: 01635 30922
Contact: Gary Billingham, Librarian
Access: By arrangement only. Access for disabled

Meridian took over the ITV franchise of the South and South East of England from Television South (TVS) in 1993. The library generally holds material from that date. Newbury produces the local ITV news for the Thames Valley and North Hampshire. The collection is strong on transport, especially Heathrow, M3, M4 and M25 (West) motorways, Newbury bypass, various regional railway companies, e.g. South West Trains, Thames Trains, Great Western and Connex South Central.

299 IWC MEDIA

St George's Studio, 93–97 St George's Road, Glasgow G3 6JA
Email: Jonathan.Warne@iwcmedia.co.uk
Web: http://www.iwcmedia.co.uk/index.html
☎ 020 7317 2230 **Fax**: 020 7317 2231
Contact: Jonathan Warne, Head of Production

Formed in May 2004, IWC Media grew out of two of the UK's most respected independent television production companies, Ideal World and Wark Clements.

300 JAZZ FM

26–27 Castlereagh Street, London W1H 5DJ
Email:info@jazzfm.com
Web: http://www.jazzfm.com
☎ 020 7706 4100 **Fax**: 020 7723 9742

Radio station. Jazz FM keeps some live sessions and recordings of shows with musicians. It has a large private music library. It does not maintain a news archive as its news is supplied by ITN.

301 JEWISH MUSEUM

The Sternberg Centre, 80 East End Road, Finchley, London N3 2SY
Email: enquiries@jewishmuseum.org.uk
Web: http://www.jewishmuseum.org.uk
☎ 020 8349 1143 **Fax**: 020 8343 2162
Contact: Sarah Jillings, Curator
Access: By arrangement only. Partial access for disabled

The Museum was founded in 1983. It has a small film/video collection relating to the growth and development of the Jewish community in London.

302 THE JOHN GRIERSON ARCHIVE

University of Stirling, Stirling, Scotland FK9 4LA
Email: g.w.willis@stir.ac.uk
Web: http://www.library.stir.ac.uk/spcoll/media/grierson.html
☎ 01786 467236
Contact: Gordon Willis
Access: By appointment

The John Grierson Archive provides a comprehensive account of the career of one of the key figures in the history of documentary filmmaking. The archive includes notebooks; correspondence; scripts and production notes; notes and transcripts of talks and lectures; articles; papers relating to various organisations for which Grierson worked including the Empire Marketing Board, GPO Film Unit, Imperial Relations Trust, National Film Board of Canada, Group 3, UNESCO, Films of Scotland Committee and Scottish Television. The archive also includes a collection of periodicals and c.500 photographs of Grierson and stills from various films.

303 JOHN RYLANDS UNIVERSITY LIBRARY OF MANCHESTER

Manchester University, 150 Deansgate, Manchester M3 3EH
Email: special.collections@manchester.ac.uk
Web: http://www.library.manchester.ac.uk
☎ 0161 275 3764 **Fax**: 0161 275 6505
Contact: Stella Butler, Head of Special Collections
Access: By prior arrangement for those outside the university

Various collections relating to British film and theatre. These include the Robert Donat archive (new acquisition, uncatalogued); the papers of Sir William Mansfield Cooper, former Manchester University Vice-Chancellor, re setting up of schools television in the early days of ITV (provisional typescript catalogue); and the archive of Basil Dean containing papers relating to Paramount Famous Lasky Corporation, RKO, Associated Talking Pictures Ltd and London Film Productions, 1928–1944.

304 JOURNEYMAN PICTURES

75A Walton Road, East Molesey, Surrey KT8 0DP
Email: info@journeyman.tv
Web: http://www.journeyman.tv
☎ 0208 941 9994 **Fax**: 0208 941 9899
Contact: Sam Goss

Journeyman Pictures is London's leading independent distributor of topical news features, documentaries and footage. Independent television producer Mark Stucke founded the company, one of the first to make the new co-production formula work for the independent sector. We market the films of many renowned independents and broadcasters and have represented, Australia's ABC, Channel 4, Germany's ZDF, Denmark's DR, Sweden's SVT and many more.

305 JUICE 107.2

170 North Street, Brighton BN1 1EA
Email: info@juicebrighton.com
Web: http://www.juicebrighton.com
☎ 01273 386107 **Fax**: 01273 273107
Contact: Marcus Patrick, Programme Controller

The radio station holds forty-two days' output to meet legal requirement. Its news team keeps scripts for this period as well.

306 JUNCTION11

RUSU Whiteknights, Reading RG6 6AZ
Email: junction11@1287am.com
Web: http://www.1287am.com
☎ 0118 986 5152
Contact: Jeff Wiley, Station Manager

Broadcasting twenty-four hours a day from studios in the Students' Union on Whiteknights Campus on 1287AM and live online, serving 15,000 students at the University of Reading with new and alternative tunes, as well as hip-hop, rock, dance, jazz, and regular news updates. Junction11 has been broadcasting for five years to students at the University of Reading from studios on Bulmershe Campus (1998–2002) and Whiteknights Campus (2002-present).

307 KICK FM

The Studios, 42 Bone Lane, Newbury, Berkshire RG14 5SD
Email: mail@kickfm.com
Web: http://www.kickfm.co.uk
☎ 01635)841600 **Fax**: 01635 841010
Contact: James O'Neil, Programme director

Kick FM covers some 200 square miles of West Berkshire, including Newbury, Thatcham, Hungerford and surrounding villages.

308 KING'S CROSS ORAL HISTORY PROJECT

King's Cross Community Development Trust, 82–84 Cromer Street,
King's Cross, London WC1H 8DG
Email: LeslieM@kings-cross.org.uk
Web: http://www.kingscrossvoices.org.uk
☎ 0207 713 7959 **Fax**: 0207 883 9268
Contact: Lesley McCartney, Project Coordinator

The King's Cross Voices Oral History Project is managed through King's Cross Community Development Trust (KCCDT). Working with community members and local partners, this project seeks to record people's memories and unique life experiences of the King's Cross area. Oral history is a vital tool in building our understanding of the recent past and is ideally suited to uncovering and sharing the hidden histories of the many diverse communities within King's Cross at this pivotal moment in its history.

309 KING'S FUND INFORMATION AND LIBRARY

11–13 Cavendish Square, London W1G 0AN
Email: library@kingsfund.org.uk
Web: http://www.kingsfund.org.uk
☎ 020 7307 2568 **Fax**: 020 7307 2805
Contact: Library Enquiry Desk,
Access: Reference library only. Videos may not be borrowed. Opening
hours – Mon-Fri, 09.30–17.30; except Wed, 11.00–17.30. Sat, 09.30–17.00

The King's Fund is an independent health charity which aims to stimulate
good practice in service provision and to influence health policy. The
Library collection covers service development and management,
particularly in health and social care settings.

310 KIRKLEES COMMUNITY HISTORY SERVICE

The Stables, Tolson Museum, Ravensknowle Park, Wakefield Road,
Huddersfield, West Yorkshire HD5 8DJ
Email: community.history.service@kirklees.gov.uk
Web: http://www.kirklees.gov.uk/news/enewsletters/history.asp
☎ 01484 223800 **Fax**: 01484 223805
Contact: Brian Haigh, Community History Manager
Access: Material is not available for loan and access is by appointment
only via Local Studies Library

Films are acquired from private individuals, local cine clubs and from
Council departments. The collection includes over 120 titles relating to the
locality which includes Huddersfield, Batley, Dewsbury, Mirfield, the Spen
Valley and the Holme and Colne Valleys. Topics covered include transport,
industry, historic events and celebrations. Acquisitions are made as they
become available.

311 KISS 100 FM

Mappin House, 4 Winsley Street, London W1N 7AR
Email: Julieanne.Toole@kiss100.com
Web: http://www.kiss100.com
☎ 020 7436 1515
Contact: Julieanne Toole, Sales/Commercial Director

Kiss FM holds programmes on video of the launch of the radio station, a
private collection of dance music, a large selection of interviews on DAT in
particular with London-based DJs and black musicians based abroad. In
addition, Kiss is planning to undertake a large archiving project.

312 KM-FM 106

9 St George's Place, Canterbury, Kent CT1 1UU
Email: mhuston@kmfm106.co.uk
Web: http://www.kmfm.co.uk
☎ 01233 895 824
Contact: Mike Huston, sales

KMFM 106 provides a mix of music, news and entertainment specifically tailored to the needs of the local potential audience of 118,000 people. The station began serving listeners in Canterbury, Whitstable and Herne Bay in September 1997 as 106CTFM. With the Kent Messenger Group's massive newsgathering operation behind it, the renamed KMFM 106 is the area's fastest source of local news and information. Holds material to meet legal requirement. Some unlogged news material is kept for in-house use only.

313 LAST REFUGE

Batch Farm, Panborough, Nr. Wells, Somerset BA5 1PN
Email: adrianwarren@lastrefuge.co.uk
Web: http://lastrefuge.co.uk
☎ 01934 712556 **Fax**: 01934 712556
Contact: Adrian Warren

The Last Refuge Stock Film Library offers footage on wildlife, environmental, aerial, time lapse, anthropological, weather and starscapes subjects, from Africa, South America and the UK. Available now are aerial shots inside and outside the spectacular Ngorongoro Crater; Mount Lengai; and the Serengeti. We also have detailed coverage of the lost world tepuis of Venezuela in South America, featuring Angel Falls, rain forest and many more. We have extensive aerial footage of cloudscapes, and a growing index for British landscapes. Wildlife footage, from East Africa, includes behaviour of serval, cheetah, lion, wildebeest, zebra, elephant, buffalo, vultures and many others.

314 LAUDER COLLEGE

Halbeath, Dunfermline, Fife KY11 8DY
Email: tmcmaster@lauder.ac.uk
Web: http://www.lauder.ac.uk
☎ 01383 845155 **Fax**: 01383 845001
Contact: Tom McMaster, Library Manager
Access: Mon-Thu, 08.30–21.00. Fri, 08.30–17.00. Sat, 10.00–13.00.

The College does not teach film and television studies specifically but there is some coverage in media studies generally.

315 LDTV PRODUCTIONS VIDEO FOOTAGE LIBRARY

PO Box 1, Mitcheldean, Glos GL17 0YT
Email: liam@ldtv.co.uk
Web: http://www.ldtvarchive.co.uk
☎ 01594 542233 **Fax**: 01594 544441
Contact: Liam Dale

An extensive range of footage covering many topics available for broadcast, commercial and educational use including documentaries, school and sell-thru formats. Specialists in education and leisure programmes. Over many years of high production value documentary making we have acquired a substantial archive of old materials as well as the acquisition of twentieth and twenty-first century location footage. Ranging from 16mm cine from the early part of the twentieth century through the High Band SP and Betacam SP eras, into the twenty-first century with DVCam footage in both 4:3 and 16:9 format, PAL or NTSC, the material is now available to documentary makers around the world.

316 LEEDS ANIMATION WORKSHOP

45 Bayswater Row, Leeds LS8 5LF
Email: law@leedsanimation.demon.co.uk
Web: http://www.leedsanimation.demon.co.uk
☎ 0113–248 4997 **Fax**: 0113–248 4997
Contact: Milena Dragic, Co-worker
Access: Mon-Thu 10.00–16.00, by prior arrangement. Staff are available to assist

Leeds Animation Workshop is a not-for-profit, cooperative company, which produces and distributes animated films and videos on social and educational issues. Holds twenty-five years of animation produced by the Workshop on social issues. The organisation began in 1976 as a group of women friends who came together to make a film about the need for pre-school childcare. After completing WHO NEEDS NURSERIES? WE DO! the group was formally established in 1978 as Leeds Animation Workshop. Since the mid-1980s the Workshop has been run by five women, who between them carry out all stages of the production process, from initial research to final distribution.

Leeds Animation Workshop

NOT TOO YOUNG TO GRIEVE (2005)

317 LEEDS INDUSTRIAL MUSEUM

Armley Mills, Canal Road, Armley, Leeds LS12 2QF
Email: armley.mills@leeds.gov.uk
Web: http://www.leeds.gov.uk/armleymills
☎ 0113 263 7861 **Fax**: 0113 263 7861
Contact: Martin Gresswell, Curator
Access: By arrangement

Armley Mills, once the world's largest woollen mill, is now an award-winning industrial museum. Exhibits dating from the eighteenth and nineteenth centuries show the history of textiles, clothing and engine and locomotive manufacture in the area. The museum also illustrates the history of cinema projections, including the first moving pictures taken in Leeds, as well as 1920s silent movies. During the regular 'working weekends' several exhibits are operated including water wheels, a steam engine and the great spinning ÚÚmules'. Film holdings are video recordings of 1888 films by Louis Le Prince, who experimented in Leeds, plus newsreels. Approximately 100 16mm films – mainly technical/training.

318 LEEDS METROPOLITAN UNIVERSITY

Woodhouse Lane, Leeds, West Yorkshire LS1 3HE
Email: s.mcdowell@leedsmet.ac.uk
Web: http://www.lmu.ac.uk
☎ 0113 283 2600 ext 3382 **Fax**: 0113 283 3123
Contact: Sandra McDowell, Learning Adviser
Access: External users, reference only. 09.00–17.00 only in vacations

The collection supports postgraduate courses in film production and scriptwriting and undergraduate courses in animation.

319 LEEDS REFERENCE LIBRARY

Central Library, Municipal Buildings, Leeds LS1 3AB
Email: pat.egan@leeds.gov.uk
Web: http://www.leeds.gov.uk
☎ 0113–247 8283 **Fax**: 0113–247 8268
Contact: Pat Egan, Central Collections Manager
Access: There are no viewing facilities on the premises

Items donated to the local studies library.

320 LEEDS UNIVERSITY

Library & Learning Resources, West Bretton, Wakefield,
West Yorkshire WF4 4LG
Email: a.j.cobb@leeds.ac.uk
Web: http://www.bretton.ac.uk/library
☎ 0113 343 9146 **Fax**: 0113 34 35561
Contact: Audrey Cobb, Academic Services, Bretton Hall Campus Library
Access: Mon, Wed, Thu, 08.30–20.30; Tue, 09.00–20.30; Sat, 09.00–17.00.
Vacations: Mon-Fri, 08.30–17.00

Film and television are not taught as subjects in their own right. Materials are purchased on these subjects to support the BA (Hons) English, Drama and Education courses. Two special collections are housed in the National Arts Education Archive (qv) and the National Media Education Archive. *Note: formerly Bretton Hall.*

321 LEEDS UNIVERSITY TELEVISION

Media Services, University of Leeds, Leeds LS2 9JT
Email: mediaservices@leeds.ac.uk
Web: http://mediant.leeds.ac.uk/vtcatalogue
☎ 0113 3432660 **Fax**: 0113 343 2669
Contact: Sally Popplewell, Sales Supervisor

University of Leeds Media Services exists to originate and edit moving images for teaching and learning in higher education. As appropriate, it also makes these available to other institutions, usually through the sale of copies of programmes, occasionally through the sale of individual sequences. It is not an archiving body, nor does it purchase materials except to contribute to its own programmes. It is not therefore generally of interest to researchers and is seldom used by them.

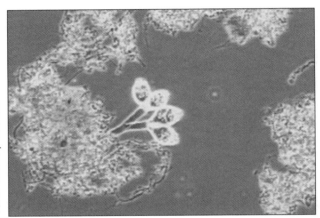

Leeds University Television

322 LEEDS UNIVERSITY/SSRC ELECTORAL BROADCASTING ARCHIVE & GULF WAR ARCHIVE

The Edward Boyle Library, Audio-Visual Section, University of Leeds, Leeds LS2 9JT
Email: a.j.depledge@leeds.ac.uk
Web: http://www.leeds.ac.uk/library
☎ 0113 233 5544 **Fax**: 0113 233 5539
Contact: Alison Depledge
Access: Through prior written application made to the Director of the Institute of Communication Studies, University of Leeds, Leeds LS2 9JT, tel: 0113 233 5800 **Fax**: 0113 233 5808. These recordings are kept for the purpose of study and research and are not for general educational purposes

The Archive originated with pre-war party films and newsreel speeches and television output from the February 1974 General Election campaign. Thereafter, grants and special licensing arrangements permitted comprehensive recording (selectively also of radio). Gifts from the Labour Party and others allowed the addition of programmes transmitted only in the London area. The Gulf War Archive consists of the round-the-clock output of BBC1 and 2, ITV, Channel 4, BSkyB and CNN, plus peak-time output of BR2 (Germany), TF1 (France), RA1 (Italy) and Gorizout (Russia), from day two of the hostilities. The Gulf War Archive is kept in the Institute of Communication Studies (qv), University of Leeds.

323 LEICESTER SOUND

6 Dominus Way, Meridian Business Park, Leicester LE19 1RP
Email: dean.roberts@musicradio.com
Web: http://leicestersound.musicradio.com/homepage.jsp
☎ 0116 256 1300 **Fax**: 0116 256 1303
Contact: Dean Roberts, News Editor

Radio station. All news output and scripts are kept for one year.

324 LEICESTERSHIRE FILM ARCHIVE

17 Kingsway, Leicester LE3 2JL
☎ 0116 289 0531 **Fax**: 0116 289 0531
Contact: Rob Foxon, Director
Access: Public film shows via the annual Bygone Leicester Moving Image
Picture Show. Film shows are also presented at the invitation of groups
and societies, schools and colleges

The Leicestershire Film Archive provides a clear identity for the Leicester
and Leicestershire collection of the TUA Film Archive (qv). It comprises
mainly amateur shot material, much of which has been blown up from
9.5mm originals, showing aspects of life in the county from around 1930 to
the present day. Film records include the 1932 Pageant of Leicester, the
1935 Silver Jubilee celebrations in Leicester, coronation parades, Royal
visits, local industry, transport, farming and country life in an area much
neglected by film-makers. There are also documentary and other
productions featuring Leicester and Leicestershire. The Archive has also
produced a small number of videos of local interest. Films can be made
available for film, video and television use, subject to copyright clearance.

325 LEICESTERSHIRE MUSEUMS SERVICE FILM ARCHIVE

Record Office for Leicestershire, Leicester & Rutland, Long Street, Wigston
Magna, Leicester LE18 2AH
Email: museums@leics.gov.uk
Web: http://www.leics.gov.uk/index/community/museums/record_
office.htm
☎ 0116–257 1080 **Fax**: 0116–257 1120
Contact: Robin Jenkins, Keeper of Archives
Access: Staff can conduct preliminary search to establish viability of
personal visit. Videos only available, except by special arrangement.
Access for disabled

The collection has been accumulated by various sections of Leicestershire
Museums, Arts & Records Service. The majority has been transferred to the
Record Office section since c.1968. The technology section at the Snibston
Discovery Park collects and copies film for its own holdings.

326 LEO & MANDY DICKINSON ADVENTURE ARCHIVE

Fudge Cottage, Dalditch Lane, Budleigh Salterton EX9 7AH
Email: info@adventurearchive.com
Web: http://www.adventurearchive.com
☎ 01395 446242 **Fax**: 01454 327686
Contact: Mandy Dickinson
Access: By arrangement. Access for disabled.

Adventure films from the last twenty-five years, including eighty completed films. Material covers rock climbing, mountaineering, ballooning, skydiving, parachuting, cave diving, caving, ice climbing, kayaking, white water rafting and wildlife in Africa. Interviews with explorers and adventurers and weather shots including time-lapse.

327 LEWISHAM LOCAL STUDIES & ARCHIVES

Lewisham Library, 199/201 Lewisham High Street, London SE13 6LG
Email: local.studies@lewisham.gov.uk
Web: http://www.lewisham.gov.uk
☎ 020 8297 0682 **Fax**: 020 8297 1169
Contact: A. J. Wait, Archivist
Access: Limited, by arrangement only

The Local History Centre collects all types of material relating to the history of Lewisham. It was established in 1960. The films held are two short length films on local events (copies supplied by *bfi*), a collection of 8mm films (forty-nine reels) of local events (particularly boys' clubs), holidays, etc., produced by Mr P. D. Dannatt, a local resident c.1937–1957, and four other 16mm films of local events. The centre also possesses four VHS videos of local plaque unveiling ceremonies and other local events.

328 LIDDELL HART CENTRE FOR MILITARY ARCHIVES

King's College London, Strand, London WC2R 2LS
Email: archives.web@kcl.ac.uk
Web: http://www.kcl.ac.uk/lhcma/home.htm
☎ 020 7873 2015 **Fax**: 020 7873 2760
Contact: Patricia Methven, Director of Archive Services
Access: By prior arrangement, including disabled. Researchers are advised to discuss their requirements with staff of the Centre in advance of a visit. All first-time readers except the staff and students of King's College London to produce a letter of introduction from a third party

The Liddell Hart Centre for Military Archives is principally an archive of personal papers of senior twentieth century British defence personnel, but it includes some film and video material, particularly research material created by television documentary production companies. The centre was founded in 1964, and the first accession of video material from a production company was received in 1989.

329 LIDDLE COLLECTION

Brotherton Library, University of Leeds, Leeds LS2 9JT
Email: r.d.davies@leeds.ac.uk
Web: http://www.leeds.ac.uk/library/spcoll/liddle
☎ 0113 343 3289 **Fax**: 0113 343 5561
Contact: Richard D Davies,
Access: Mon-Thu, 09.00–19.00. Fri, 09.30–19.00. Sat, 10.00–13.00 (vacation etc, variations). Access for disabled

Founded thirty years ago to collect, preserve and make available for research all forms of evidence of personal experience of World War I. *Soldiers in Khaki 1914–1918: British and Commonwealth Experience on the Western Front* is a CD-ROM containing images, text and sound clips compiled from materials in the Liddle Collection. It is available for use in the Special Collections Reading Room on request.

330 LIGHT HOUSE

The Chubb Buildings, Fryer Street, Wolverhampton WV1 1HT
Email: info@light-house.co.uk
Web: http://www.light-house.co.uk
☎ 01902 716055 **Fax**: 01902 717143
Contact: Frank Challenger, Chief Executive
Access: Library is open at specified times and by appointment

Light House houses the region's only dedicated media reference library which comprises a comprehensive selection of film, television and media books, journals, periodicals, industry guides, study packs and film directories. In addition, there is a collection of over 3,000 film portfolios for the 1960s to the present and a collection of film posters. There is also a somewhat eclectic collection of programmes on video tape (various formats) which comprises the majority of the Arts Council's films about art and related matters, independent productions from the region, documentaries on local issues, and programmes made on the Light House's training courses.

Light House video production

331 LINCOLNSHIRE & HUMBERSIDE FILM ARCHIVE

PO Box 140, Boston, Lincolnshire PE22 0ZP
Email: info@lincsfilm.co.uk
Web: http://www.lincsfilm.co.uk
☎ 01775 725631 **Fax**: 01205 751031
Contact: Peter Ryde, Archivist (for general enquiries and details of title contents)
Access: Staff are available to assist

Formed in 1986 to locate, preserve and make accessible film on all aspects of life and work in historic Lincolnshire (Lincolnshire and South Humberside), especially pre-1960, though later items are not refused. Professional access: viewing on or off the premises (VHS only). Material selected by client supplied on Beta-SP or DVCAM. Charges for facilities and rights available on request. Public access: viewing on premises only, except by special arrangement. Viewings on projected video arranged off premises for societies, etc. Numerous compilations on VHS or DVD available for public sale.

Lincolnshire & Humberside Film Archive

Opening the new Municipal buildings, Boston 1904

332 LINDSAY ANDERSON COLLECTION

Stirling University Library, Stirling, Scotland FK9 4LA
Email: karl.magee@stir.ac.uk
Web: http://www.stir.ac.uk
☎ 01786 466619 **Fax**: 01786 466866
Contact: Karl Magee, Archivist

Correspondence, production notes, scripts, photographs, promotional material and press cuttings relating to all of Lindsay Anderson's films including THIS SPORTING LIFE, IF...., O LUCKY MAN and BRITANNIA HOSPITAL and forty of his theatre productions; correspondence and scripts relating to unrealised film projects; general correspondence (1970s-90s); correspondence and minutes of Royal Court Theatre; correspondence with the British Film Institute (1974–94); correspondence with the BBC (1977–94); personal diaries and working papers; theatre and film posters; scrapbooks; awards and memorabilia. The collection also includes Anderson's personal library of books (mainly on film and theatre).

333 LIVERPOOL JOHN MOORES UNIVERSITY

Aldham Robarts Learning Resource Centre, Mount Pleasant,
Liverpool L3 5UZ
Email: leasstre@livjm.ac.uk
Web: http://cwis.livjm.ac.uk/lea/info/arts/dva.htm
☎ 0151 231 3104 **Fax**: 0151 707 1307
Contact: Sheena Streather, Senior Information Officer
Access: Recorded items only available for loan by members of the
University. May be viewed on premises on production of HE ID at
Learning & Information Services' discretion

The content of the collection reflects its primary purpose, to support
courses in Media and Cultural Studies, Screen Studies, Drama, Musical
Theatre, Literature and Cultural History, and Languages. Comprises mainly
feature films of which there are over 400, including contemporary popular,
plus foreign, classic and silent films; some television series and sample
episodes of series, including drama, comedy, BBC Shakespeare productions,
televised plays and musicals; also a few documentary and factual videos on
these subject areas, including Pathe newsreels and other historical footage,
theatrical techniques and film and television production training videos.

334 LIVERPOOL RECORD OFFICE & LOCAL HISTORY DEPARTMENT

Liverpool Libraries & Information Services, Central Library, William Brown
Street, Liverpool L3 8EW
Email: recoffice.central.library@liverpool.gov.uk
Web: http://archive.liverpool.gov.uk
☎ 0151 233 5817 **Fax**: 0151 233 5886
Contact: David Stoker, Manager, Record Office

We subscribe to the North West Sound Archive (qv) and originals will
normally be transferred there for storage, preservation and cataloguing.
Copies for access will be made for consultation in Liverpool Record Office,
as at present we have no specialist facilities for the storage and preservation
of sound archives. At present, investigation and consultation are being
carried out into the various options for providing a film archive service
including the possibility of a service from the North West Film Archive (qv).
We will accept film archives if they are in danger of being lost or destroyed,
although at the moment we have no specialist facilities for film archives.

335 LLANELLI PUBLIC LIBRARY

Vaughan Street, Llanelli, Wales SA15 3AS
Email: MJewell@carmarthenshire.gov.uk
☎ 01554 773538 **Fax**: 01554 750125
Contact: Mark Jewell, Llanelli Regional Librarian
Access: Tue, Wed, 09.30–18.00. Mon, Thu, Fri, 09.30–17.00. Sat,
09.30–17.00. Bona fide researchers should write to the Llanelli Regional
Librarian

The collection is primarily being developed as a film archive of Llanelli for
posterity as a part of the extensive collection of conventional local
material. Started in 1957 when a camera was purchased to record the
making of tinplate by hand in Llanelli, before the last of a large number of
mills, which had operated for almost a century, closed. This arose out of a
decision to collect film (movie and still) as local history archive material.

336 LONDON CANAL MUSEUM

12/13 New Wharf Road, London N1 9RT
Email: val@canalmuseum.org.uk
Web: http://www.canalmuseum.org.uk
☎ 020 7713 0836 **Fax**: 020 7689 6679
Contact: Val Pindar, Librarian/Archivist/Curatorial

The museum's collections include objects related to canals, social history, industry, and art. The museum also includes archives which contain papers, maps, photographs, audio and video tapes. The London Canal Museum is participating in an Inland Waterways Heritage Network project to collect recordings of people talking about the old days of the inland waterways. Our particular interest is in the canals of the London area although we would also include, as part of a national project, someone living in London whose memories related to another part of the UK.

London Canal Museum

Traditional canal painting displayed at the museum

337 LONDON FILM ARCHIVE

78 Mildmay Park, Newington Green, London N1 4PR
Email: info@londonfilmarchive.org
Web: http://www.londonfilmarchive.org
☎ 020 7923 4074 **Fax**: 020 7241 4929
Contact: Robert Dewar, Archivist
Access: By appointment

In 1996 the trustees of the London Film Archive became aware that Greater London had no film repository and local film focus of its own. Accordingly, the Archive was constituted as a charity. As with most other regional archives, the aims of the Trust are to collect, preserve and make accessible moving image materials that document life in the city, since the first films of 1895 to the present day. With an emphasis on documentary films, both professional and amateur, the archive attempts to illustrate the social and economic changes of the capital, as well as encapsulating London's position as a major centre for the sciences and the arts.

338 LONDON FIRE BRIGADE

Room 520, Hampton House, 20 Albert Embankment, London SE1 7SD
Email: libraryservices@london-fire.gov.uk
Web: http://www.london-fire.gov.uk
☎ 020 7587 6340 **Fax**: **Fax**: 020 7587 6086
Contact: Gail Parlane, Library Resources Centre Manager
Access: Limited, by appointment only

Wartime material is held at the Imperial War Museum. The National Film and Television Archive (qv) is holding material of the 1950s. The IWM's and NFTVA's respective charges apply for duplicating and searching. London Fire Brigade charges apply for copyright.

339 LONDON JEWISH CULTURAL CENTRE FILM DEPARTMENT ARCHIVE

Ivy House, 94–96 North End Road, London NW11 7HU
Email: admin@ljcc.org.uk
Web: http://www.ljcc.org.uk
☎ 020 8457 5000 **Fax**: 020 8455 5024
Contact: Stuart Libson, Archive Curator
Access: Mon-Fri 09.30–17.30. Access for disabled

The collection started in 1994 to fulfil the educational requirements of this Institute for the study of Jewish history and culture.

340 LONDON METROPOLITAN UNIVERSITY, HOLLOWAY ROAD LEARNING CENTRE

236–250 Holloway Road, London N7 6PP
Email: c.partridge@londonmet.ac.uk
Web: http://www.londonmet.ac.uk/services/sas/library-services
☎ 020 7133 2720
Contact: Crispin Partridge, Film Librarian

The university offers a broad range of undergraduate film modules, some television modules and postgraduate courses in the digital moving image. The collection, based at two site libraries, reflects these demands.

341 LONDON NEWS NETWORK LIBRARY

c/o ITN Source, Independent Television News Ltd, 200 Gray's Inn Road, London WC1X 8XZ
Email: sales@itnsource.com
Web: http://www.itnsource.com
☎ 020 7430 4480 **Fax**: 020 7430 44563
Contact: ITN Source
Access: 09.00–17.30. Staff are available to assist

London News Network was established by Carlton and LWT in 1992 as a seven-day-a-week regional news, features and sport service for London. The library holds transmitted stories and selected rushes/stock shots in a wide range of subject areas including the arts, crime, events, leisure, locations, social issues, and sport. The collection covers the period from autumn 1992 to date. Also some access to LWT news material 1990–1992. We also have an extensive collection of worldwide location footage e.g. Cuba, Jerusalem, Maldives and many others. Absorbed by ITN in 2004.

342 LONDON'S TRANSPORT MUSEUM

39 Wellington Street, London WC2E 7BB
Email: simon.murphy@ltmuseum.co.uk
Web: http://www.ltmuseum.co.uk
☎ 020 7379 6344 **Fax**: 020 7565 7252
Contact: Simon Murphy, Assistant Curator, Film & Photo Collections
Access: By appointment, Mon-Tue only

The collection includes films and videos made for/by London's public transport companies and their predecessors for a general audience, plus some more specialist training and instructional films. The earliest film is a Metropolitan Railway production of 1905. There are silent films of the 1920s but the bulk of the collection dates from the post Second World War era up to the late 1960s – the heyday of Edgar Anstey's British Transport Films, productions rich in social history and 'behind the scenes' detail. The Museum also holds for reference only a small selection of relevant off-air programmes, etc, and video copies of feature films featuring London Transport subjects.

343 LUTON CENTRAL LIBRARY FILM AND SOUND ARCHIVE

Luton Central Library, St Georges Square, Luton LU1 2NG
Email: referencelibrary@luton.gov.uk
Web: http://www.luton.gov.uk/internet/Education_and_learning/Libraries/Archives.htm
☎ 01582 547420 **Fax**: 01582 547450
Contact: Mark Stubbs, Team Librarian/Information Services
Access: By arrangement only. Access for disabled

The Luton Central Library Film Archive consists of video copies of films donated by the Luton Borough Council archives and by individuals. The collection includes films of local interest, locally produced European travelogues from the 1960s and miscellaneous material. Much of the material was taken by amateurs. The originals are now located at the East Anglian Film Archive (qv).

344 LUX DISTRIBUTION

3rd Floor, 18 Shacklewell Lane, Dalston, London E8 2EZ
Email: mike@lux.org.uk
Web: http://www.lux.org.uk
☎ 020 7503 3980 **Fax**: 20 7503 1606
Contact: Mike Sperlinger, Head of Distribution
Access: By arrangement only

Lux Distribution is Europe's largest distributor of artists' film and video, with an expanding collection of over 3,500 titles. Alongside the large collection of British works are key pieces from the United States, Latin America, Japan and Australia. All works in the catalogue are available for hire to museums, galleries, cinemas and colleges worldwide, and Lux can offer curatorial support and educational advice for those seeking access to the collection. Much of the collection is available for purchase by museums and educational institutions, and Lux operates as a sales agent for broadcast, internet and video publishing.

Lux distribution

345 MAGIC 105.4

Mappin House, 4 Winsley Street, London W1W 8HF
Web: http://www.magic1054.co.uk
☎ 020 7504 7000 **Fax**: 020 7504 78001
Contact: Trevor White, Programme Manager

The Magic radio stations, owned by EMAP Radio Ltd, share large private music collections.

346 MAGIC 1161

Commercial Road, Hull, Yorkshire HU1 2SG
Email: reception@magic1161.co.uk
Web: http://www.magic1161.com
☎ 01482 325141 **Fax**: 08546 382967
Contact: Mike Bawden, Programme Director

The radio station holds forty-two days' output only to meet legal requirement. The Magic stations, owned by EMAP Radio Ltd, share large private music collections.

347 MAGIC 1170

Radio House, Yales Crescent, Thornaby, Stockton-on-tees,
Cleveland TS17 6AA
Email: catherine.ellington@magicradio.com
Web: http://www.magic1170.com
☎ 01642 888222 **Fax**: 01642 868288
Contact: Catherine Ellington

The radio station holds forty-two days' output only to meet legal requirement. The Magic stations, owned by EMAP Radio Ltd, share large private music collections.

348 MAGIC 999

St Paul's Square, Preston, Lancashire PR1 1YE
Email: Andy.Stratton@rockfm.co.uk
Web: http://www.magic999.com
☎ 01772 556301 **Fax**: 01772 201917
Contact: Rob Kelly, Programme Director

The radio station holds forty-two days' output only to meet legal requirement. The Magic stations, owned by EMAP Radio Ltd, share large private music collections.

349 MAGIC AM

Radio House, 900 Herries Road, Sheffield, South Yorks S6 1RH
Email: adrian@magicam.co.uk
Web: http://www.magicam.co.uk
☎ 0114 285 2121 **Fax**: 0114 285 3159
Contact: Adrian Serle, Programme Director

The radio station holds forty-two days' output only to meet legal requirement. The Magic stations, owned by EMAP Radio Ltd, share large private music collections.

350 MANCHESTER ARTS LIBRARY

Central Library, St Peter's Square, Manchester M2 5PD
Email: arts@libraries.manchester.gov.uk
Web: http://www.manchester.gov.uk/libraries/central/arts/index.htm
☎ 0161 234 1974 **Fax**: 0161 234 1961
Contact: Jeannette Canavan, Arts Coordinator
Access: Mon-Thu, 13.00–20.00, Fri-Sat, 13.00–17.00. Proof of ID (name and address) may be required for some material

The library service in Manchester was established in 1852. The Arts Library was established as a separate department in the Central Library in 1960, covering the performing arts as one of its subject areas. There is a full set of *Radio Times* as well as other journals. The Manchester Theatre Collection contains *The Manchester Programme of Entertainment and Leisure* (1897–1934), a weekly journal which records the early days of cinema in Manchester.

351 MANCHESTER JEWISH MUSEUM

190 Cheetham Hill Road, Manchester M8 8LW
Email: don@manchesterjewishmuseum.com
Web: http://www.manchesterjewishmuseum.com
☎ 0161 834 9879 **Fax**: 0161 832 7353
Contact: Don Rainger, Administrator
Access: 10.30–16.00 Mo -Thu, Friday by appointment only. Closed
Saturdays. Open Sundays 11.00–17.00

The museum opened in 1984 and the holdings include photographs and an
oral history collection, including recollections of the anti-Jewish pogroms
from the beginning of the twentieth century. There are also video
recordings of events and weddings.

352 MANCHESTER'S MAGIC 1152

Castle Quay, Castlefield, Manchester M15 4PR
Email: simon.lowe@magicradio.com
Web: http://www.magicmanchester.co.uk
☎ 0161 288 5000 **Fax**: 0161 288 5001
Contact: Simon Lowe, Head of Magic 1152

The radio station holds forty-two days' output to meet legal requirement.
The Magic stations, owned by EMAP Radio Ltd, share large private music
collections.

Emao Radio Ltd

Spencer Macdonald and Mike Maguire of MACDONALD AND
MAGUIRE AT BREAKFAST

353 MANSFIELD 103.2

Samuel Brunts Way, Mansfield, Nottinghamshire NG18 2AH
Email: info@mansfield103.co.uk
Web: http://www.mansfield103.co.uk
☎ 01623 646666 **Fax**: 01623 660606
Contact: Katie Trinder, Programme Director

The radio station holds forty-two days' output only to meet legal requirement.

354 MANX NATIONAL HERITAGE

Manx National Heritage Library, Kingswood Grove, Douglas IM1 3LY
Email: library@mnh.gov.im
Web: http://www.gov.im/mnh
☎ 01624–648000 **Fax**: 01624–648001
Contact: R.M.C. Sims, Archivist
Access: Mon-Sat, 10.00–17.00. Access for disabled

The collection was begun in the late 1980s to provide a home for film and video material relating to the Isle of Man.

355 MANX RADIO

PO Box 1368, Douglas, Isle of Man IM99 1SW
Email: chriswilliams@manxradio.com
Web: http://www.manxradio.com
☎ 01624 682 600 **Fax**: 01624 682 604
Contact: Chris Williams, Programme Director

Manx Radio first went on air in June 1964, long before commercial radio became part of everyday life in Britain. This was made possible because the Isle of Man has internal self-government: it is a Crown Dependency and is not part of the United Kingdom. But Manx Radio did need a licence from the UK authorities and this was eventually agreed to. Manx Radio transmits from four sites around the Isle of Man. For technical reasons they each use a different frequency. One site, located at Foxdale, broadcasts on the AM (Medium Wave) band and covers the whole Island. Three sites, however, are needed for Island-wide coverage on the FM (VHF) band.

356 MARINE BIO-IMAGES

We are based aboard Maria, a 42' gaff rigged ketch currently near Exeter, South West England
Email: colin-m@marine-bio-images.com
Web: http://www.marine-bio-images.com
☎ 01392 275839,
Contact: Colin Munro

Several hundred hours of high quality video footage are held, shot in DV format, 4:3 aspect ratio. The volume and range of the library is increasing all the time.

357 MARYLEBONE CRICKET CLUB (MCC) LIBRARY

Lord's Cricket Ground, St John's Wood, London NW8 8QN
Email: museum@mcc.org.uk
Web: http://www.lords.org/mcc/about-mcc
☎ 020 7616 8656 **Fax**: 020 7616 8659
Contact: Stephen Green, Curator
Access: MCC gives access in special cases but does not have the facilities at the moment to make the collection readily available

A small collection of cricket films and videos.

358 MASSEY FERGUSON, AUDIOVISUAL SERVICES

Massey Ferguson Ltd, Audio Visual Services, B8, Banner Lane, Coventry, Warwickshire CV4 9GF
Email: uksales@uk.agcocorp.com
Web: http://www.masseyferguson.com/agco/mf/uk/home.htm
☎ 024 7669 4400 **Fax**: 024 7685 2495
Contact: Ivor L. Clarke, Audiovisual Specialist
Access: Limited, by arrangement only

The film library holds 16mm films, dating from 1945 to 1985, most of which are from Massey-Harris-Ferguson, with many on the original Ferguson TE20 tractor and implements. The video library holds U-matic and Betacam-SP video, from 1984 to the present, on all of the company's products.

359 MAVERICK ENTERPRISES

31 Dobree Avenue, London NW10 2AD
Email: ghizela@totalise.co.uk
☎ 020 8459 3858 **Fax**: 020 8459 3895
Contact: Ghizela Rowe, Director
Access: Available

The collection was set up as a specialist music film library and concentrates on the 1960s up to the late 1970s, with live concert and promo material on numerous British and American rock/pop/soul/punk acts. The 1960s footage also covers a wide range of personalities in interviews and at work, with many visual profiles on the leading pop artists such as Hockney, etc. Films on the Columbia state riots, surfing and the Indyatlantic motor races, etc. from the same area are also held. Also includes all the material of the 1960s' filmmaker, Peter Whitehead, and Peter Clifton's pre-1978 material, before the demise of Notting Hill Studios, an active London-based production company.

360 MCKINNON FILMS

17 Norfolk Road, London NW8 6HG
Email: mckinnonfilms@dial.pipex.com
Web: http://www.mckinnonfilms.com
☎ 020 7449 0329 **Fax**: 020 7483 2319
Contact: Anna James
Access: By prior permission

The film archive contains more than 200 hours of a diverse range of natural history, environmental and cultural footage of the Arabian Peninsula and surrounding seas. It includes a comprehensive collection of Arabian wildlife species and locations accumulated during the production of over seventy films in the past twenty-five years: Major series such as Channel 4's THE ARABS, BBC/Discovery's ARABIA: SAND SEA AND SKY and National Geographic's TIDES OF WAR and RETURN OF THE UNICORN. The collection also contains new Gulf cities and the oil and chemical industries. Material was shot on 16mm, super 16mm film and Digibeta. All is available on Beta SP and Digibeta and cleared for copyright.

361 MEDIA AND COMMUNICATION RESEARCH ARCHIVE (MACRA)

Loughborough University, Ashby Road, Loughborough,
Leicestershire LE11 3TU
Email: p.b.riley-jordan@lboro.ac.uk
Web: http://www.lboro.ac.uk/departments/ss/MACRA.htm
☎ 01509 223877 **Fax**: 01509 223944
Contact: Peter Riley-Jordan, Technician
Access: By prior permission

The purpose of MACRA is to resource research and teaching in the mass media. The main holding within MACRA is an extensive newspaper archive, consisting of the national broadsheets from 1998 to date, and the national tabloids from 1992 to date. It also houses a special collection of historic newspapers. Its digital collection of media materials consists of all broadsheet newspapers (plus *Daily Mail/Mail on Sunday*) on CD-ROM from 1992 to date. Special collections of media broadcast materials include political media coverage from 1992–1993; and broadcast news coverage on BBC 1, ITV and Channel 4 from 1996–1998.

362 MEDIA ARCHIVE FOR CENTRAL ENGLAND (MACE)

1 Salisbury Road, University of Leicester, Leicester LE1 7RQ
Contact: James Patterson, Director
Access: Mon-Fri 09.00-17.00, by appointment. Note: The Archive moved from Nottingham to Leicester as this book was going to press. For full contact and access details, see the Media Archive of Central England's entry on the Researcher's Guide Online, http://www.bufvc.ac.uk/rgo.

The Archive was established in 2000 as the English regional moving image archive covering the East and West Midlands. The collections of film, videotape and digital media span the entire era of moving image production from the mid-1890s to the present day. The material held is primarily non-fiction and is a mix of amateur and professional. The largest single holding at the time of writing is the regional news and programme collection of ATV and Central Television, spanning a period from 1956 to about 1990. The television collections number some 24,000 reels of film or videocassettes representing news inserts for the entire period and regional programmes principally from the 1980s.

363 MEDISCAN

2nd Floor Patman House, 23–27 Electric Parade, George Lane, South Woodford, London E18 2LS
Email: info@mediscan.co.uk
Web: http://www.mediscan.co.uk
☎ 0871 220 5256 **Fax**: 020 8989 7795
Contact: Anthony Bright, Production Director

Mediscan provides medical media to the home user, publisher or professional. The collection consists of over one million images and 2,000 hours of broadcast quality film footage. The medical television unit offers a comprehensive range of solutions from digital to analogue, filming on location or in a studio environment. If a QuickTime movie is required to be embedded in a PowerPoint presentation or a series of digital frames lifted from video, we have the expertise and the technology to do it. Our design team has a wealth of experience in all types of illustrative work and the production of scientific posters and exhibitions.

364 MERCURY 102.7 FM

PO Box 1, Crawley, West Sussex RH10 2SE
Email: dan.jennings@musicradio.com
Web: http://mercuryfm.musicradio.com/homepage.jsp
☎ 01293 519161 **Fax**: 01293 565663
Contact: Dan Jennings, Programme Manager/Controller

Radio station. Holds output to meet legal requirement.

365 MERIDIAN BROADCASTING

ITV Meridian, Solent Business Park, Whiteley, Hampshire PO15 7PA
Email: paul.johnson.meridian@granadamedia.com
Web: http://www.itvregions.com/meridian
☎ 01489 442000 **Fax**: 01489 442000
Contact: Paul Johnson
Access: By arrangement only

Meridian took over the ITV franchise of the South and South East of England from Television South in 1993. The franchise holder before Television South was Southern Television. The collection includes many of the regional programmes made by Television South between 1982 and 1992, and the news/magazine programmes back to 1970. In late 2004 ITV Meridian moved out of its Southampton premises to a new regional production centre at Whiteley, equipped with the latest digital technology.

366 MERIDIAN BROADCASTING NEWS LIBRARY

Footage sales c/o ITN Source (qv), 200 Gray's Inn Road, London WC1X 8XZ
Email: sales@itnsource.com
Web: http://www.itnsource.com
☎ 020 7389 8664 **Fax**: 020 7430 4453
Contact: Liz Cooper
Access: via ITN Source

Meridian News holds all edited items transmitted by former company (TVS) between 1982–1992, and by Meridian from 1993 to the present. This includes selected rushes and stock shots from stories relating to Kent, Sussex and parts of Essex. Separate news centres at Southampton and Newbury store material relating to the South and Thames Valley areas of the Meridian region.

367 METRO RADIO

55 Degrees North, Pilgrim Street, Newcastle Upon Tyne NE1 6BF
Email: sharron.dennis@metroandmagic.com
Web: http://www.metroradio.co.uk
☎ 0191 420 0971 **Fax**: 0191 488 9222
Contact: Sharron Dennis, Head of Production

Radio station. Holds forty-two days' output to meet legal requirement. Local news items and recent interviews are kept on minidisc for one year.

368 MFM 103.4

The Studios, Mold Road, Gwersyllt, Nr Wrexham, Clywd LL11 4AF
Email: Lisa.marrey@musicradio.com
Web: http://mfm.musicradio.com
☎ 01978 752202 **Fax**: 01978 759701
Contact: Lisa Marrey, Programme Controller

The radio station holds forty-two days' output only to meet legal requirement.

369 MICHAEL ESSEX-LOPRESTI

c/o Huntley Film Archives, 22 Islington Green, London N1 8DU
Email: films@huntleyarchives.com
Web: http://www.huntleyarchives.com
☎ 020 7226 9260 **Fax**: 020 7359 9337
Contact: Amanda Huntley
Access: via Huntley Film Archives (qv)

The collection comprises approximately 150 titles of mainly medical films dating from 1897 to 1970, from silent black and white to colour sound. Also included are some semi-professional and amateur sound films made by the South London Film Society.

370 MIGRANT MEDIA ARCHIVE

Migrant Media, PO Box 47412, London N13 5WG
Email: migrantmedia@pop3.poptel.org.uk
Web: http://homepages.poptel.org.uk/migrantmedia/docs/migrant.htm
☎ 020 8889 7080 **Fax**: 020 8889 6160
Contact: Ken Fero, Coordinator
Access: By arrangement

Since 1985 documenting experiences of migrant refugee and black communities in the UK and Europe. Focus on issues of self-defence, racist attacks, labour struggle and state human rights violations.

371 MINSTER FM

PO Box 123, Dunnington, York YO1 5ZX
Email: studio@minsterfm.com
Web: http://www.minsterfm.com
☎ 01904 488888 **Fax**: 01904 481088
Contact: John McCray, Station Manager

Radio station. Holds forty-two days' output to meet legal requirement.

372 MORAY COLLEGE

Moray Street, Elgin, Moray IV30 1JJ
Email: angie.mackenzie@moray.uhi.ac.uk
Web: http://www.moray.ac.uk
☎ 01343 576000 **Fax**: 01343 576001
Contact: A. Mackenzie
Access: During library opening hours only

A collection of books and videos to support college courses; video production, audio-visual presentation, photography.

373 MORAY FIRTH RADIO

Scorguie Place, Inverness, Scotland IV3 8UJ
Email: mfr@mfr.co.uk
Web: http://www.mfr.co.uk
☎ 01463 224433 **Fax**: 01463 243224
Contact: Gary Robinson, Programme Controller

From 1982 material of local history value has been archived, e.g. weekly interview series with local celebrities (on reel to reel and cassette), and also, from recent years, major news series and documentaries which will be available for researchers. Scripts are kept for about two years.

374 MOSAIC

1A Flaxman Court, London W1A 0AU
Email: colin@mosaicfilms.com
Web: http://www.mosaicfilms.com
☎ 020 734 7224 **Fax**: 020 287 4810
Contact: Colin Luke
Access: Limited

Mosaic has been producing documentaries all over the world for the past twenty years. The collection is made up of rushes from these productions. The library comprises international general views which are constantly being up-dated and is particularly strong on Russia.

375 MOVING IMAGE COMMUNICATIONS

Maidstone Studios, Vinters Park, Maidstone, Kent ME14 5NZ
Email: mike@milibrary.com
Web: http://www.milibrary.com
☎ 01622 684 569 **Fax**: 01622 687 444
Contact: Michael Maloney, Director

Moving Image Communications represents different collections from international film libraries, national organisations, film and television producers, cinematographers and independent archive sources. The library covers an ever increasing range of subjects both archival and contemporary with material originating from film and video. Footage ranges from early silent movies to celebrity chat shows; from newsreels to travelogues. Collections include: TV-AM (1983–1992), Wild Islands, Flying Pictures, Skyworks, Filmfinders, Channel X, British Tourist Authority (1930-present day), Freud home movies, Jazz on Film, National Trust Film Archive, Cuban Archives and more. All collections are extensively logged in our regularly updated database.

376 THE MUSEUM OF ENGLISH RURAL LIFE

University of Reading, Redlands Road, Reading RG1 5EX
Email: merl@rdg.ac.uk
Web: http://www.ruralhistory.org
☎ 0118 378 8660 **Fax**: 0118 378 5632
Contact: J.H. Brown, Archivist
Access: Tue-Fri 10.00–16.30, by appointment. Access for disabled

The museum acts as the national information centre for rural and agricultural history. About half of the 1,000 original film reels are from the Ministry of Agriculture, the rest being primarily from agricultural engineering firms such as Ransomes, International Harvester and Ford New Holland. The earliest films are from the 1920s but the majority is from post-1945. Almost all items are listed, and catalogue records are available online for several collections. Particular subject strengths are tractors, harvesting machinery, dairying, agrochemicals and agricultural aviation. As well as advertisements, there are training films and general interest newsreels.

377 MUSEUM OF RUGBY, TWICKENHAM

Twickenham Stadium, Rugby Road, Twickenham, Middlesex TW1 1DZ
Email: jedsmith@rfu.com
Web: http://www.rfu.com/microsites/museum
☎ 0870 405 2001 **Fax**: 0870 405 2002
Contact: Jed Smith, Museum Curator

The Museum of Rugby is a museum of international rugby history, and the collection includes objects from all over the globe. Since the birth of the Rugby Football Union in 1871 a variety of rugby memorabilia has been collected. The collection includes dusty minute books, faded letters, early match programmes and tickets for memorable games. More recently the collection has developed to include historical and contemporary photographs, videos, artworks, equipment and other miscellaneous objects. Holdings include a small number of items of rugby football-related film footage. Mainly rugby matches in progress, but also training and the social side of the game.

378 MUSEUM OF SCIENCE AND INDUSTRY IN MANCHESTER ARCHIVES: FERRANTI COLLECTION

Collections and Learning Department, Liverpool Road, Manchester M3 4FP
Email: archive@msim.org.uk
Web: http://www.msim.org.uk/ferranti/index.html
☎ 0161 6060127 **Fax**: 0161 6060186
Contact: Jan Hargreaves, Senior Archivist
Access: Tue-Thu 10.00–16.30

The museum holds the archive collections of some of Manchester's most famous companies. The type of material ranges from company minute books, order books, sample books and letters to engineering drawings, photographs, films and oral history recordings. Ferranti Ltd formed the Ferranti Archive in 1960, and a large proportion of the Archive comprises marketing and publicity material for Ferranti Ltd products, including over 10,000 photographs. The company's archives and over 1,500 Ferranti objects were presented to the museum in 1995. Holdings include dozens of corporate, recruitment, advertising and promotional video materials.

379 MUSEUM OF WELSH LIFE

St Fagans, Cardiff CF5 6XB
Email: mari.gordon@nmgw.ac.uk
Web: http://www.museumwales.ac.uk/en/stfagans
☎ 029 573427 **Fax**: 029 573490
Contact: Meinwen Ruddock, Assistant Curator, Audiovisual Collections
Access: Most material is accessible to bona fide researchers by prior appointment. Staff are available to assist

A collection of films from various sources, some dating from the 1930s, but mainly fieldwork recordings dating from the 1960s dealing with various aspects of the folk life of Wales. The rate of acquisition is slow. Also a small collection of off-air video recordings of broadcasts relating to Welsh life.

380 MUSIC MALL

1 Upper James Street, London W1F 9DE
Email: andi@musicmall.co.uk
Web: http://www.musicmall.co.uk
☎ 020 7534 1444 **Fax**: 020 7534 1440
Contact: Andi Baron, Production Manager
Access: Mon-Fri 09.00–17.30

Music Mall, a division within VPL, sources and supplies music videos to a range of clients. The repertoire ranges from vintage clips of the 1970s right up to the latest releases. If the single has been released in the UK it is very likely that its video will be available through our service – this includes many international artists and bands. Because of our contacts with record companies and the access we have to their archives, Music Mall can provide a very quick and efficient service, particularly for older titles which can be very difficult to find. On the website a selection of 20,000 music videos titles can be searched.

381 MUSIC PRESERVED

Barbican Music Library, Barbican Centre, Silk Street, London EC2Y 8DS
Email: mp@musicpreserved.org.uk
Web: http://www.musicpreserved.org
☎ 020 7638 0672 **Fax**: 01730 895052
Contact: Tim Appleyard
Access: Mon, Wed: 09.30–17.30; Tue, Thu: 09.30–19.30; Fri, 09.30–14.00;
Sat, 09.30–16.00

Formerly the Music Performance Research Centre, Music Preserved holds over 1,500 archive recordings of live performances, audio and video interviews, from the 1930s to the present day. There are on-site archive recordings made by the MPRC at concert halls and opera houses and off-air recordings of public performances, donated to the MPRC, dating from 1934 to the present. The archive includes recordings that to the best of its knowledge cannot be heard elsewhere. It holds recorded conversations with international conductors, soloists, singers and orchestral musicians and video archive recordings made from 1951 onwards, including a collection provided by the BBC Libraries and Archives Division.

382 NAPIER UNIVERSITY LEARNING INFORMATION SERVICES

Sighthill Court, Edinburgh EH11 4BN
Email: g.forbes@napier.ac.uk
Web: http://www.napier.ac.uk
☎ 0131 455 3558 **Fax**: 0131 455 3566
Graeme Forbes, Head of Resource Management and Development

The film and video collection includes several dozen titles. The Head of Resource Management and Development also manages seven other learning centres in Edinburgh, Livingston and Melrose.

383 NAPIER UNIVERSITY MERCHISTON LEARNING CENTRE

10 Colinton Road, Edinburgh EH10 5DT
Email: m.kirton@napier.ac.uk
Web: http://nulis.napier.ac.uk
☎ 0131 455 2581 **Fax**: 0131 455 2377
Contact: Marian Kirton, Information Services Advisor
Access: Consultation open to all

Off-air collection of videos covers all subjects taught at the University. Among these are approximately 3,000 titles relating to motion pictures, television and radio, of which a handful are commercial recordings rather than off-air. Most of these are simply cassettes containing one or two motion pictures.

384 NATIONAL ARCHIVE FOR THE HISTORY OF COMPUTING

Centre for the History of Science, Technology and Medicine, Manchester
University, Maths Tower, Manchester M13 9PL
Email: nahc@fs1.li.man.ac.uk
Web: http://www.chstm.man.ac.uk/nahc
☎ 0161 275 5850 **Fax**: 0161 275 5699
Contact: Jon Agar, Associate Director
Access: By arrangement

The National Archive for the History of Computing was created in 1987 to
collect, preserve and make accessible to historians documents relating to
the history of computing. The films and videos are part of the National
Archive for the History of Computing collection.

385 NATIONAL ARMY MUSEUM

Royal Hospital Road, Chelsea, London SW3 4HT
Email: info@national-army-museum.ac.uk
Web: http://www.national-army-museum.ac.uk
☎ 020 7730 0717 ext 2241/2214 **Fax**: 020 7823 6573
Contact: A. W. Massie, Head of Archives, Photographs, Film and Sound
Access: By prior appointment, preferably on Mondays. Access for disabled

The museum has acquired film on a piecemeal basis since the 1960s but has
recently begun to collect more actively, particularly amateur footage of the
British and Indian armies in the 1930s and 1940s. The films show almost
every aspect of army life at that time, including the introduction of
mechanisation, training, engineering work, social life, and sports. In some
cases they carry a soundtrack added by the original cameraman when the
film was copied. Film collections of the Middlesex Regiment and Women's
Royal Army Corps museums have recently been acquired, as have a number
of Ministry of Defence recruiting and information films.

386 NATIONAL CENTRE FOR ENGLISH CULTURAL TRADITION

University of Sheffield, 9 Shearwood Road, Sheffield S10 2TN
Email: j.redford@shef.ac.uk
Web: http://www.shef.ac.uk/natcect
☎ 0114 222 0195
Contact: Jill Redford, Archivist
Access: Given the lack of any working copy tapes access to the collection
is severely limited

The video collection is held in the Archives of Cultural Tradition,
established in 1964 to preserve material collected through the Centre's
ongoing survey of language and folklore. The core of the collection
comprises original field recordings of traditional customary events, made in
the 1970s and early 1980s in and around the Yorkshire region. New
accessions are now mainly fieldwork recordings submitted by students to
accompany under- and post-graduate research projects in folklore studies.

387 NATIONAL CO-OPERATIVE FILM ARCHIVE

Co-operative College, Holyoake House, Hanover Street,
Manchester M60 0AS
Email: archives@co-op.ac.uk
Web: http://archive.co-op.ac.uk/filmarchive.htm
☎ 0161 246 2925 **Fax**: 0161 246 2946
Contact: Gillian Lonergan, Archivist
Access: Limited, by prior arrangement only. Access for disabled

The archive was established in 1992 to coordinate information regarding the films of the British Consumer Cooperative Movement. It aims to preserve all film and photographic material relating to the consumer co-operative movement, to promote the use of archive films in co-operative education and to stimulate research into the movement's use of film. Films are not stored at the Archive, but where possible video copies are.

388 NATIONAL EDUCATIONAL VIDEO LIBRARY

Arfon House, Bontnewydd, Caernarfon, Gwynedd LL54 7UN
Email: tryfannevl@aol.com
☎ 01286 676001. Mobile: 07768 105467 **Fax**: 01286 676001
Contact: John Lovell, Head of Library
Access: Mon-Fri 09.00–17.00

16mm films and videotapes produced by the Educational Foundation for Visual Aids between 1950 and 1978.

389 NATIONAL ELECTRONIC AND VIDEO ARCHIVE OF THE CRAFTS (NEVAC)

University of the West of England, Bower Ashton Campus, Kennel Lodge Road, Bristol BS3 2JT
Email: matthew.partington@uwe.ac.uk
Web: http://www.media.uwe.ac.uk/nevac
☎ 0117 3284746
Contact: Matthew Partington, Director

The National Electronic and Video Archive of the Crafts – NEVAC – gathers materials which will act as a resource for those researching the nature of the crafts. These materials are characteristically in the form of digital video and sound recordings of people who have been intimately associated with the development of the crafts in Britain. There are currently 271 hours of interviews with 123 people, (including ceramists, textile artists, wood-workers, print-makers, enamel artists and curators).

390 NATIONAL FAIRGROUND ARCHIVE

The Library, University of Sheffield, Sheffield S10 2TN
Email: l.a.allen@sheffield.ac.uk
Web: http://www.shef.ac.uk/nfa
☎ 0114 222 7231 **Fax**: 0114 222 7290
Contact: Vanessa Toulmin, Research Director
Access: Mon-Fri, 09.30–16.30. Prior appointment necessary

The NFA is a unique collection of photographic, printed, manuscript, fairground ephemera and audio-visual material covering all aspects of the culture of travelling showpeople in the United Kingdom, their organisation as a community, their social history and everyday life and, the artefacts and machinery of fairgrounds. From Easter to October over 200 fairs are held weekly in the UK and the holdings present a comprehensive record of these events from the 1890s onwards. Additional collections include the Showmen's Guild Records and the Malcolm Airey Circus and Theatre Collection with many items of interest to people studying the transition of music hall artistes to film actors.

391 NATIONAL FILM AND TELEVISION ARCHIVE (NFTVA)

21 Stephen Street, London W1T 1LN
Email: http://www.bfi.org.uk/help/contact
Web: http://www.bfi.org.uk/nftva
☎ 020 7255 1444 (switchboard) **Fax**: 020 7436 0165
Contact: Darren Long, Head of Collections and Information
Access: By arrangement, Mon-Fri 10.00–17.30

The NFTVA began its existence in May 1935 to 'maintain a national repository of films of permanent value'. Its role is to select, acquire, preserve, document and make available for research, study and screening a collection of films and television programmes of all kinds, exhibited and transmitted in the UK, of British and foreign origin. As no statutory deposit for film, television and video production exists yet in the UK, material is acquired primarily by voluntary donation. The Archive's main source of finance is from the *bfi*'s annual government grant. It also receives funding from television companies for the preservation of ITV, Channel 4 and Five programmes. Specialist collections include sport, advertising films, political propaganda and material from industrial companies such as Courtaulds, British Steel, National Coal Board and British Transport form an important element of the Archive's collection.

392 NATIONAL FOOTBALL MUSEUM

Sir Tom Finney Way, Deepdale, Preston PR1 6RU
Email: malcolm@nationalfootballmuseum.com
Web: http://www.nationalfootballmuseum.com
☎ 01772 908 425 **Fax**: 01772 908 433
Contact: Malcolm MacCallum, Curatorial and Research
Access: Currently, due to restricted funding in this area, the research facility is unavailable but it is hoped that it will be fully operational in the near future.

The objective of the National Football Museum is to preserve, conserve and interpret the greatest collections of football memorabilia in the world. Holdings include archival material such as books, booklets and brochures, scrapbooks, newspapers, magazines, photographs, programmes, video and audio recordings and other commemorative items.

393 NATIONAL GEOGRAPHIC DIGITAL MOTION

First Floor, National House, 60/66 Wardour Street, London W1F 0TA
Email: psmith@ngs.org
Web: http://www.ngtlibrary.com
☎ 0207 734 9159 **Fax**: 0207 287 1043
Contact: Patrick Smith, Sales Manager, Europe, Middle East, Africa

Unparalleled moving images of the world, wildlife, adventure and exploration, people and cultures, natural phenomena, and human origins are the treasure inside National Geographic Digital Motion. Right now, more than 250,000 hours of dramatic footage – from National Geographic videos, films, and their production outtakes, as well as from our partner libraries – are available for licensing. The Film Library is actively seeking news and educational partners to expand the depth and breadth of the Library's wholly owned and licensed film properties through its commercial sales. Formerly National Geographic Film Library.

National Geographic

DOLPHINS – THE WILD SIDE (1999)

394 NATIONAL MARITIME MUSEUM FILM ARCHIVE

National Maritime Museum, Greenwich, London SE10 9NF
Email: films&filming@nmm.ac.uk
Web: http://tinyurl.co.uk/6gqb
☎ 020 8312 6727/8522 **Fax**: 020 8312 6599/6533
Contact: Nell Carrington
Access: By appointment, Mon-Fri 10.00–17.00

National archive built up over the past fifty years. The collection grew from education requirements and gifts of special material as well as the Museum's involvement with productions for broadcast television. It is a varied archive of maritime related film. The National Maritime Museum holds a fascinating collection of over 1,500 documented films dating back to 1910. These provide a rich insight into Britain's relationship with the sea. There are also some unique views of coastal resorts and ports both at home and abroad at the start of the twentieth century.

395 NATIONAL MOTOR MUSEUM FILM & VIDEO LIBRARY

National Motor Museum, Beaulieu, Hampshire SO42 7ZN
Email: filmandvideo@beaulieu.co.uk
Web: http://www.beaulieu.co.uk/motorlibrary/filmlibrary.cfm
☎ 01590 614664 **Fax**: 01590 612655
Contact: J. Stephen Vokins, Film and Video Librarian/Telecine Facilities Manager
Access: Limited, by appointment only

The film archive was created in 1976 by the Trustees of the National Motor Museum, and was formally established with the appointment of a Sound and Film Archivist in November 1979. Since the Montagu Motor Museum was established in 1952, a number of films have been donated to Beaulieu, mostly from industrial sources. This material is now being fully catalogued, along with newer additions to the archive. The Library is further enhanced by its own in-house broadcast standard telecine facilities and standards conversion, which it is also able to offer to outside users.

396 NATIONAL MUSEUM OF PHOTOGRAPHY, FILM & TELEVISION

Pictureville, Bradford, Yorks BD1 1NQ
Email: p.goodman@nmsi.ac.uk
Web: http://www.nmpft.org.uk
☎ 01274 202 030 Direct line: 01274 203378 **Fax**: 01274 723 155
Contact: Paul Goodman, Head of Collections
Access: Open every day except Monday

Founded in 1983, the Museum aims to help the public understand and enjoy the history and contemporary practice of photography, film and television. The Cinematography Collection houses material relevant to filmmaking processes, the historical development of its technology and its 'delivery' methods. It contains around 13,000 objects. Early camera technology is strongly represented. The Television Collection comprises around 19,000 items of equipment and artefacts. The Printed Materials and Ephemera Collection records and illustrates the development of photography, film and television and it helps to interpret the relationship between the visual media.

397 NATIONAL MUSEUM OF PHOTOGRAPHY, FILM & TELEVISION (TELEVISION COMMERCIALS COLLECTION)

Pictureville, Bradford BD1 1NQ
Email: talk.nmpft@nmsi.ac.uk
Web: http://www.nmpft.org.uk
☎ 01274 773399 **Fax**: 01274 723155
Contact: Ian Potter, TV Heaven Curator
Access: By arrangement only

The film library comprises two collections: 1) Television Commercials Collection, originally belonged to the BBTA (British Bureau of Television Advertising). When the BBTA closed down in 1975 the library was taken over by the ITCA (now the ITV Association), which continued to add to the collection. In 1993 the collection was taken over by the National Museum of Photography, Film & Television. 2) Film Samples Collection, consists of about 200 frame samples illustrating film formats and processes from 1896 onwards, compiled since the 1930s by the Science Museum and the Kodak Museum. Over 900 programmes can be viewed free of charge in our TV Heaven gallery.

398 NATIONAL RESOURCE CENTRE FOR DANCE (NRCD)

University of Surrey, Guildford GU2 5XH
Email: chris.jones@surrey.ac.uk
Web: http://www.surrey.ac.uk/NRCD
☎ 01483 879316 **Fax**: 01483 879500
Contact: Chris Jones, Manager
Access: Appointment required

The Centre was established in 1982 to provide support services for dance research and education and as part of a major development in dance studies at the University of Surrey and throughout the UK. It is the sole national archive for dance and movement in the UK. The NRCD's thirty-six special collections and substantial core collection contain a variety of materials, including film/video, sound recordings, personal papers, photographs, books, periodicals, artwork, notation/music scores, programmes, posters, cuttings, and other ephemera. The special collections represent the life and work of dance companies, organisations, choreographers, movement theorists, educationalists, and critics.

399 NATIONAL SCREEN AND SOUND ARCHIVE FOR WALES

Unit 1, Aberystwyth Science Park, Cefn Llan, Aberystwyth, Wales SY23 3AH
Email: iola@sgrin.co.uk
Web: http://screenandsound.llgc.org.uk/index.htm
☎ 01970 626007 **Fax**: 01970 626008
Contact: Iola Baines, Film Development Officer
Access: 09.00–17.30, by arrangement only. Staff are available to assist. Access ramp and toilets for disabled available

The collection comprises the film and video deposits and donations of film-makers and production companies, individuals, groups, organisations and corporate bodies. All commonly used film and video formats are represented, with 16mm the most common for film. Television material is acquired via the collections of individual production companies and producers, rather than systematically from broadcasters or off-air, although Welsh-language fourth channel S4C deposits selected drama material. Non-fiction, being the largest category of material held, includes newsreels and topicals, television and film documentaries, educational films and home movies and other amateur productions.

400 NATIONAL TRAMWAY MUSEUM

The Tramway Museum Society, Crich, Matlock, Derbyshire DE4 5DP
Email: enquiries@tramway.co.uk
Web: http://www.tramway.co.uk
☎ 01773 852565 **Fax**: 01773 852326
Contact: Roger Benton, Member of the Board of Management
Access: By arrangement only, 09.00–17.00

British tramway history began c.1860 with horse tramways. Steam and cable trams followed and the development of the electric tramcar commenced in 1885. The modes overlapped, with the earlier propulsion systems being phased out mainly by about 1920, leaving electric tramcars dominant. Nevertheless the earlier systems survived long enough to have been captured by early cinematographers and many examples have survived. Film collecting began in 1973, sources being varied and often obscure. The earliest film dates from 1896.

401 NATIONAL VIDEO ARCHIVE OF STAGE PERFORMANCE

Theatre Museum, 1E Tavistock Street, London WC2E 7PA
Email: tmenquiries@vam.ac.uk
Web: http://www.theatremuseum.org
☎ 020 7943 4727 **Fax**: 020 7943 477
Contact: Claire Hudson, Head of Library and Information Services
Access: Tue-Fri 10.30–16.30, by arrangement only. All researchers are welcome to watch the recordings and look at associated materials. A list of the recordings is available

The National Video Archive of Performance is the outcome of a unique agreement between the Federation of Entertainment Unions and the Theatre Museum enabling the Museum to make high quality archival recordings of live performance without payment of artists' fees. These recordings can be viewed by researchers and used in our educational workshops and in our exhibitions. The collection started in 1992 with trial recordings to establish best techniques and formats for recording live performance in front of an audience. There are now over 160 recordings, largely drama and some opera, musical theatre and pantomime.

402 NATIONAL VIEWERS' AND LISTENERS' ASSOCIATION COLLECTION

Special Collections, Albert Sloman Library, University of Essex, Wivenhoe Park, Colchester CO4 3SQ
Email: nigelct@essex.ac.uk
Web: http://libwww.essex.ac.uk/speccol.htm#NVALA
☎ 01206 873172 **Fax**: 01206 872289
Contact: Nigel Cochrane, Deputy Librarian
Access: Mon-Fri 08.00–10.00, Sat 9.00–18.00, Sun 14.00–19.00, though times vary throughout the year

The National Viewers' and Listeners' Association was established in 1965 by a group including Mary Whitehouse. The archive includes a considerable body of correspondence by Mary Whitehouse, to leading politicians and key persons in various successive UK governments and television stations, as well as letters of complaint by members of the public. Also included are notes for books and publications by NVALA, newsletters both local and foreign, newspaper cuttings, photographs of Mary Whitehouse's overseas tours, and audio-visual material.

403 NESCOT – NORTH EAST SURREY COLLEGE OF TECHNOLOGY

Reigate Road, Ewell, Epsom, Surrey KT17 3DS
Email: ghodge@nescot.ac.uk
Web: http://www.nescot.ac.uk
☎ 020 8394 3174 **Fax**: 020 8394 3030
Contact: Graeme Hodge, Library Services Manager

Media students studying courses at Nescot benefit from a major studio complex, which provides state of the art equipment for them to use. This includes a digital audio studio, voice over, vocal and drum booths, a ProTools digital audio control room, digital editing suite and two Avid digital video editing suites.

404 NEVIS RADIO

Ben Nevis Estate, Fort William, Scotland PH33 6PR
Email: sales@nevisradio.co.uk Web: http://www.nevisradio.co.uk
☎ 01397 700007 **Fax**: 01397 700007
Contact: William Cameron, Director of Programming

Nevis Radio is a community oriented music and information station based in Fort William. Nevis Radio does not maintain an archive. Its website won the Radio Academy Award for technical innovation in 1999.

405 NEW HALL

Huntingdon Road, Cambridge, Cambs, CB3 0DF
Email: library@newhall.cam.ac.uk
Web: http://www.newhall.cam.ac.uk
☎ 01223 762202
Contact: Alison Wilson, Librarian
Access: Not normally open to non-members

New Hall has recently begun a video archive, planning to interview members of the college from its foundation in 1954 onwards. Eight people have been interviewed so far. There is film of the building of the college in 1964 (now a listed building) and a programme made for BBC East's MATTER OF FACT series about women's education. A CD-ROM was made for graduates of 1999 and there is a graduation video of the sixties. Funding is being sought for cataloguing.

406 NEW STYLE RADIO

339 Dudley Road, Winson Green, Birmingham B18 4HB
Email: webmaster@newstyleradio.co.uk
Web: http://www.newstyleradio.co.uk
☎ 0121 456 3826 **Fax**: 0121 678 6030

Community radio station developed as one of the Afro-Caribbean Millennium Centre (ACMC) projects, serving the Birmingham area.

407 NEWHAM ARCHIVES AND LOCAL STUDIES LIBRARY

Stratford Library, 3 The Grove, Stratford, London E15 3EL
Email: richard.durack@newham.gov.uk
Web: http://tinyurl.co.uk/p44u
☎ 020 8430 6881
Contact: Richard Durack
Access: By arrangement. Access for disabled

The Local Studies Library collects material, including film and video, relating to the London borough, the former county boroughs of East and West Ham, and Essex and London materials where relevant. The library was opened in Stratford Reference Library in 1978.

408 THE NEWSMARKET

10–11 Percy Street, London W1T 1DA
Email: info@thenewsmarket.com
Web: http://www.thenewsmarket.com/GateWay/GateWay.aspx
☎ 020 7580.8330 **Fax**: 020 7580 8335

The NewsMarket is a pioneering broadcast news distribution service that brings newsmakers and journalists together via a single Web-based platform to create a more efficient environment for the exchange of video news content. More than 4,000 media outlets in seventy-five countries log on to www.thenewsmarket.com to find, preview and retrieve broadcast-standard video and other multimedia content. Registered news organisations include CNN, CNBC, BBC, EuroNews, Bloomberg TV and Reuters Television. Locations: New York (headquarters), San Francisco, London, Munich, Singapore, Hong Kong and Mumbai.

409 NORTH NORFOLK RADIO

The Studio, Breck Farm, Stody, Norfolk NR24 2ER
Email: info@northnorfolkradio.com
☎ 01263 860808 **Fax**: 01263 860809
Contact: Jeff Thomas, Station Manager & Sales Manager

North Norfolk's very own radio station serving the local population and holidaymakers with a mix of local news, information and classic hits from the 1960s to today. Began broadcasting in 2003.

410 NORTH WEST FILM ARCHIVE

Manchester Metropolitan University, Minshull House, 47–49 Chorlton Street, Manchester M1 3EU
Email: n.w.filmarchive@mmu.ac.uk
Web: http://www.nwfa.mmu.ac.uk
☎ 0161 247 3097 **Fax**: 0161 247 3098
Contact: Jo Abley, Collections Assistant
Access: Mon-Fri 09.00–17.00. User-search of online Film & Video Catalogue recommended in advance; assistance available

The North West Film Archive is a public regional collection holding material from early 'animated' pictures to contemporary productions. The collection dates from 1897 and includes cinema newsreels, documentaries, educational and training films, travelogues, advertising and promotional material, corporate videos and regional television programmes. A wide range of subject matter is represented: work and local industry, sport and leisure, holidays, local traditions and celebrations, transport, housing, healthcare and wartime experiences. The archive's collection of amateur films is particularly extensive and includes family home movies.

411 NORTH WEST SOUND ARCHIVE

Clitheroe Castle, Clitheroe, Lancashire BB7 1AZ
Email: nwsa@ed.lancscc.gov.uk
Web: http://www.lancashire.gov.uk/education/record_office/about/
archive.asp
☎ 01200 427897 **Fax**: 01200 427897
Contact: Andrew Schofield, Sound Archive Officer
Access: Mon-Fri, 09.00–17.00

The collection holds c.40,000 radio broadcasts from BBC Radio Blackburn, BBC Radio Manchester and GMR and Radio Piccadilly from the establishment of the stations in 1988. The recordings cover all aspects of the stations' output, including news reports, local history series, music programmes, sports reports and programmes, and 'celebrity' interviews.

412 NORTHAMPTONSHIRE LIBRARIES & INFORMATION SERVICE, NORTHAMPTONSHIRE STUDIES COLLECTION

Northamptonshire Central Library, Abington Street,
Northampton NN1 2BA
Email: ns-centib@northamptonshire.gov.uk
Web: http://www.northamptonshire.gov.uk/Leisure/Libraries/local.htm
☎ 01604 462 040 ext 222 **Fax**: 01604 462 055
Contact: Terry Bracher, Local History Librarian
Access: Only available on written application to the Local Studies
Librarian

The Northamptonshire Studies Collection is the county's main collection of printed and pictorial material on the history of Northamptonshire, comprising books, pamphlets, maps, photographs, illustrations, parish registers and census records. Fourteen films held of local interest, plus c.200 cassette tapes relating to interviews and programmes broadcast by BBC Northampton Radio.

413 NORTHAMPTONSHIRE RECORD OFFICE

Wootton Hall Park, Northampton NN4 8BQ
Email: archivist@northamptonshire.gov.uk
Web: http://www.northamptonshire.gov.uk/Community/record/
about_us.htm
☎ 01604 762129 **Fax**: 01604 767562
Contact: Sarah Bridges, County Archivist
Access: By arrangement. Access for disabled. Anglia Television films
cannot be used for commercial purposes without consent

The Record Office aims to ensure the safe preservation of archives and to make those archives available for research. The archives date from the twelfth century to modern times and come in many different formats including court rolls, deeds, parish and nonconformist registers, maps, letters, diaries, accounts, minute books, wills, photographs, films, paper, parchment and modern media. The records relate primarily to the county of Northamptonshire.   However, the records of the diocese of Peterborough covering Northamptonshire, the Soke of Peterborough and Rutland, and some records relating to other counties are also held.

414 NORTHANTS 96

19–21 St Edmund's Road, Northampton NN1 5DY
Email: reception@northants96.musicradio.com
Web: http://northants96.musicradio.com
☎ 01604 795600 **Fax**: 01604 795601
Contact: Mark Jeeves, Programme Controller

The radio station holds forty-two days' output to meet legal requirement.

415 NORTHERN REGION FILM AND TELEVISION ARCHIVE

School of Law, Arts and Media, University of Teesside, Middlesbrough,
Tees Valley TS1 3BA
Email: leo@nrfta.org.uk
Web: http://www.nrfta.org.uk
☎ 01642 384049 **Fax**: 01642 384099
Contact: Leo Enticknap, Director
Access: Mon-Fri, 09.00–16.00. By appointment

The NRFTA is the moving image archive serving County Durham, Cumbria,
Northumberland, Tyne and Wear and the Tees Valley. It was formed in 1998
as a consortium of a number of organisations which held existing film and
television collections in the region, and became a limited company in 2003.
Our major collections include an almost complete run of filmed inserts
from the regional BBC news programme LOOK NORTH from 1957–1991,
news and documentary footage from Tyne Tees, and industrial collections
which include Trade Films' output and the ICI corporate collection. We also
hold educational, promotional and training films and a large collection of
amateur 'home movie' footage.

ROAD SAFETY

416   NORTHSOUND 1

Abbotswell Road, Aberdeen, West Tullos AB12 3AJ
Email: iain.mckenna@northsound.co.uk
Web: http://www.northsound1.co.uk
☎ 01224 337000 **Fax**: 01224 400003
Contact: Iain McKenna, Managing Director

The radio station maintains on disc a news archive of major local and national news items. Everything else is held to meet legal requirement (in English, not Scottish).

417 NORTHUMBERLAND COUNTY LIBRARY

County Central Library, The Willows, Morpeth NE61 1TA
Email: pahallam@northumberland.gov.uk
Web: http://www.northumberland.gov.uk/cs_libraries.asp
☎ 01670 534524 **Fax**: 01670 534513
Contact: Pat Hallam, Adult Services Librarian
Access: Library opening hours

The Film Collection is housed in the County Central Library in Morpeth. It comprises over 3,000 books and an archive of periodicals on all aspects of the cinema: actors, directors, production, scripts, social and political history, world cinema, genres, theory and criticism. Some screenplays are also acquired. As far as can be ascertained there is no other public collection like the Teesside Film Collection in the UK (the British Film Institute considers it has no parallel elsewhere in Britain). Its scope includes all significant work published in the UK. The collection is divided into ten areas and has its own classification scheme.

418 NORWOOD FILM ARCHIVE

Email: info@norwoodfilms.com
Web: http://www.norwoodfilms.com
☎ 01843 220 348 **Fax**: 01843 220 348

Based in the south east of England, Norwood Films specialises in all aspects of visual entertainment from classic clips to the latest digital imagery. Norwood Film Archive has been supplying clips for the film, television and video industry for over twenty years. The collection includes over 3,000 films. Archive includes: vintage film clips for terrestrial, cable and satellite television productions, commercials-advertising- pop promo-corporate etc; wacky aircraft, crazy automobiles, life-threatening stunts, famous movie stars, forgotten heroes, almost extinct animals, former life styles, historic recreations, battles of two world wars, defunct adverts etc. Everything is held everything on 16mm film.+

419 NOVA FILM & VIDEOTAPE LIBRARY

62 Ascot Avenue, Cantley, Doncaster DN4 6HE
Email: library@novaonline.co.uk
Web: www.novaonline.co.uk/library.html
☎ 0870 765 1094 **Fax**: 0870 169 2982
Contact: Gareth Atherton, Head of Library

An extensive and unrivalled collection of unique archive material of Britain and the world. The library holds a huge selection of amateur cine film documenting the changing social life of Britain dating back to 1944 and has a dedicated collection of transport footage from 1949 to the present day. The library also holds a wide selection of specially shot modern footage and interviews. A catalogue and showreel are available, and a selection of video clips are available from the website.

420 OBAN FM

132 George Street, Oban, Argyll PA34 5NT
Email: tom_obanfm@lineone.net
Web: http://www.obanfm.org
☎ 01631 570057 **Fax**: 01631 570530
Contact: Ian Mackay, Station Manager

Oban FM Radio is a community radio station, based in Oban, and broadcasting to much of North Argyll in the Highlands of Scotland. The Oban FM group was founded in 1972. Oban FM is run largely by volunteers. As a community radio station, our first priority is our community, who are our source of news, our focus, our audience, and our staff. Nobody is paid for broadcasting on Oban FM. The radio station holds forty-two days' output to meet legal requirement.

421 OCTAGON CSI

Octagon House, 81/83 Fulham High Street, London SW6 3JW
Email: octagonarchive@octagon.com
Web: http://www.octagon.com
☎ 0208 944 4221 **Fax**: 0208 944 4132
Contact: Ian Childs, Managing Director – Octagon Movie and Media

Great events in history, sport, art, music, lifestyle, politics and war; our library houses more than 70,000 hours of footage covering a vast range of people and events. Using a custom-built database, the highly skilled and experienced researchers collate material to an unrivalled level of detail for both its visual and commercial impact. The result is access to a myriad of images at the touch of a button, from classic moments to top athletes and dramatic scenes in contemporary history, to countless examples of corporate branding and almost endless supplies of stock footage of cities and places around the world.

422 OLYMPIC TELEVISION ARCHIVE BUREAU (OTAB)

4th Floor, McCormack House, Burlington Lane, London W4 2TH
Email: pmoore@otab.com
Web: http://www.otab.com
☎ 020 8233 5353 **Fax**: 020 8233 5354
Contact: Philippa Moore, Sales Manager

In 1995 the International Olympic Committee (IOC) established the Olympic Television Archive Bureau (OTAB) to manage and market the IOC's extensive Olympic Games Archive. The Archive now contains over 20,000 hours of film, television and newsreel material dating back to the turn of the twentieth century, with additional Olympic Games material being researched, restored and added regularly to the Archive through the IOC's Acquisitions Programme, in co-operation with the Olympic Museum in Lausanne. Management of the International Olympic Committee's 'one stop shop' Archive of Moving Imagery, involving administration of licensing procedures, tape duplication and delivery of material. This also includes administration of OTAB's website.

423 OMNIMOVI

Email: sales@omnimovi.com
Web: http://www.omnimovi.com
☎ 020 8347 6555 **Fax**: 020 8347 6555
Contact: Spencer Rowell

OmniMovi is an expanding collection of Rights Protected moving sequences made specifically for commercial use. It covers generic lifestyle footage and can be compiled using our unique Omniboard Pro storyboard software. OmniMovi can be used to make presentations, terrestrial or satellite commercials, plasma screen advertising, and for Internet and corporate use. OmniMovi is a very flexible and versatile collection of images that can be used for endless permutations and purposes. Our footage is photographed on Fuji 35mm motion picture film with Panavision cameras. With our association with Extreme Music, we are able to provide music to match the clips.

424 ONEWORD RADIO

Landseer House, 19 Charing Cross Road, London WC2H 0ES
Email: info@oneword.co.uk
Web: http://www.oneword.co.uk
☎ 020 7976 3030 **Fax**: 020 7930 9460
Contact: Paul Ken, Programme Director

Jointly owned by Channel 4 Television and UBC Media. Features the best in spoken word entertainment – book serialisations, drama, comedy and discussion. BETWEEN THE LINES is the UK's only daily author interview show, hosted by Paul Blezard and features the biggest names in books reading from their latest works. CINEMASCOPE is Oneword radio's weekly film review and movie news show.

425 OPEN UNIVERSITY LIBRARY

Learning Resources Centre, The Open University Library, Walton Hall, Milton Keynes MK7 6AA
Email: c.m.tucker@open.ac.uk
Web: http://library.open.ac.uk/waltonhall/lrc/video_footage.html
☎ 01908 652366 **Fax**: 01908 653571
Contact: Christine Tucker, Teaching Materials Officer
Access: Mon and Wed 08.30–19.30, Tue and Thu 08.30–21.00, Fri 08.30–17.00, Sat 09.00–17.00

The Learning Resources Centre holds a wide range of Open University teaching materials, including audio-visual resources, printed course materials, multimedia resources and digital video. These include Open University television and radio programmes from 1971 onwards; audio cassettes from 1978 and video cassettes; CDs and DVDs; production transcripts and programme synopses, a slide collection. Programme material covers the Faculties of Arts, Social Sciences, Mathematics and Computing, Science, Technology, Education and Language Studies, Law, the Business School, Health and Social Care, and Institute of Educational Technology. Also, general information about the Open University.

426 OPEN UNIVERSITY WORLDWIDE

Michael Young Building, Walton Hall, Milton Keynes MK7 6AA
Email: S.L.Mccormack@open.ac.uk
Web: http://www.ouw.co.uk
☎ 01908 659083 **Fax**: 01908 858787
Contact: Sarah McCormack, Business Development Manager
Access: By prior permission

Learning resources from Open University undergraduate and business courses, including print, video and software.

427 OVERSEAS FILM AND TELEVISION CENTRE

2 The Quadrant, 135 Salusbury Road, London NW6 6RJ
Email: research@film-images.com
Web: http://www.film-images.com
☎ 020 7624 3388 **Fax**: 020 7624 3377
Access: Appointments necessary. Access for disabled. Research can be carried out on behalf of customers

The Overseas Film and Television Centre (OFTVC) is a collection of historically important films showing Britain's former colonies, mainly Africa and the Caribbean. Its main purpose was to promote economic and social development and for all the colonial countries to obtain their own independent film units with technical help from the organisation. Also includes films from other clients, including Milk Marketing Board, Gullick (mining equipment manufacturer), RSPCA, Young's Brewery, Castrol Oil, Crawfords Advertising Agency, Conservative Party, and the British Travel Association. There are also commercials made by the OFTVC for clients such as Ovaltine, Barclays Bank and Guinness.

428 OXFAM FILM ARCHIVE

Oxfam – Information Services, 274 Banbury Road, Oxford OX2 7DZ
Email: cwebb@oxfam.org.uk
Web: http://www.oxfam.org.uk/about_us/archive.htm
☎ 01865 313764 **Fax**: 01865 313770
Contact: Chrissie Webb, Archivist
Access: By arrangement only. Staff are available to assist. Access for disabled

The collection comprises films – documentary, educational and promotional – from about 1958–1990, relating to Oxfam's work, made by or on behalf of Oxfam. It holds copies of television programmes and other films about Oxfam or on subjects closely related to its interests.

429 OXFORD BROOKES UNIVERSITY AND ROYAL COLLEGE OF PHYSICIANS MEDICAL SCIENCES VIDEO ARCHIVE

Headington, Oxford OX3 0BP
Email: dmarshall@brookes.ac.uk
Web: http://www.brookes.ac.uk/schools/bms/medical
☎ 01865 483 146 **Fax**: 01865 483 998
Contact: Donald Marshall, Audio Visual Librarian
Access: Available for viewing by researchers by appointment

The archive was founded in 1984 by Sir Gordon Wolstenholme and Dr Max Blythe and funded by Oxford Brookes University until 1992. By the beginning of 1999, 187 major interviews had been completed and edited. Transcripts have slightly lagged behind with about ninety now completed. International developments have involved a collaboration with the Australasian Academy of Science which arranged a first short series of television broadcasts in 1998, based on interviews conducted in Australia. The Oxford Brookes University and Royal College of Physicians Medical Science Video Archive resources are held by the University and are available for viewing by researchers, by appointment.

430 OXFORD SCIENTIFIC (OSF)

Network House, Station Yard, Thame, Oxon OX9 3UH
Email: footage@osf.co.uk
Web: www.osf.co.uk
☎ 01844 262 370 **Fax**: 01844 262 380
Contact: James Cape, Sales Director
Access: By arrangement only

Oxford Scientific was founded in the early 1960s and offers the highest quality time-lapse and real-time stock footage imagery. Custom shots for feature films, commercials, music videos and other video projects are also a specialty. As well as over 350,000 still images the library also consists of over 2,000 hours of stock footage and specialises in wildlife, science, special effects, time-lapse, slow motion, macro and micro cinematography. Content includes clouds, skyscapes of all descriptions, suns, moons, lightning and star fields; landscapes, cityscapes, moving shadows, deserts and mountains, fire and fog; transportation, traffic, crowds, children and Americana.

431 PASSION 107.9

270 Woodstock Road, Oxford, Oxon OX2 7NW
Email: info@passion1079.com
Web: http://www.passion1079.com
☎ 01865 315980 **Fax**: 01865 315981
Contact: Andy Green, Programme Controller

Radio station. Holdings: three months' output. Also keeps topical news stories, large news stories (audio and script), a large private music collection, and commercials. Holds minidisc copies of film clips. A new large internet music service is also being provided covering different genres of music, and there are services for students on a twenty-four hour basis. The station aims to expand its archive. *Note: formerly Oxygen 107.9 FM.*

432 PATRICK STANBURY COLLECTION

12 Laurel Crescent, Woodham Lane, Woking, Surrey GU21 5SS
☎ 01932 345924
Email: photoplay@compuserve.com
Contact: Patrick Stanbury
Open to all researchers

Extensive collection of silent features and short subjects (fiction and documentary), American and European, and animation material. Official representative for the Blackhawk Library, a long established US-based 16mm collection of silent and early sound material, much of it rare and unobtainable elsewhere. The collection is expanding on a consistent basis.

Mike Hill/Oxford Scientific (OSF)

433 PHIL SLATER ASSOCIATES

Video House, Ash Street, Fleetwood, Lancashire FY7 6TH
Email: info@slater.uk.com
Web: http://www.slater.uk.com
☎ 01253 770510 **Fax**: 01253 776729

Phil Slater Associates and its sister companies, Video House and Yellow Productions, were formed in the late 1970s, and have produced and provided programmes to television broadcasters located in every territory of the world. From specialised niche documentaries and light entertainment series for mainstream terrestrial television, to easily translatable travel programmes that cater for the global mass market. Holdings include over twenty-five years of archived footage from exotic holiday destinations to heavy industry and just about everywhere in between.

434 PHILOSOPHY LIBRARY, OXFORD UNIVERSITY

10 Merton Street, Oxford, Oxon OX1 4JJ
Email: hilla.wait@bodley.ox.ac.uk
Web: http://www.bodley.ox.ac.uk/boris/guides/philosophy
☎ 01865 276927 **Fax**: 01865 276932
Contact: Hilla Wait, Philosophy Librarian

The Philosophy Library is developing a collection of philosophy videos, with a preference for current philosophical debate rather than as standard lecture substitutes. It holds the set of PHILOSOPHERS IN CONVERSATION (Donald Davidson, Willard Quine, Peter Strawson), and a video debate between Jürgen Habermas and Richard Rorty. These were all obtained commercially. The Library has no unpublished material.

435 PHOTOPLAY PRODUCTIONS

21 Princess Road, London NW1 8JR
Email: photoplay@compuserve.com
☎ 020 7722 2500 **Fax**: 020 7722 6662
Contact: Patrick Stanbury
Access: Research advice can be provided to aid locating material from other sources. Available to all researchers. All enquiries by telephone or letter in the first instance

Specialising in silent material, the company handles films from the private collections of its founders as well as material acquired in the course of making major television documentaries on silent film history.

436 PLANNED ENVIRONMENT THERAPY TRUST ARCHIVE AND STUDY CENTRE

Church Lane, Toddington, Gloucestershire GL54 5DQ
Email: craig@pettarchiv.org.uk
Web: http://www.pettarchiv.org.uk
☎ 01242 620125 **Fax**: 01242 620125
Contact: Craig Fees, Archivist
Access: Limited, by arrangement only. Staff are available to assist. Access and facilities provided for disabled

The film/video collection forms part of the archive of The Planned Environment Therapy Trust. The archive was founded in 1989 in order to gather and protect the papers of individuals and organisations involved in environment therapy, milieu therapy and therapeutic communities.

437 PLATO VIDEO

3 Poole Road, Bournemouth, Dorset BH2 5QJ
Email: lionel@platovideo.com
Web: http://www.plato-video.co.uk
☎ 01202 554382 **Fax**: 01202 761227
Contact: Lionel Fynn, Video Librarian
Access: By arrangement

The collection includes 8mm, 9.5mm and 16mm film and video material, from the 1920s to the present day. Subjects include aviation, liquor licensing (pubs, etc), rural and urban planning and design; shipping, including paddle steamers, cross channel ferries, hovercraft (including last day of cross-channel operation), liners (including pre-war cruise liner Bremen) and Southampton Docks in the 1930s; aviation, including biplane airliner flight to Paris from Croydon, air shows going back to the 1950s, flights in World War II aircraft and Concorde. Also includes 16mm film of London and Paris in the late 1930s and video of rural and urban locations in the UK, Paris, Venice and the USA.

438 PLYMOUTH COLLEGE OF ART AND DESIGN

Tavistock Place, Plymouth PL4 8AT
Email: lharding@pcad.ac.uk
Web: http://www.pcad.ac.uk/fin/index.html
☎ 01752 203 412 **Fax**: 01752 203 444
Contact: Linda Harding, Learning Resource Centre Manager

Small independent College of Art library serving about 1,800 students and 100 staff. Subject specialisation is in Fine Art, Interior Design, Graphic Design, Fashion, Photography, Film and Media. Courses range from ND level through to BA. Stock is mainly books, periodicals, videos and CD-ROMs. The Critical Studies Group of the college of which the Librarian is Chair has produced a useful student study guide which includes advice on referencing and compiling a bibliography for film and video material plus illustrations.

439 PLYMOUTH LIBRARY SERVICE – LOCAL STUDIES AND NAVAL HISTORY LIBRARY

Plymouth Central, Plymouth, PL4 8AL
Email: localstudies@plymouth.gov.uk
Web: http://tinyurl.co.uk/ej21
☎ 01752 305909 **Fax**: 01752 305905
Contact: Joyce Brown, Local Studies and Naval History Librarian

The collection comprises videos of local events, areas and people, mostly of historic nature as well as videos of naval information concerning training, recruitment and commercials.

440 PORT OF LONDON AUTHORITY FILM COLLECTION, MUSEUM IN DOCKLANDS

Unit C14, Poplar Business Park, 10 Prestons Road, London E14 9RL
Email: raspinall@museumofdocklands.org.uk
Web: http://www.museumindocklands.org.uk/English
☎ 020 7515 1162 **Fax**: 020 7538 0209
Contact: R.R. Aspinall, Museum in Docklands Librarian and Archivist
Access: By arrangement only. Access for disabled

The Port of London Authority is responsible for the management and administration of the River Thames from Teddington to the Nore. The first PLA film was made around 1921. Films were made at regular intervals. Probably the best known films relating to the Port of London, CITY OF SHIPS and WATERS OF TIME, are in the collection. However, all the early nitrate stock, as well as the masters for the later films, are held by the National Film and Television Archive (qv). The collection spans roughly sixty years (1920–1980). A number of recent films about modern cargo handling facilities at Tilbury Docks are held.

441 PORTHCURNO TELEGRAPH MUSEUM: CABLE AND WIRELESS ARCHIVE

Eastern House, Porthcurno, Cornwall TR19 6JX
Email: mary.godwin@cw.com
Web: http://www.porthcurno.org.uk
Contact: Mary Godwin

The PK Trust was set up in 1997 by Cable & Wireless to preserve the important historical buildings and collections at Porthcurno, the home of the British Empire's first international telecommunications network. The Trust's two major activities are operation of the award-winning Porthcurno Telegraph Museum and the management of the Cable & Wireless historic archive of photographs, films and documents. In addition the museum also runs a database of historical photographs and an oral history project, both relating to the parish of St Levan.

442 PORTSMOUTH CITY MUSEUM AND RECORDS OFFICE

Museum Road, Portsmouth, Hampshire PO1 2LJ
Email: searchroom@portsmouthcc.gov.uk
Web: http://www.portsmouthrecordsoffice.co.uk
☎ 023 9282 7261 **Fax**: 023 9287 5276
Contact: John Stedman, Local History Officer
Access: Through searchroom at the City Museum and Records Office

Substantial oral history collections (over 1,100 recordings) relating to Portsmouth history and to D-Day, subjects including Portsmouth dockyard, the Home Front in WW2, leisure, the Chinese, Bangladeshi and Caribbean communities, corset making, ferry workers, local rock musicians, D-Day and the Battle for Normandy. Also the Richard Lancelyn Green Collection of film, books, archives, sound recordings and stills, etc, relating to Sherlock Holmes and Sir Arthur Conan Doyle. There are film items presented to the city from time to time by individuals. All film acquired before 2004 has been transferred to the Wessex Film and Sound Archive, Winchester (qv).

443 POWELL-COTTON MUSEUM

Quex Park, Birchington, Kent CT7 0BH
Email: powell-cotton.museum@virgin.net
Web: http://www.era.anthropology.ac.uk/Era_Resources/Era/P-C_Museum
☎ 01843 842168 **Fax**: 01843 846661
Contact: Malcom Harman, Curator
Access: By arrangement only

In the 1930s Major P.H.G. Powell-Cotton and his daughter Dr Diana Powell-Cotton made several ethnographic films in Africa, chiefly in Italian Somaliland and southern Angola, and mostly illustrating local crafts. In the 1950s and 1960s other members of the family made ethnographic and wildlife films in Kenya and Uganda. The museum has over thirty of these films, the earliest dating from 1922 and made in the Cameroons. We have additional films from Frank Varian who was an engineer in Angola from about 1911. Films and the 20,000 photographs are available for commercial use, rates quoted on application.

444 PRAXIS ARCHIVE

Praxis Films Ltd, PO Box 290, Market Rasen, Lincolnshire LN3 6BB
Email: archive@praxisfilms.com
Web: http://www.praxisfilms.com
☎ 01472 399976 **Fax**: 01472 399976
Contact: Sue Waterfield, Archivist
Access: All research done in-house. No external researchers

Built up over twenty years through purchase and shooting own material in Eastern and Northern England. The collection began with a series of rural, sea-fishing and industrial films. Current affairs, documentary and educational films made in Northern England, throughout the UK and internationally are continually being added to the holdings.

445 THE PRESS ASSOCIATION

292 Vauxhall Bridge Road, London SW1V 1AE
Email: broadcasting.info@pa.press.net
Web: http://services.press.net/pressnet/tvnewsclip/index.jsp
☎ 020 7963 7000

BBC Worldwide has formed a partnership with The Press Association as its global distributor for BBC news footage. This includes all news footage from the BBC's three main terrestrial daily news bulletins. The Press Association is the distributor of the latest news footage from the BBC. The website includes the past ninety days' output from the BBC as well the entire catalogue of news footage from The Press Association. The Press Association's Video News Library is updated on a daily basis with the latest television news footage from the UK and around the world. The service is available to broadcasters and production companies in the UK and abroad who may like to purchase the footage.

446 PRISM DIGITAL COMMUNICATIONS

15 Marden Road, Staplehurst, Kent TN12 0NF
Email: stevebergson@mac.com
☎ 01580 891683 **Fax**: 01580 890143
Contact: Steve Bergson, Director
Access: Limited, by arrangement. Access for disabled

Mainly rushes from productions – broadcast, corporate, home video and multimedia.

447 PUBLIC RECORD OFFICE OF NORTHERN IRELAND (PRONI)

66 Balmoral Avenue, Belfast, Northern Ireland BT9 6NY
Email: proni@dcalni.gov.uk
Web: http://www.proni.gov.uk
☎ 028 9025 5905 **Fax**: 028 9025 5999
Contact: Valerie Adams, Principal Record Officer
Access: Access to film collection under review at present

A collection of about 200 films, the earliest dating from the 1920s, from private and official sources; contains documentary footage, some newsreels, tourist promotional films, and amateur footage.

448 Q101.2 FM WEST

42A Market Street, Omagh, Co Tyrone, Northern Ireland BT78 1EH
Email: Manager@q101west.fm
Web: http://www.q101west.fm
☎ 028 8224 5777 **Fax**: 028 8225 9517
Contact: Frank McLaughlin, Managing Director/Programme Controller

Broadcasting around the Co's of Tyrone and Fermanagh – AC, Hot AC, traditional music, specialised music at weekend, local and international news and sports. The radio station holds forty-two days' output to meet legal requirement. Special events programmes may be kept.

449 Q102.9 FM

The Riverside Suite, 87 Rossdowney Road, Waterside, Londonderry,
Northern Ireland BT47 5SU
Email: Manager@q102.fm
Web: http://www.q102.fm
☎ 028 7134 4449 **Fax**: 028 7131 1 77
Contact: Frank McLaughlin, Managing Director/Programme Controller

Q102.9FM broadcasts twenty-four hours per day around the North West
region of Northern Ireland with CHR and AC music – local and international
news and sports – also on the Northern Ireland DAB. The radio station
holds forty-two days' output to meet legal requirement. Special events
programmes may be kept.

450 Q96FM 96.3

65 Sussex Street, Glasgow, Scotland G41 1DX
Email: mike.richardson@q-fm.com
Web: http://www.q96.net/index.shtml
☎ 0141 429 9430 **Fax**: 0141 429 9431
Contact: Mike Richardson, Programme Controller

Radio station. Local Paisley/local Glasgow news collection held.

451 Q97.2 FM

24 Cloyfin Road, Coleraine, Londonderry, Northern Ireland BT52 2NU
Email: Manager@q972.fm Web: http://www.q972.fm
☎ 028 7035 9100 **Fax**: 028 7032 6666
Contact: Frank McLaughlin, Managing Director/Programme Controller

Broadcasting around the Causeway Coast region of Northern Ireland
including Coleraine, Portrush, Portstewart, Ballymoney, AC and Hot AC and
specialised music, community information, local and international news
and sports. The radio station holds forty-two days' output to meet legal
requirement. Special events programmes may be kept.

452 QUEEN MARGARET UNIVERSITY COLLEGE

Corstorphine Campus, Clerwood Terrace, Edinburgh EH12 8TS
Email: bsmith@qmuc.ac.uk
Web: http://www.qmced.ac.uk/lb
☎ 0131 317 3301/3303 **Fax**: 0131 339 7057
Contact: Barbara Smith, Faculty Librarian (Arts)
Access: Open to the public for reference only

The library is a key resource for staff, students and researchers and our aim
is to provide an information service which is effective, dynamic, up-to-date
and responsive to the needs of our users.

453 QUEEN'S UNIVERSITY OF BELFAST

Main Library, University Square, Belfast, Northern Ireland BT7 1LS
Email: s.rawson@qub.ac.uk
Web: http://www.qub.ac.uk/lib
☎ 028 9027 3831 **Fax**: 028 9032 3340
Contact: Stuart Rawson, Head of Acquisitions and Cataloguing
Access: Many items for use in library only

The moving image collection is mainly designed to support the Film Studies course.

454 RADIO ACADEMY

5 Market Place, London W1N 7AH
Email: info@radioacademy.org
Web: http://www.radioacademy.org
☎ 020 7255 2010
Contact: John Bradford, Director

The Radio Academy is a forum for the British radio industry. Its website covers industry news, skills and studies in radio, marketing information, conference, festival and events information and the Sony Radio Awards. An A-Z Radio Stations Listing is included and details are given of a number of useful organisations in the field. Its Hall of Fame (still in development) is the Academy's tribute to those figures in the public eye who have made an outstanding contribution to the radio industry and radio in the UK.

455 RADIO AUTHORITY (see OFCOM)

Web: http://www.ofcom.org.uk/radio
☎ 020 7981 3000 **Fax**: 020 7981 3333
Note: OFCOM has now absorbed the Radio Authority. An archive of the old Radio Authority website can be accessed at:
http://www.ofcom.org.uk/static/archive/rau/textindex.html.

456 RADIO BORDERS

Tweedside Park, Galashiels, Scotland TD1 3TD
Email: http://www.radioborders.com/contactus.asp
Web: http://www.radioborders.com
☎ 01896 759444 **Fax**: 01896 759494
Contact: Danny Gallagher, Programme Controller

Radio station. Holds forty-two days' output to meet legal requirement. Some sports broadcasts and special items may be kept.

457 RADIO CEREDIGION

Yr Hen Ysgol Gymraeg, Ffordd Alexandra, Aberystwyth,
Ceredigion SY23 1LF
Email: admin@ceredigionfm.co.uk
Web: http://www.ceredigionfm.co.uk
☎ 01970 627999 **Fax**: 01970 627206
Contact: Dan Griffiths

Radio station. Regional news programmes kept. Notable events are stored at the National Library of Wales (audio is stored on videotape.) These include news bulletins for the past eight years. Local programming is recorded every week. Recordings are largely in the Welsh language; some may be in English.

458 RADIO MALDWYN

The Studios, The Park, Newtown, Powys SY16 2NZ
Email: sales@magic756.net
Web: http://www.magic756.net
☎ 01686 623555 **Fax**: 01686 623666
Contact: Austin Powell, Programme Controller

Radio Maldwyn came on air on 1 July 1993. Serving the bulk of mid-Wales, the radio station holds forty-two days' output to meet legal requirement. A few scripts for news items are kept.

459 RADIO SOCIETY OF GREAT BRITAIN

Lambda House, Cranborne Road, Potters Bar, Herts, EN6 5HU
Email: GM.Dept@rsgb.org.uk
Web: http://www.rsgb.org.uk
☎ 01707 659015 **Fax**: 01707 645105
Contact: John Crabbe, Librarian/Museum Curator, AM Radio Department
Access: Mon and Thu, 10.00–16.00, or with prior permission

Amateur radio allows millions worldwide to communicate with each other. Radio amateurs even have their own satellites and can transmit television pictures from their own homes. The RSGB is the UK's internationally recognised national society for all radio amateurs. Videos and some films of amateur radio activities; sound recordings of lectures etc. on amateur radio-related topics.

460 RADIO XL 1296 AM

KMS House, Bradford Street, Birmingham B12 0JD
Email: info@radioxl.net
Web: http://www.radioxl.net
☎ 0121 753 5353 **Fax**: 0121 753 3111
Contact: Barry Curtis, Programme Controller

Radio station. Holds forty-two days' output to meet legal requirement. Maintains a private library of South Asian music on hard disc.

461 RAM FM

35–36 Irongate, Derby DE1 3GA
Email: james.daniels@musicradio.com
Web: http://ramfm.musicradio.com/homepage.jsp
☎ 01332 205599 **Fax**: 01332 851188
Contact: James Daniels, Programme Controller

The radio station holds forty-two days' output to meet legal requirement. Special events, e.g. charity events, and slices of the BREAKFAST SHOW are kept for a year.

462 RAMBERT DANCE COMPANY ARCHIVE

94 Chiswick High Road, London W4 1SH
Email: jp@rambert.org.uk
Web: http://www.rambert.org.uk/index_a.html
☎ 020 8630 0608 **Fax**: 020 8747 8323
Contact: Jane Pritchard, Archivist
Access: Appointments may be made for weekdays 10.30–16.30. As space is limited personal access to the Archive is not available for those undertaking school project work although enquiries will be responded to when possible

Rambert Dance Company is the oldest dance company in Britain, dating its existence from 1926. It is also Britain's flagship modern dance company, employing a larger group of artists than any other modern dance company in the UK. The Rambert Dance Company Archive was established in 1982 with financial assistance from the Calouste Gulbenkian Foundation, the Pilgrim Trust and the Radcliffe Trust. It exists to ensure a complete and accurate record of the work of Britain's oldest active dance company. Its primary function is to serve the Company but it also responds to enquiries from outside the organisation.

463 RAPIDO TELEVISION

2 Halkin Street, London SW1X 7DJ
Email: richard.jeffs@rapidotelevision.com
Web: http://www.rapidotelevision.com
☎ 020 7486 1450
Contact: Richard Jeffs

BAFTA-winning Rapido is one of the UK's best known television companies. Our archive is the largest collection of youth culture, cult, sexy mass-broadcast material in the world. In addition to clips from over 100 popular shows, ranging from interviews with the world's biggest film stars, to performances by rock star legends, the Rapido archive also boasts a large volume of original edited short-stories or story-clips, from our clip based shows including: EUROTRASH, FORTEAN TV, BAADAAS TV, GIRLIE SHOW, YANKY PANKY SUBJECTS, PASSENGERS, FREAK OUT, NAKED CITY. Rapido's massive and unmatched library consists of 35,000+ broadcast tapes.

464 RAY HOOLEY 'RUSTON' COLLECTION

16 Alexandra Avenue, North Hykeham, Lincoln LN6 8NR
Email: rehooley@tiscali.co.uk
Web: http://www.oldengine.org/members/ruston/front.htm
☎ 01522 682406 (evenings and weekends) **Fax**: 01522 512929
Contact: Ray Hooley
Access: By arrangement

A small collection of 16mm and 35mm films of Ruston and Hornsby (Engineers) of Lincoln and Grantham (oldest film dated 1908).

465 REACT

Russell House, Ely Street, Stratford-upon-Avon, CV37 6LW
Email: phil@eaglereact.co.uk
Web: http://www.eaglereact.com
☎ 01789 268627
Contact: Phil Lloyd, Head of Archive

React is the archive arm of Eagle Media Productions, which is a television and film production company supplying all the world's major broadcasters with documentaries on a wide range of subjects and genres including history, travel, transport, famous people, music, war, art and lifestyle. React is an archive specialising in images of re-enactments of famous battles, figures and eras from history for use by educationalists, researchers, production companies, ad agencies, librarians and artists who are looking for top quality period footage or stills of actual or imagined events from the dawn of time to the advent of film.

466 READING UNIVERSITY LIBRARY – SPECIAL COLLECTIONS

Whiteknights, PO Box 223, Reading, Berks RG6 6AE
Email: g.m.c.bott@rdg.ac.uk
Web: http://www.library.rdg.ac.uk/colls/special/index.html
☎ 0118 378 8776 **Fax**: 0118 378 6636
Contact: Mike Bott

Special collections include the papers of the author and screenwriter Elinor Glyn. The collection includes typescripts of many of her books, articles and scripts, notes on film-making, correspondence, publishers' agreements and agreements with film associates. Some of the correspondence relates to her two companies, Elinor Glyn Ltd and Talkicolor Company Ltd.

467 RED DRAGON FM

Atlantic Wharf, Cardiff Bay, Cardiff, Wales CF10 4DJ
Email: david.rees@reddragonfm.co.uk
Web: http://www.reddragonfm.co.uk
☎ 029 2066 2066 **Fax**: 029 2066 2067
Contact: David Rees, Programme Controller

The radio station holds first broadcasts and maintains a news archive for each year for the past fifteen years.

468 REID KERR COLLEGE

Renfrew Road, Paisley, Renfrewshire PA3 4DR
Email: stephenjgrant@yahoo.co.uk
Web: http://www.reidkerr.ac.uk
☎ 0141 581 2222 **Fax**: 0141 581 2204
Contact: Stephen Grant, Librarian
Access: 09.00–17.00, term time

The college has two libraries /learning resource centres which provide an excellent information, lending and reference service for all courses offered by the college. The Centre offers computers with internet/intranet access, study areas, books, magazines, IT support (word processing, presentations, cv preparation etc.), scanning, photocopying, and colour printing facilities, music and electronic resources (CD-ROM, Internet Subscription Services).

469 REUTERS TELEVISION LIBRARY

c/o ITN Source, Independent Television News Ltd, 200 Gray's Inn Road,
London WC1X 8XZ
Email: sales@itnsource.com
Web: http://www.itnsource.com
☎ 020 7430 4480 **Fax**: 020 7430 44563
Contact: ITN Source
Access: 09.00–17.30. Staff are available to assist

Reuters Television, the international news agency, provides a daily
syndicated news service to more than 400 broadcasters in eighty-four
countries. Since 1998 ITN Archive (now ITN Source) has held world-wide
rights to the entire Reuters Television library, making it the largest news
archive in the world. A network of cameramen, staff and stringers,
numbering approximately 400 works for Reuters Television throughout the
world. In addition, Reuters Television has access to all news material shot
by its owner-organisations. Special arrangements also exist for acquiring
news material from television organisations in Africa, Eastern and Western
Europe, South America, China, Japan and elsewhere.

470 ROLLS-ROYCE PLC, IMAGE RESOURCE DEPARTMENT, FILM AND VIDEO ARCHIVE

Rolls-Royce, PO Box 31, Derby DE24 8BJ
Email: footage@rolls-royce.com
Web: http://www.rolls-royce.com/media/video/default.jsp
☎ 01332 242424 **Fax**: 01332 249936
Contact: Malcolm Thomas

The Rolls-Royce Image Resource film archive covers the ninety years of the
company's involvement in aero-engine manufacture and the airframes and
airlines associated with it. These include both military and civil applications
in airframes, aviation, ships and shipping, transport, technology, energy,
engineering, education. Recent footage includes the Allison aero-engine of
the USA. Other footage includes the Rolls-Royce Industrial Power Group
with subject matter including diesel engines and power generation
systems.

471 RONALD GRANT ARCHIVE

The Cinema Museum, The Master's House, The Old Lambeth Workhouse,
2 Dugard Way, London SE11 4TH
Email: pixdesk@rgapix.com
Web: http://www.rgapix.com
☎ 020 7840 2200 **Fax**: 020 7840 2299
Contact: Martin Humphries
Access: By arrangement only. Applications from students and serious
researchers are encouraged

The collection was started by Mr Grant as a schoolboy in the 1940s
collecting small rolls of 35mm film. The archive has grown from this modest
beginning to be of interest now at international level. The collection
embraces the important and early material collected by the late Graham
Head between 1918 and 1980, and original camera negatives 1899–1906 of
Mitchell and Kenyon's fiction films.

472 ROSE BRUFORD COLLEGE

Lamorbey Park Campus, Burnt Oak Lane, Sidcup DA15 9DF
Email: enquiries@bruford.ac.uk
Web: http://www.bruford.ac.uk/home.htm
☎ 020 8308 2626 **Fax**: 020 8308 0542
Contact: John Collis, College Librarian
Access: Prior permission by phone

The Rose Bruford College Library video collection is made up mainly of off-air recordings. Its particular subject strengths are films and plays, arts documentaries, opera, musicals and dance, and programmes about writers/dramatists.

473 ROTHAMSTED FILMS

c/o British Universities Film & Video Council, 77 Wells Street,
London W1T 3QJ
Email: ask@bufvc.ac.uk
Web: http://www.bufvc.ac.uk
☎ 020 7393 1503 **Fax**: 020 7393 1555
Contact: Geoffrey O'Brien, Assistant Director
Access: By arrangement

A small collection of material shot, mainly by Chris Doncaster, at the Rothamsted Experimental Station and passed to the BUFVC. The earliest material dates from 1959.

474 ROTHERHAM METROPOLITAN BOROUGH COUNCIL

Archives & Local Studies Service, Central Library & Arts Centre, Walker Place, Rotherham S65 1JH
Email: archives@rotherham.gov.uk
Web: http://www.rotherham.gov.uk
☎ 01709 823616 **Fax**: 01709 823650
Access: Tue, Wed, Fri 10.00–17.00; Thu 13.00–19.00; Sat 09.30–13.00; 14.00–16.00. Access for disabled. We recommend that you contact us in advance of your visit

Acquired in a haphazard manner over the years, the collection comprises twenty films. It includes newsreel items of local events, civic films and some amateur footage.

475 ROYAL AIR FORCE MUSEUM FILM COLLECTION

Grahame Park Way, London NW9 5LL
Web: http://www.rafmuseum.org/hendon/collections/film-sound/film_collections.cfm
☎ 020 8205 2266 **Fax**: 020 8200 1751
Contact: Film Archivist
Access: Limited

The Royal Air Force Museum was established in 1963 to collect, preserve and display all forms of material recording the history of the Royal Flying Corps, the Royal Navy Air Service, the Royal Air Force and aviation generally. It is the only national museum concerned solely with aviation. The Royal Air Force Museum Film Collection was formally established in April 1974 although the museum did have a small number of films prior to this date. Since 1988 the collection has formed part of the Visual Arts Department of the museum. It includes industrial, amateur, promotional, training and various documentary films.

476 ROYAL ANTHROPOLOGICAL INSTITUTE

50 Fitzroy Street, London W1T 5BT
Email: film@therai.org.uk
Web: http://www.therai.org.uk
☎ 020 7387 0455 **Fax**: 020 7383 4235
Contact: Susanne Hammacher, Film Officer
Access: Hiring and sale of films and videos for non-commercial educational purposes only

The Royal Anthropological Institute's film library was set up in 1971. The major part of the collection is contemporary (i.e. 1960 to present). Most of Granada Television's DISAPPEARING WORLD series is held. The RAI sponsors an Ethnographic Film Festival every two years, which is held at different hosting institutions each time.

DIVORCE IRANIAN STYLE (1998)

477 ROYAL BALLET VIDEO ARCHIVE

Royal Ballet Company, Royal Opera House, Covent Garden, London WC2E 9DD
Email: robert.jude@roh.org.uk
Web: http://www.royalballet.org.uk
☎ 020 7240 1200 **Fax**: 020 7212 9121
Contact: Robert Jude, Company Manager
Access: Presently very limited, based on individual application

A collection of rehearsals on stage of the repertoire of the Royal Ballet. Since 1956 all productions have been recorded. Recordings between 1956–1970 were made on 16mm film – now lodged with the NFTVA (qv), but video copies remain in the collection. Small amounts of in-house non-broadcast recordings of interviews and master classes, educational resources material, etc.

478 ROYAL FOREST OF DEAN COLLEGE

Five Acres Campus, Berry Hill, Coleford, Gloucestershire GL16 7JT
Email: judy_o@rfdc.ac.uk
Web: http://www.rfdc.ac.uk
☎ 01594 838 522 **Fax**: 01594 837 497
Contact: Judy Offord, Librarian
Access: Phone first

RFDC is a further education college and does not specialise in the moving image. It records or purchases items appropriate to its courses.

479 ROYAL GEOGRAPHICAL SOCIETY PICTURE LIBRARY

1 Kensington Gore, London SW7 2AR
Email: images@rgs.org
Web: http://images.rgs.org/movingfootage.aspx
☎ 020 7591 3060 **Fax**: 020 7591 3001
Contact: Justin Hobson, Picture Library Manager
Access: Mon-Fri by appointment

Photographs and artwork from the 1830s onwards include a variety of subjects such as anthropology, landscapes (e.g. polar regions and deserts), colonial empire, climbing, indigenous peoples, and remote destinations. The focus of the collection is the portrayal of human kind's resilience, adaptability and mobility around the world. Artwork includes a range of sketches, watercolours, pastels, portraits and oil paintings by amateur and established artists. And the largest private map collection in the world. Our collection contains a small amount of moving footage, including a film of the 1922 Everest expedition led by Brigadier-General Charles Granville Bruce (NFTVA, qv).

Edward Mendell / Royal Geographical Society

Tribesman, Papua New Guinea

480 ROYAL HIGHLAND FUSILIERS REGIMENTAL MUSEUM

RHQ RHF, 518 Sauchiehall Street, Glasgow, Scotland G2 3LW
Email: assregsec@rhf.org.uk
Web: http://www.rhf.org.uk
☎ 0141 332 0961 **Fax**: 0141 353 1493
Contact: Major W. Shaw, Curator
Access: By arrangement only. The collection is accessible to researchers, students, etc. All enquiries should be sent to Major W. Shaw.

This is a collection of films and videos ranging from 1915 to the present day. It covers various aspects of regimental life including parades, royal visits, war and training. The films form part of a larger collection of regimental property held at Regimental Headquarters and in the Regimental Museum.

481 ROYAL HOLLOWAY LIBRARY

University of London, Egham Hill, Egham TW20 0EX
Email: g.firth@rhbnc.ac.uk
Web: http://www.lb.rhbnc.ac.uk
☎ 01784 444 065 **Fax**: 01784 477 670
Contact: Graham Firth, Liaison Librarian
Access: See web pages

One hundred years ago, in 1900, both Bedford and Royal Holloway were admitted as Schools of the University of London, when it was constituted as a teaching university. Today, the University of London is made up of over sixty colleges and institutes and offers the widest range of higher education opportunities in Britain. The newly merged Royal Holloway and Bedford New College was inaugurated in 1986. The library holds thousands of off-air videos, DVDs, LPs and CDs.

482 THE ROYAL INSTITUTION OF GREAT BRITAIN

21 Albemarle Street, London W1S 4BS
Email: cwashbrook@ri.ac.uk
Web: http://www.rigb.org/rimain/index.jsp
☎ 020 7409 2992 **Fax**: 020 7629 3559
Contact: Corinna Washbrook, Collections Assistant
Access: By appointment only

Most of the moving image collection relates to videos and audio recordings of lectures held at the Royal Institution. There are two main subsets: the Christmas Lectures (the video recordings date back to the 1960s), and the Friday Evening Discourses (FED). Audiotapes and digital recordings of the FED go back to the 1950s to present. The RI holds tapes of about 90% of the series. There are also video recordings of some of the FED, these are produced in-house and commence about 1970. In addition there are a small number of miscellaneous audio and visual recordings relating to various activities of the Royal Institution.

483 ROYAL LONDON HOSPITAL ARCHIVES AND MUSEUM

The Royal London Hospital, Whitechapel, London E1 1BB
Email: jonathan.evans@bartsandthelondon.nhs.uk
Web: http://www.bartsandthelondon.nhs.uk/aboutus/museums_and_
archives.asp
☎ 020 7377 7608 **Fax**: 020 7377 7413
Contact: Jonathan Evans, Archivist
Access: Mon-Fri 10.00–16.30. Staff are available to assist researchers.
Access for disabled

Film collections have been built up since the 1930s by the Royal London Hospital for public information, recruitment and educational purposes. The Archives and Museum has brought collections together and deposited originals at the National Film and Television Archive (qv) since 1988. The medical film unit was begun c.1950 at the London Hospital and produced approximately 100 films about surgery and medicine up to the 1970s. Films also made by London Hospital Dental Film Unit and London Hospital School of Nursing. Queen Elizabeth Hospital for Children films (1930s +) also held. Various scientific films, (USA, France, Germany, 1930s-1970s).

484 ROYAL MARINES MUSEUM ARCHIVES

Southsea, Hampshire PO4 9PX
Email: info@royalmarinesmuseum.co.uk
Web: http://www.royalmarinesmuseum.co.uk/services.htm
☎ 023 9281 9385 **Fax**: 023 9283 8420

Our archives consist of manuscripts, letters, documents, diaries and some Royal Marines historical administrative material dating back to the 18th century, plus a tape and video collection. Although the Museum does not hold its film collection, on site, video and DVD reference copies are available of originals now held in the Wessex Film and Sound Archive (qv). The sound collection is comprised of oral history recordings, as well as recordings of the Royal Marine Band Service. Recorded music is in the form of CD, 78rpm shellac, vinyl and audio tapes of varying formats. The collection covers the 1920s to the present day and constitutes a very substantial music library.

485 ROYAL NATIONAL INSTITUTE FOR THE BLIND VOCATIONAL COLLEGE

RNIB, Radmoor Road, Loughborough, Leicestershire LE11 3BS
Email: enquiries@rnibvocoll.ac.uk
Web: http://www.rnib.org.uk/voccoll/welcome.htm
☎ 01509 611077 **Fax**: 01509 232013
Contact: Susan Sutton, Learning Resource Centre Supervisor
Access: Mon-Fri, 09.00–17.00. Loan to members

RNIB Vocational College is a national, specialist college welcoming people with disabilities aged 16 to 63 on a residential or day basis. Most but not all our learners have a sight problem. Large collection of purchased audiotapes includes a number of RNIB productions.

486 ROYAL NORTHERN COLLEGE OF MUSIC

124 Oxford Road, Manchester M13 9RD
Email: anna.smart@rncm.ac.uk
Web: http://www.rncm.ac.uk
☎ 0161 907 5241 **Fax**: 0161 273 7611
Contact: Anna Smart, Librarian
Access: By appointment

The RNCM is a conservatoire which prepares gifted students of all backgrounds and nationalities for a professional career in music. The main emphasis is on preparation for a career in performance (including composition) but a balanced education in music is provided. The library supports the teaching programme of the college and its collection of commercial videos and off-air recordings, which focuses on classical music, comprises the following: operas, off-air recordings, commercial recordings and concerts/documentaries.

487 ROYAL PHOTOGRAPHIC SOCIETY

The Octagon, Milsom Street, Bath BA1 1DN
Email: enquiries.nmpft@nmsi.ac.uk
Web: http://www.rps.org
☎ 01274 202030
Contact: The Collection Department
Access: Membership is open to everyone with a real interest in photography. Gallery opening hour seven days a week, 09.30–17.30

The photographic collection dates from 1827 to the present day. The most important, best known, best researched and most seen collections are those of the major photographers, but there is an equal wealth of material amongst the lesser known items, such as early colour, large collections of hitherto unprinted glass negatives, albums, lantern slides, etc, which relate to and support the main bodies of work by putting them in context. *Note. The collection has now transferred to the National Museum of Photography, Film & Television in Bradford (qv).*

488 ROYAL SOCIETY AUDIOVISUAL ARCHIVE

6 Carlton House Terrace, London SW1Y 5AG
Email: joanna.corden@royalsoc.ac.uk
Web: http://www.royalsoc.ac.uk/library
☎ 020 7541 2605 **Fax**: 020 7930 2170
Contact: Joanna M. Corden, Archivist
Access: By appointment during opening hours

The audiovisual archive covers the period 1931 to the present and consists of audio-visual recordings by or about Fellows of the Royal Society. The bulk of the collection consists of audio material, in particular cassette recordings of the Society's named lectures which have been preserved in this manner since 1974. The remainder of the series has been acquired as supplementary material to the personal records, although there are a few items which predate those autobiographies. The series is arranged chronologically. Several items are dictabelts for which the Society has no suitable playback facilities. It is intended to reproduce these as standard cassettes.

489 ROYAL TELEVISION SOCIETY LIBRARY AND ARCHIVE

100 Grays Inn Road, London WC12X 8AL
Email: clarecolvin@blueyonder.co.uk
Web: http://www.rts.org.uk
☎ 020 7430 1000 **Fax**: 020 7430 0924
Contact: Clare Colvin, Archivist
Access: By written application to the Archivist

The archives of the Society document its history from 1927 to today and provide a resource for historians and members researching the diverse aspects of the history of the television. The archive holds written, photographic and audio-visual material. The majority of the collections are housed in stores off-site, but can be accessed with reasonable notice. In addition to maintaining the archive and answering enquiries, the Archivist co-ordinates applications for the Shiers Trust, an annual research award for the history of television, and represents the Society on its History and Archives Group.

490 ROYAL VETERINARY COLLEGE HISTORICAL COLLECTIONS

Royal College Street, London NW1 0TU
Email: kwarner@rvc.ac.uk
Web: http://www.rvc.ac.uk
☎ 020 7468 5162 **Fax**: 020 7468 5162
Contact: Kate Warner, Assistant Librarian
Access: By appointment only

Many reels of film of various sizes, unidentified and some damaged, are held in basement vault. Subjects include students' research trips to Africa, etc., and operations, veterinary procedures, etc.

491 THE RSPB FILM COLLECTION

The Royal Society for the Protection of Birds, The Lodge, Sandy, Bedfordshire SG19 2DL
Email: lynda.whytock@rspb.org.uk
Web: http://www.rspbfilmcollection.com
☎ 01767 680551 **Fax**: 01767 683262
Contact: Lynda Whytock, Film Library Manager

The best source of bird-related footage for professionals in news, television and film production.

492 S4C

Parc Ty Glas, Llanishen, Cardiff CF4 5DU
Email: jennifer.pappas@s4c.co.uk
Web: http://www.s4c.co.uk/e_index.html
☎ 029 20 741 431 **Fax**: 029 20 754 444
Contact: Jennifer Pappas, Library Manager

The S4C archive contains material from programmes commissioned from independent production companies (mostly through the medium of Welsh) since the channel's launch in November 1982. While offering material relating to Wales and the Welsh our collection also reflect a wider and more general range of programme strands and content whose themes are universal and appeal to all audiences from pre-school to adults.

493 SAVE THE CHILDREN ARCHIVES

1 St John's Lane, London EC1M 4AR
Email: archivist@savethechildren.org.uk
Web: http://www.savethechildren.org.uk
☎ 020 7716 2269 **Fax**: 020 7708 2508
Contact: Susan Sneddon, Archivist
Access: By prior arrangement, Mon-Fri 10.00–17.30, Staff are available to assist

Save the Children has been using film as a resource for education and fundraising since 1921. In 1995 all the organisation's films were transferred to the National Film and Television Archive (qv) in London. No films have been produced since 1985.

494 SCENE CHANGE

Top Floor, Emerson Studios, 4 –8 Emerson Street, London SE1 9DU
Email: nigels@scene-change.com
Web: http://www.scene-change.com
☎ 020 7960 0261
Contact: Nigel Sadler

Scene Change holds over 10,000 royalty free clips from collections such as the Artbeats Digital Film Library, Digital Juice Jumpbacks, the Digital Vision Motion Clip Library and Scene Change's own specialised collections, all available via a fully searchable online image database. Artbeats Digital Film Library is one of the largest single collections of royalty-free stock footage available. Digital Vision, one of the UK's premier publisher of royalty-free stock footage, brings to Scene Change a great collection of royalty-free motion video content, including clips from all sectors of everyday life, effects footage and a collection of animated backgrounds.

495 SCHOOL OF ART CERAMIC ARCHIVE

University of Wales Aberystwyth, Buarth, Aberystwyth, Wales SY23 1NG
Email: neh@aber.ac.uk
Web: http://www.aber.ac.uk/ceramics
☎ 01970 622399 **Fax**: 01970 622404
Contact: Neil Holland, Curator of Collections

The group comprises reel-to-reel audio tape, cassette and mini-disc recordings of interviews with potters, collectors and others, many of which were conducted as part of the 'Interviews with Potters Working in Wales' Project, along with recordings of lectures delivered by potters. The group also includes video recordings of exhibitions, pottery festivals and television programmes relating to ceramics; photographs and slides of potters, potteries and ceramic works, and digitised images of ceramics from the university collections.

496 SCOTT POLAR RESEARCH INSTITUTE

Cambridge University, Lensfield Road, Cambridge CB2 1ER
Email: rkh10@cam.ac.uk
Web: http://www.spri.cam.ac.uk
☎ 01223 336555 **Fax**: 01223 336549
Contact: Robert Headland, Archivist
Access: By appointment

Includes the Sir Michael Balcon collection, relating to the making of the
1948 film SCOTT OF THE ANTARCTIC, the Ealing Studios collection and the
Herbert Ponting collection, which includes material on the making of his
documentary of the Scott expedition.

497 SCOTTISH LIFE ARCHIVE – GORDON-MORE COLLECTION OF AGRICULTURAL FILMS

Royal Museum of Scotland, Chambers Street, Edinburgh EH1 1JF
Email: d.kidd@nms.ac.uk
Web: http://www.nms.ac.uk/nms/collections/sla.asp?m=5&s=7
☎ 0131 247 4076 / 4346 **Fax**: 0131 247 4312
Contact: Dorothy Kidd
Access: Mon-Fri, by appointment

The collection comprises about sixty films made by the Edinburgh School of
Architecture (c.1935–1950) which have all been copied onto U-matic and
VHS tapes.

498 SCOTTISH ORAL HISTORY CENTRE

Department of History, University of Strathclyde, Glasgow G1 1XQ
Email: a.mcivor@strath.ac.uk
Web: http://www.strath.ac.uk/Departments/History
☎ 0141 548 2227 **Fax**: 0141 552 8509
Contact: Dr. Arthur McIvor, Director

The Scottish Oral History Centre was set up in 1995 within the Department
of History at the University of Strathclyde to support the use of oral history
within the academic community and in cognate areas such as archives and
museums. The Centre is building up an archive of oral history transcripts
which it uses in teaching and which it makes available for *bona fide*
researchers. The archive already holds the transcripts of more than 200
interviews. These are all held in hard-copy form, and some are in disc
format.

499 SCOTTISH SCREEN

2nd floor, 249 West George Street, Glasgow G2 4QE
Email: info@scottishscreen.com
Web: http://www.scottishscreen.com
☎ 0141 302 1700/1730 **Fax**: 0141 302 1711
Contact: Isabella Edgar, Information Manager
Access: Mon-Thu 10.00–17.00; Fri, 10.00–16.30

The Scottish Screen Information Service aims to provide for the information
needs of organisations and individuals concerned with the moving image
in Scotland.

500 SCOTTISH SCREEN ARCHIVE

39–41 Montrose Avenue, Hillington Park, Glasgow, G52 4LA
Email: archive@scottishscreen.com
Web: http://www.scottishscreen.com/archive
☎ 0845 366 4600 (local rate) **Fax**: 0845 366 4601
Contact: Annie Docherty, Production Library Administrator
Access: Mon-Fri 09.00–12.30 and 14.00–17.00, by prior appointment

The Scottish Screen Archive was established in November 1976. The film collection was inherited in part from its parent body, the Scottish Film Council, and has subsequently been enlarged through acquisitions from private and public sources in Scotland. The material dates from 1896 to the present day and concerns aspects of Scottish social, cultural and industrial history.

SEAWARDS THE GREAT SHIPS (1960)

501 SCOTTISH TELEVISION FILM & VIDEOTAPE LIBRARY

Scottish TV, 200 Renfield Street, Glasgow G2 3PR
Email: francesca.scott@smg.plc.uk
Web: http://www.scottishtv.co.uk
☎ 0141 300 3122 **Fax**: 0141 300 3546
Contact: Francesca Scott, Head of Library Sales
Access: Bona fide researchers only, by arrangement. Access for disabled

Scottish Television has held the ITV franchise for Central Scotland since 1957. The library is responsible for the storage and cataloguing of all programme output on film, videotape or videocassette and also maintains the company's advertising commercials library and acquired materials trafficking.

502 SHAKESPEARE CENTRE LIBRARY

The Shakespeare Birthplace Trust, Henley Street, Stratford-upon-Avon, Warwickshire CV37 6QW
Email: library@shakespeare.org.uk
Web: http://www.shakespeare.org.uk/library.htm
☎ 01789 201803 **Fax**: 01789 296083
Contact: Senior Librarian
Access: Mon-Fri, 10.00–17.00. Sat, 09.30–12.30. Staff are available to assist. Access for disabled. Please telephone in advance

The Shakespeare Birthplace Trust Library (founded 1862) and the Library of the Royal Shakespeare Theatre (founded 1880) were amalgamated in 1964. The Library is a research collection on Shakespeare's life, work and times, and on the stage history of his plays. Film and television materials have been added since the late 1970s. The Library purchases videos of Shakespeare films, television documentaries or productions relating to Shakespeare and to the Royal Shakespeare Company, as its budget allows. RSC archive includes production videos received on deposit since the 1980s.

503 SHAKESPEARE INSTITUTE LIBRARY

Information Services, University of Birmingham, Church Street, Stratford-upon-avon, Warwickshire CV37 6HP
Email: J.A.Shaw@bham.ac.uk
Web: http://www.is.bham.ac.uk/shakespeare
☎ 01789 293384 **Fax**: 01789 292021
Contact: James Shaw, Librarian
Access: Limited opening hours

The Shakespeare Institute Library aims to collect films and sound recordings relating to English drama 1564–1642, particularly the works of William Shakespeare. Includes commercially available recordings and off-air television and radio recordings. Archive collections include unpublished Shakespeare film scripts and the archive for the SHAKESPEARE: ANIMATED TALES series. Significant holdings of secondary criticism on Shakespeare on film, television, and radio.

504 SHARK BAY FILMS

The Stables, St.Martin's, Isles Of Scilly TR1 111
Email: john@sharkbayfilms.demon.co.uk
Web: http://www.sharkbayfilms.com
☎ 01326 563811
Contact: John Boyle

Shark Bay Films has an extensive underwater stock footage library with hundreds of hours of footage compiled during fifteen years of filming throughout the oceans of the world. John is a trustee of The Shark Trust, international co-ordinator of the Seychelles Underwater Film Festival SUBIOS, and a regular guest presenter at film festivals worldwide.

505 SHEFFIELD HALLAM UNIVERSITY

Learning Centre, Psalter Lane, Sheffield , South Yorks S11 8UZ
Email: r.a.swift@shu.ac.uk
Web: http://www.shu.ac.uk/services/lc
☎ 0114 225 2721 **Fax**: 0114 225 2717
Contact: Richard Swift, Senior Information Adviser
Access: Mon-Thu, 08.45–21.00. Fri, 08.45–18.00. Sat, 10.00–17.00. Sun,
13.00–20.00. Reduced hours in vacations

The Learning Centre collection supports Sheffield Hallam University's
undergraduate and postgraduate courses in film and media. It contains key
reference books and the journals are a mixture of the popular (e.g. *Empire*,
Premiere), critical (e.g. *Sight & Sound*, *Screen*, *Cahiers du Cinema*) and
trade (e.g. *Variety*, *Broadcast*). A number of early journal titles (e.g. *The
Bioscope*, *Kinematograph Weekly*) are also available on microfilm.
Collection strengths include British cinema, biography, and broadcasting
history and policy. There is a significant collection of approximately 200
items (including videocassettes of feature films) relating to Alfred
Hitchcock.

506 SHEFFIELD LIBRARY AND INFORMATION SERVICES

Central Library, Surrey Street, Sheffield S1 1XZ
Email: localstudies.library@sheffield.gov.uk
Web: http://www.shef.ac.uk/~lib/intro/one.html
☎ 0114 273 5067 **Fax**: 0114 273 5009
Contact: Doug Hindmarch, Senior Local Studies Librarian
Access: By arrangement. Access for disabled.

The Sheffield Libraries collection incorporates material held by the Local
Studies Library, Sheffield Archives and the former South Yorkshire Record
Office. Items relating mainly to Sheffield, particularly the steel industry.

507 SHELL FILM AND VIDEO UNIT

Visual Media Services, Shell Centre, London SE1 7NA
Email: jane.poynor@shell.com
Web: http://www.shell.com
☎ 020 7934 3318 **Fax**: 020 7934 4918
Contact: Jane Poynor, Archive Sales
Access: Disabled visitors have to be accompanied

It contains almost all the films made by the Shell Film Unit since it was set
up in 1934. It also contains copies of films made by and for Shell companies
overseas, but these are not part of the main collection. Most of the films
made during the war when the Shell Film Unit was working for the
Ministry of Information are held by the Imperial War Museum (qv). Since
the collection is really only the work of the Shell Film and Video Unit it can
only expand by taking in the new productions as they are made.

508 SHOTBANK MEDIA LIBRARY

The Old Studios, Kings Yard, Fordinbridge, Hampshire SP6 1AB
Email: orders@shotbank.co.uk
Web: http://www.videofootagelibrary.com
☎ 01722 711 111 **Fax**: 01425 652 111
Contact: Kim McKay, Head of Facility

Shotbank is one of the United Kingdom's leading royalty-free video footage providers. We offer a huge variety of individual video clips and collections to media professionals. Clips are available in PAL or NTSC format as MPEG, AVI, QuickTime and can be downloaded via e-mail or sent to your facility on CD/DVD. Shotbank can also supply media clips on a variety of tape formats. All media clips and collections can be ordered on-line. Includes stock footage of London and European locations, vehicles, transport, sport.

509 SKY NEWS LIBRARY SALES

British Sky Broadcasting Ltd, Unit One, Grant Way, Isleworth, Middlesex TW7 5QD
Email: libsales@bskyb.com
Web: http://www.sky.com/skynewslibsales
☎ 020 7585 4490 or 020 7585 4485 **Fax**: 020 7585 4454
Contact: Susannah Owen, Senior News Library Sales Picture Researcher
Access: By appointment only. Access for disabled

Extensive coverage of world news and current affairs since 1989. Footage includes: the Gulf War, Balkans conflicts, South Africa, Russia and the British Royal Family, entertainment and showbiz. Detailed shotlists are available of all footage – both rushes and cut stories.

510 SOCIAL DEMOCRATIC PARTY (SDP) ARCHIVES

Special Collections, Albert Sloman Library, University of Essex, Wivenhoe Park, Colchester CO4 3SQ
Email: robert@essex.ac.uk
Web: http://libwww.essex.ac.uk
☎ 01206 873477 **Fax**: 01206 873598
Contact: Robert Butler, Librarian

The very substantial archives of the SDP were acquired between 1988 and 1994. The collection consists of some 80 m. of SDP committee minutes and papers, administrative records, publications (including policy papers and Council for Social Democracy records), local SDP files, speeches of the 'Gang of Four', a newspaper cuttings collection, and a small number of video tapes. The archives cover the period 1980–1987.

511 SOCIETY FOR CO-OPERATION IN RUSSIAN AND SOVIET STUDIES

320 Brixton Road, London SW9 6AB
Email: ruslibrary@scrss.org.uk
Web: http://www.scrss.org.uk/theatrekino.htm
☎ 020 7274 2282 **Fax**: 0207274 3230
Contact: John Cunningham
Access: Mon-Fri, 10.00–13.00 and 14.00–18.00. Appointment necessary

The SCRSS library's theatre and cinema collection covers the entire Soviet period, with detailed materials on the 1920s-30s. It includes the writings of theatre practitioners (Meyerhold, Stanislavsky, Vakhtangov, and Nemirovich-Danchenko) and film practitioners (Eisenstein, Pudovkin and Romm), biographies of directors and artistes, histories of theatres, theatre and film criticism. The collection is backed up by a superb visual resource comprising photographs and Russian and Soviet regalia.

512 SOLENT TV

The Media Centre, Lower St James Street, Newport, Isle of Wight, PO30 5
Email: omar@solent.tv
Web: http://www.solent.tv/index.aspx
☎ 01983 522344
Contact: Production team

Solent TV is the first not-for-profit local television station in the UK and was awarded the RSL Isle of Wight (Rowridge) Licence by the then ITC – now OFCOM – to broadcast to the Isle of Wight from 31 October 2002. Solent TV actively encourages local groups to make contact make use of the services it can provide. Solent TV supports a key number of community and charity events throughout the year such as the Isle of Wight Garlic Festival, Ryde Arts Festival and is also the 2005 sponsor of Ryde Carnival. One off VHS copies of the programmes produced by Solent TV can be purchased, including editions of SOLENT TONIGHT, TOP STORY and AFTERNOON LIVE.

513 SOUTH EAST FILM & VIDEO ARCHIVE (now SCREEN ARCHIVE SOUTH EAST)

University of Brighton, Grand Parade, Brighton, East Sussex BN2 2JY
Email: screenarchive@brighton.ac.uk
Web: http://www.brighton.ac.uk/screenarchive
☎ 01273 643213 **Fax**: 01273 643128
Contact: Frank Gray, Curator
Access: By arrangement only. Access for disabled. Conservation Centre at the West Sussex Record Office: County Hall, Orchard Street, Chichester, West Sussex PO19 1RN, tel: 01243 533911 **Fax**: 01243 533959

The South East Film & Video Archive was established in 1992 to locate, collect, preserve and promote films and videotapes made in the counties of Kent, Surrey, East Sussex and West Sussex and the unitary authorities of Medway and Brighton & Hove. The archive is split between two sites: the West Sussex Record Office in Chichester houses the master film material, the University of Brighton focuses on video production Web-site development, educational projects and research. The collection includes newsreels, corporate documentaries, amateur and publicity material. It incorporates material previously held by the Hastings Museum & Art Gallery and the West Sussex Record Office.

514 SOUTH WALES COALFIELD COLLECTION

The South Wales Miners' Library, Hendrefoelan House, Gower Road,
Swansea, Wales SA2 7NB
Email: miners@swan.ac.uk
Web: http://lisweb.swan.ac.uk/swcc/
☎ 01792 518603 **Fax**: 01792 518694
Contact: Sian Williams, South Wales Miners' Librarian
Access: By appointment only

The South Wales Coalfield Collection (SWCC) was established in 1969 to
preserve the documentary records of the mining community of South
Wales. The video recordings consist mainly of interviews, including some
with such figures as Dai Francis, Emlyn Williams and Phil Weekes. Also
included are conferences arranged by the National Union of Mineworkers,
the Trades Union Congress, Llafur and others along with recordings of the
cultural activities of the mining communities; recordings of various news
reports, including American news coverage of the 1984–85 miners strike;
and various documentaries recorded from television broadcasts, including
topics such as the Spanish Civil War.

515 THE SOUTH WEST FILM AND TELEVISION ARCHIVE

Melville Building, Royal William Yard, Stonehouse, Plymouth,
Devon PL1 3RP
Email: elayne@tswfta.co.uk
Web: http://www.tswfta.co.uk
☎ 01752 202650 **Fax**: 01752 205025
Contact: Elayne Hoskin, Director
Access: Mon-Fri, 09.00 to 17.00, by arrangement only. Staff are available
to assist. Access for disabled

The South West Film and Television Archive was founded in 1993. Its
holdings are from 1898 to the present day and its core collections are the
Television South West Film and Video Library (which includes all ITV
material for the area from 1961 to 1992) and the BBC South West Film
Collection (dating from 1961 onward). In addition the Archive also holds
many other amateur and professional collections. The Archive is committed
to providing access to the collections it safeguards. The Archive is a
member of the Film Archive Forum.

516 SOUTHAMPTON CITY ARCHIVES

Southampton City Archives Office, Southampton City Council,
Civic Centre, Southampton SO14 7LY
Email: city.archives@southampton.gov.uk
Web: http://www.southampton.gov.uk/leisure/archives/default.asp#0
☎ 023 8083 2251 **Fax**: 023 8083 2156
Contact: Sue Woolgar, Archives and Services Manager
Access: By arrangement or via the Wessex Film and Sound Archive (qv).
Opening hours: Tue-Fri, 09.30–16.30 (one late evening per month by
appointment)

Collection of a few films which have been deposited in the City Archives
Office (which deals primarily with written material) since 1954, by different
depositors. There is no connection between them and there is no definite
policy for collecting film material, but it is possible that additional items
may be received occasionally.

517 SOUTHAMPTON SOLENT UNIVERSITY

East Park Terrace, Southampton, Hampshire SO14 0YN
Email: john.moore@solent.ac.uk Web: http://www.solent.ac.uk
☎ 023 8031 9248 **Fax**: 023 8031 9697
Contact: John Moore, Head of Library
Access: ERA membership of academic institution. Prior permission
required

Previously known as the Southampton Institute. The Mountbatten Library
serves the whole of the city campus and offers a modern, spacious study
environment with a floor space of 4,500 square metres. It combines
collections of print and multimedia materials with access to an electronic
library that offers fast and comprehensive information both on and off
campus, allowing students to study at times and in places convenient to
themselves. Includes the Ken Russell Collection, a unique archive of
photographs, stills, slides, scripts and personal memorabilia donated by
one of Britain's most innovative directors.

518 SOUTHERN CO-OPERATIVES

44 High Street, Fareham, Hampshire PO16 7BN
Email: link@southernco-op.co.uk
Web: http://www.southernco-op.co.uk
☎ 01329 223000 **Fax**: 01329 223022
Contact: Gerard Blair, Corporate Relations Department
Access: Available to any reputable and recognised research body,
educational/business organisation

The collection is mostly made up of 16mm black and white film (and some
early Agfa colour) produced 1935–39. It records the various commercial
(retailing and productive) undertakings of the Co-operative Society. There
are also film sequences dealing with dairy processing; the bakery; building,
coach building, sign writing; early motor transport, servicing, etc. In
addition there is some coverage of the social, recreational and leisure
involvement within the Co-operative Membership. Some interesting
background material is recorded (City building, e.g. Portsmouth Guildhall –
local parks and recreation areas, which were later damaged or destroyed
during World War II).

519 SOUTHWARK LOCAL STUDIES LIBRARY

211 Borough High Street, London SE1 1JA
Email: local.studies.library@southwark.gov.uk
Web: http://www.southwark.gov.uk
☎ 020 7403 3507 **Fax**: 020 7403 8633
Contact: Ruth Jenkins, Local Studies Librarian
Access: By arrangement only. Disabled access

Inheritance from former Metropolitan Boroughs of Bermondsey,
Southwark and Camberwell. Original material mostly held at the National
Film and Television Archive (qv); video copies are held at the library. The
collection comprises also copies from broadcasts, mainly news and
documentaries regarding the area and copies of commercially produced
videos on events, etc.

520 SPECTRUM RADIO

International Radio Centre, 4 Ingate Place, London SW8 3NS
Email: enquiries@spectrumradio.net
Web: http://www.spectrumradio.net
☎ 020 7627 4433 **Fax**: 020 7627 3409

Does not archive news items as it uses ITN. Occasionally keeps interviews, e.g. with Jeffrey Archer, Michael Barrymore. Maintains a private music library of world music.

521 SPROUT

Gainsborough House, 2 Sheen Road, Richmond-upon-Thames YW9 1AE
Email: dan.atkins@sprout-media.com
Web: http://www.sprout-media.com
☎ 020 8973 2440 **Fax**: 020 8973 2441
Contact: Dan Atkins

Specialist in action sports footage, previously known as Chillimedia.

522 ST ANDREWS UNIVERSITY LIBRARY

North Street, St Andrews, Fife KY16 9TR
Email: jmy@st-andrews.ac.uk
Web: http://www-library.st-andrews.ac.uk
☎ 01334 462294 **Fax**: 01334 462282
Contact: Jean Young, Electronic Resources
Access: No special restrictions when library open

The library holds a small but growing collection of DVDs, videocassettes and audiocassettes. The existing collection of around 400 videocassettes is held near the Microform area, on Level 3 of the University Library. There are also a large number of videos of Spanish language films, used for teaching purposes. In addition, a small collection of Italian language audiocassettes is held. All these DVDs, videocassettes and tapes are separately listed in SAULCAT, the Library's online catalogue.

523 ST CATHARINE'S COLLEGE LIBRARY

Trumpington Street, Cambridge CB2 1RL
Email: librarian@caths.cam.ac.uk Web:
https://dragon.caths.cam.ac.uk/liberty3/opac
☎ 01223 338343 **Fax**: 01223 338340
Contact: Suzan Griffiths, Assistant Librarian
Access: Current members of college only

The video collection comprises films of mainly foreign directors.

524 ST GEORGE'S CHAPEL, WINDSOR CASTLE

St George's Chapel Archives, The Cloisters, Windsor Castle,
Windsor SL4 1NJ
Email: archives@stgeorges-windsor.org
Web: http://www.stgeorges-windsor.org/archives/arch_index.asp
☎ 01753 865538 **Fax**: 01753 620165
Contact: Dr Eileen Scarff, Archivist
Access: By arrangement only

No collecting policy; donations or the result of special occasions.

525 ST GEORGE'S UNIVERSITY OF LONDON

AV Services, Hunter Wing, Cranmer Terrace, London SW17 0RE
Email: rpinhasi@sgul.ac.uk
Web: http://www.sgul.ac.uk/depts/is/library/spec_coll/av.htm
☎ 020 8725 0855 **Fax**: 020 8725 5377
Contact: Rita Pinhasi, Acquisitions Co-ordinator
Access: Term time: Mon-Fri, 08.00–22.00; Sat 09.00–17.00. Vacation: Mon-Fri, 09.00–21.00; Sat, closed

The reference collection covers medical, nursing and other health related subjects.

526 STAFFORDSHIRE FILM ARCHIVE

Staffordshire University, Nelson Library, Beaconside, Stafford ST18 0AD
Email: mc4@staffs.ac.uk
Web: http://www.staffs.ac.uk/services/library_and_info/library.html
☎ 01782 294547 / 01785 353219 **Fax**: 01782 295799
Contact: Mick Chalmers
Access by arrangement. Staff are available to assist. Access for disabled

Housed at Staffordshire University, the collection was set up in 1980 and features footage of the industrial background and social history of the Staffordshire area. Included in the collection is footage of many of the local trades once found in the locality such as pottery making, the entire Rubery Owen Archive (including British racing motors 1950–1964) and the British Commercial Vehicle Museum Archive (lorries and buses).

527 STAFFORDSHIRE UNIVERSITY

Thompson Library, College Road, Stoke On Trent, Staffs ST4 2XS
Email: d.e.roberts1@staffs.ac.uk
Web: http://www.staffs.ac.uk/services/library_and_info/library.html
☎ 01782 294809 **Fax**: 01782 295 799
Contact: Debbie Roberts, Senior Subject & Learning Support Librarian

Special collections include the Staffordshire Film Archive (qv) as well as hundreds of video and DVD titles and related publications.

528 STATES OF GUERNSEY FILM & SOUND ARCHIVE

Island Archives Service, 29 Victoria Road, St Peter Port, Guernsey GY1 1HU
Email: archives@gov.gg
Web: http://user.itl.net/~glen/archgsy.html
☎ 01481 724512 **Fax**: 01481 715814
Contact: D.M. Ogier, Administrative Assistant
Access: 09.30–16.30

Collection arising from: films of royal visits, etc. acquired from 1921; film deposits, 1915 onwards; films/sound tapes prepared for the Education Department, 1970s; and the production of tapes (for sale) from collection of private films, 1930s onwards.

529 STEVENSON COLLEGE

Bankhead Avenue, Edinburgh, Lothian EH11 4DE
Email: mcampbell@stevenson.ac.uk
Web: http://www.stevenson.ac.uk
☎ 0131 535 4739 **Fax**: 0131 535 4666
Contact: Morag Campbell, Head of Faculty, Creative Arts
Access: College hours, by arrangement

Large college producing a continuous stream of student created moving image material, from drama to factual. College provides training in audio-visual technology, television operations and production and degree foundation film and television. The work is a microcosm of students' perceptions of life in its variegated forms as seen through the lens of student film-makers. It ranges from documentary to location drama, from pop promos to sport. Many graduates work behind the camera in various capacities with BBC, ITV, independents, and major film studios in the UK and abroad.

530 SUFFOLK RECORD OFFICE, BURY ST EDMUNDS BRANCH

77 Raingate Street, Bury St Edmunds IP33 2AR
Email: bury.ro@suffolkcc.gov.uk
Web: http://www.suffolk.gov.uk/LeisureAndCulture/Libraries
☎ 01284 352352 **Fax**: 01284 352355
Contact: S. Reed, Public Services Manager
Access: Limited. Access for disabled

Cine-films deposited for preservation by private or institutional depositors. Future deposits, unless part of a larger archive, would probably be referred to the East Anglian Film Archive (qv).

531 SUFFOLK RECORD OFFICE, IPSWICH BRANCH

Gatacre Road, Ipswich IP1 2LQ
Email: Gwyn.Thomas@libher.suffolkcc.gov.uk
Web: http://www.suffolkcc.gov.uk/libraries_and_heritage/sro
☎ 01473 584541 **Fax**: 01473 548533
Contact: Gwyn Thomas, Senior Archivist
Access: By arrangement only. Access for disabled

Cine-films deposited for preservation by private or institutional depositors. Future deposits, unless part of a larger archive, would probably be referred to the East Anglian Film Archive (qv).

532 SUFFOLK RECORD OFFICE, LOWESTOFT BRANCH

Central Library, Clapham Road, Lowestoft NR32 1DR
Email: lowestoft.ro@suffolkcc.gov.uk
Web: http://tinyurl.co.uk/2fix
☎ 01502 405357 **Fax**: 01502 405350
Contact: L. Clarke, Public Service Manager
Access: Limited. Access for disabled

Videos deposited for preservation by private or institutional depositors. Future deposits, unless part of a larger archive, would probably be referred to the East Anglian Film Archive (qv).

533 SUNDERLAND CITY LIBRARY AND ARTS CENTRE

Fawcett Street, Sunderland, Tyne and Wear SR1 1RE
Email: julie.mccann@sunderland.gov.uk
Web: http://www.sunderland.gov.uk/libraries/City-Library-and-Arts-Centre.asp
☎ 0191 5148424 **Fax**: 0191 514 8444
Contact: Julie McCann, Principal Librarian (E-Resources & Information Services)

General collection relating to film, radio, television and new technologies.

534 SUNRISE RADIO

Sunrise House, Sunrise Road, Southall, Middlesex UB2 4AU
Email: reception@sunriseradio.com
Web: http://www.sunriseradio.com
☎ 020 8574 6666 **Fax**: 020 8813 9700
Contact: Tony Lit, Managing Director

Sunrise Radio launched on Monday 5 November 1989, to service West London's Asian community. It was the UK's first twenty-four hour Asian radio station and in fact the first independent twenty-four hour Asian radio station in the world. Sunrise London was launched on 1 January 1994, transmitting on 1458 AM to Greater London and the Home Counties. Holds forty-two days' output to meet legal requirement. All commercials are archived. Maintains a large private collection of South Asian music.

535 SUNSET & VINE

30 Sackville Street, London W1S 3DY
Email: nickv@sunsetvine.co.uk
Web: http://www.sunsetvine.co.uk
☎ 020 7478 7356 **Fax**: 020 7478 7407
Contact: Nick Vance, Head of Library Sales

Handles a variety of collections pertaining to music and sport – the library also includes the Music Box library of around 7,000 music interviews and access to over 12,000 music promo clips. Clients include VH-1, NEVERMIND THE BUZZCOCKS (BBC2), I LOVE THE…80s (BBC1), TOP 10s (C4).

536 SURREY HISTORY CENTRE

130 Goldsworth Road, Woking, Surrey GU21 6ND
Email: shs@surreycc.gov.uk
Web: http://www.surreycc.gov.uk/surreyhistoryservice
☎ 01483 518737 **Fax**: 01483 518738
Contact: Michael Page, Head of acquisitions and processing
Access: Open

The film and video held by Surrey History Centre forms part of the growing collection of archive and local studies material relating to the county of Surrey. All original films deposited with the centre are transferred to the South East Film & Video Archive (SEFVA, qv). Video copies of films relevant to Surrey are held at Surrey History Centre and are available for public viewing. Also, new compilation VHS/DVD produced jointly with SEFVA, SURREY ON FILM 1914–1953: A COMMUNITY IN PEACE AND WAR traces community life in the county from peacetime through the trauma of two world wars and closes with the coronation celebrations of Queen Elizabeth II in 1953.

From Joseph Emberton's family films EMBERTON FAMILY LIFE, late 1930s

537 SURREY INSTITUTE OF ART & DESIGN – ANIMATION RESEARCH CENTRE ARCHIVE

Faculty of Arts & Media, Falkner Road, Farnham, Surrey GU9 7DS
Email: jwalker@surrart.ac.uk
Web: http://www.surrart.ac.uk/arc
☎ 01252 892 806 **Fax**: 01252 892 787
Contact: Jim Walker, ARC Archive Manager
Access: The collections are currently housed off-site. Researchers are
welcome to make an appointment to view and peruse the collections

The ARC aims to promote, contribute to and support the under-researched
discipline of animation theory. The aims of the archive are to maintain and
expand holdings of UK animation and to develop and produce teaching
and other support materials for animation curricula and other disciplines
affiliate with international archival institutions. The library has a significant
collection of animation films on video as a research resource for students
and scholars. These videos represent one of the largest animation film
study collections in England.

538 SURVIVAL – ANGLIA (SURCAT)

c/o ITN Source, 200 Gray's Inn Road, London WC1X 8XZ
Email: sales@itnsource.com
Web: http://www.surcat.com
☎ 020 7430 4480 **Fax**: 020 7430 4453
Contact: Kathey Battrick, Research Manager
Access: 09.00–17.30. Staff are available to assist. Access for disabled

The Survival Unit has produced over 1,000 natural history documentaries for
the ITV Network since 1961. The Library exists to service stock shot sales and
is now known as SURCAT. Footage sales are now handled by ITN Source (qv).

539 SWANSEA SOUND

PO Box 1170, Victoria Road, Gowerton, Swansea, Wales SA4 3AB
Email: reception@swanseasound.co.uk
Web: http://www.swanseasound.co.uk
☎ 01792 511170 **Fax**: 01792 511171
Contact: Andy Griffiths, Programme Director

The radio station holds forty-two days' output to meet legal requirement.
Does not maintain an archive but holds a private music library.

540 SWINDON FM

Old Town Court, 10–14 High Street, Old Town, Swindon SN1 3EP
Email: studio@swindonfm.co.uk Web: http://www.swindonfm.co.uk
☎ 01793 509700
Contact: Sean McHugh, Director

Swindon FM was born out of a very real and genuine passion for a local
Swindon radio. Swindon FM is now broadcasting seven days a week on
DAB Digital radio between 6am and 10pm. The station is also available
online.

541 TALK SPORT

18 Hatfields, Southwark, London SE1 8DJ
Email: jyoung@thewirelessgroup.net
Web: http://www.talksport.net
☎ 020 7959 7800 **Fax**: 020 7959 7804
Contact: Jonathan Young, Head of Creative

Formerly Talk Radio. The station holds forty-two days' output to meet legal requirement. Retrieval of items within this period is possible. Recordings of major sports events, e.g. Euro 2000, are usually kept. Some Talk Radio recordings are held.

542 TATE BRITAIN

Education Department, Tate Gallery, Millbank, London SW1 4RG
Email: ben.hick@tate.org.uk
Web: http://www.tate.org.uk/research/researchservices/archive
☎ 020 7887 8757 **Fax**: 020 7887 8762
Contact: Ben Hick, Audiovisual and Film Manager
Access: Access for disabled. By written arrangement

Collection began on an occasional basis from 1962, and then on a permanent basis from 1971. The collection includes manuscripts, correspondence, diaries, notebooks, sketchbooks and other artworks, photographs, press cuttings, some printed ephemera and posters, film and sound recordings, and administrative records. It very selectively collects material relating to earlier British art and twentieth century foreign artists when they relate closely to Tate's collection. In addition to acquired collections, the archive also houses supporting material in three artificial collections comprising c.100,000 photographs, over 2,000 posters and over 3,000 audio-visual accessions.

543 TAY FM

6 North Isla Street, Dundee DD3 7JQ
Email: tayfm@srh.co.uk
Web: http://www.tayfm.co.uk
☎ 01382 200800 **Fax**: 01382 423252
Contact: Arthur Ballingall, Programme Director

Radio station. A variety of programmes are kept from the last twenty years. In particular, these include interviews with local celebrities and community-based interviews and programmes. News items are not really archived.

544 TEESSIDE ARCHIVES

Exchange House, 6 Marton Road, Middlesbrough TS1 1DB
Email: teessidearchives@middlesbrough.gov.uk
Web: http://www.middlesbrough.gov.uk/ccm/portal
☎ 01642 248321 **Fax**: 01642 248391
Contact: David Tyrell, Archivist
Access: Mon, Wed, Thu 09.00–17.00 Tue 09.00–21.00 Fri 09.00–16.30.
Access for disabled

Teesside Archives is responsible for collecting and preserving archival material from official and private sources in the areas served by the councils of Middlesbrough, Redcar and Cleveland, Stockton and Hartlepool. Holds seven hours of video: documentary and oral history material, and four films.

545 THAMES VALLEY UNIVERSITY

Walpole House, 18–22 Bond Street, Ealing, London W5 5AA
Email: elizabeth.ward@tvu.ac.uk   Web: http://www.tvu.ac.uk
☎ 020 8231 2648 **Fax**: 020 8231 2631
Contact: Liz Ward, Audio Visual Librarian
Access: No external access to slide collection, electronic databases (or PCs), or ERA licensed off-air recordings. External access for students is allowed via SCONUL scheme and UK Libraries Plus. Otherwise by written arrangement, but restricted

The main collection supporting media-related pathways is located in the St Mary's Road Learning Resources Centre. It supports media arts and creative arts and technologies pathways, not just film and television. Subjects include broadcasting, cinema and film, communications, film industry, media studies, radio, television and video production. There is a large film collection on video, mainly off-air recordings, which covers all genres, independent and classic films and some foreign feature films; there is also a growing collection of films in DVD format. There is a collection of about sixty radio programmes, particularly plays, comedies, and some illustrating the history of radio.

546 THREE S FILMS – ACTION SPORTS IMAGE LIBRARY

12 Regent Square, Penzance TR18 4BG
Email: john@threesfilms.com   Web: http://www.threesfilms.com
☎ 01736 367912 **Fax**: 01736 350957
Contact: John Adams, Managing Director
Access: Mon-Fri 10.00–17.00

Archive and contemporary collection of surfing films on video. Action Sports Image Library originated in 16mm, 35mm and Beta. The Library holds also *Made in Cornwall*, a collection of films and programmes concerning Cornwall.

547 TIBET FOUNDATION

1 St James Market, London SW1Y 4SB
Email: getca@tibet-foundation.org
Web: http://www.tibet-foundation.org/index.php
☎ 020 7930 6001 **Fax**: 020 7930 6002
Contact: Phuntsog Wangyal, Director
Access: By arrangement

The Tibet Foundation holds video material relating to Tibetan Buddhist teachings and Tibetan cultural programmes.

548 THE TIBETAN KNOWLEDGE CONSORTIUM (TKC)

The Orient Foundation, 15 Gay Street, Bath BA1 2PH
Email: admin@tibetanknowledge.org
Web: http://www.tibetanknowledge.org
☎ 020 7278 2576
Contact: Graham Coleman, Co-Director

The Tibetan Knowledge Consortium is the coming together of three of the world's leading Tibetan cultural conservancy organisations, which includes the major Tibetan monastic universities, libraries, medical colleges and arts schools of India, Nepal and Inner Asia. It is integrating into a single multimedia digital library: the world's largest collection of digitized classical Tibetan texts and the largest collection of recordings of oral commentarial explanations to key Tibetan texts, together with the world's most comprehensive video archive of Tibetan arts skills, created by the Orient Foundation (UK and India).

549 TOWER FM

The Mill, Brownlow Way, Bolton, Greater Manchester BL1 2RA
Email: michaelbenjamin@towerfm.co.uk
Web: http://www.towerfm.co.uk
☎ 01204 387000 **Fax**: 01204 534065
Contact: Michael Benjamin, Station Director

Tower FM started life nine years before getting the full transmission licence as Bury Sound. The station was granted various RSL licences these normally for a period of one month. In 1999 however the Radio Authority granted the station a full licence to serve Bolton & Bury and Tower FM was born. The radio station holds forty-two days' output to meet legal requirement.

550 TOWER HAMLETS LOCAL HISTORY LIBRARY AND ARCHIVES

Bancroft Library, 277 Bancroft Road, London E1 4DQ
Email: localhistory@towerhamlets.gov.uk
Web: http://www.towerhamlets.gov.uk
☎ 020 7364 1289 **Fax**: 020 7364 1292
Contact: Chris Lloyd, Local History Librarian
Access: Tue, Thu, 09.00–20.00. Fri 09.00–18.00. Sat 09.00–17.00. Access for disabled. There is a ramp to the front door of the building and a lift

Library formed by amalgamating the local history collections of three former metropolitan boroughs of Bethnal Green, Poplar and Stepney in 1965. Some films of local interest in the Poplar and Stepney collections have been added to in recent years with films mostly copied from those in the National Film and Television Archive (qv).

Tibetan Knowledge Consortium

551 TRAINING SERVICES

Brooklands House, 29 Hythegate, Werrington, Peterborough PE4 7ZP
Email: tipton@trainingservices.demon.co.uk
Web: http://www.trainingservices.demon.co.uk
☎ 01733 327337 **Fax**: 01733 575537
Contact: Christine Tipton, Proprietor
Access: 09.00–17.00

Library of approximately 100 titles on management, health and safety training video packages.

552 TREADWELL

Now part of Footage Farm (qv), 22 Newman Street, London W1T 1PH
Email: English@footagefarm.co.uk
Web: http://www.footagefarm.co.uk
☎ 020 7631 3773 **Fax**: 020 7631 3774
Contact: Orly Yadin, Managing Director
Office open 9.00–18.00; please phone in advance

The Treadwell collection was acquired by Footage Farm in 2001 and has been absorbed into it. The collection specialised in represented materials from the United Kingdom, Russia and Germany.

553 TRILITH RURAL VIDEO UNIT

Corner Cottage, Brickyard Lane, Bourton, Gillingham, Dorset SP8 5PJ
Email: johnholman@hopstep.demon.co.uk
Web: http://www.farmradio.co.uk
☎ 01747 840750 or 01747 840727
Contact: John Holman, Joint Director
Access: By prior arrangement

Trilith is a media charity; its general activities include video, television and radio production and community media training. Trilith has gathered an extensive collection of moving images, mainly of Dorset but also from Wiltshire, dating from 1905 to the present day, both amateur and professional. There is also a steadily growing amount of audio material which is being produced by the various community radio production projects run by Trilith. This mainly consists of short, documentary type material but also includes some original short drama.

554 TUA FILM COLLECTION

17 Kingsway, Leicester LE3 2JL
☎ 0116 289 0531 **Fax**: 0116 289 0531
Contact: Rob Foxon, Owner

The TUA Film Collection was established in the 1970s to support Rob Foxon's archive railway film shows. It has subsequently developed to encompass other forms of transport (road, aircraft, shipping etc.) and British history. The collection dates from 1895 to the present day and forms the source material for Rob's nationwide *Railways Remembered* and *Bygone Britain* archive film shows. The local history collection is now formed into the Leicestershire Film Archive (qv). The specialised 16mm railway collection is probably one of the finest in the UK and covers all aspects of British and world railway operations. It includes pioneer footage from the birth of the cinema, melodrama, publicity, documentary and instructional films, together with footage of amateur shot railway film records.

555 TUC LIBRARY COLLECTIONS

Holloway Road Learning Centre, London Metropolitan University, 236 Holloway Road, London N7 6PP

Email: c.coates@londonmet.ac.uk

Web: http://www.londonmet.ac.uk/libraries/tuc

☎ 020 7133 2260 **Fax**: 020 7133 2529

Contact: Christine Coates

Access: Mon-Fri, 09.15–16.45. By appointment only

The TUC Library Collection was transferred to the University of North London, now London Metropolitan University, in 1996. The collection was first established in 1922 for the use of the TUC and affiliated unions, but its specialisation led to its parallel development as a major research library in the social sciences. Major strengths of the library are the large holdings of pamphlets and other ephemera from unions, pressure groups and campaign movements which have survived here as in few other comparable libraries. The majority of this material dates from the 1920s onwards, although some earlier pamphlets date back to the nineteenth century.

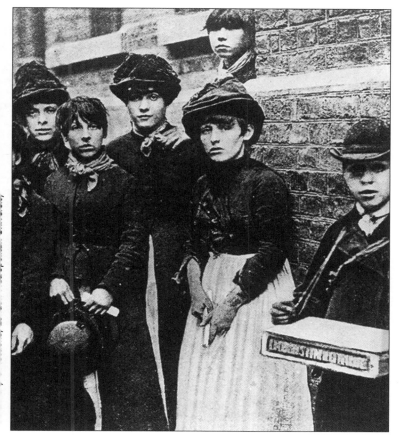

Match Workers at the Bryant and May Factory, London, 1888

556 TWI ARCHIVE

McCormack House, Burlington Lane, London W4 2TH
Email: chope-dunbar@imgworld.com
Web: http://www.twiarchive.com
☎ 020 8233 5500 **Fax**: 020 8233 5301
Contact: Charles Hope-Dunbar, Sales Director

Extensive experience in archive management, acquisitions and commercial exploitation of the rights to many of the world's most prestigious sporting events. The collection includes major sporting federations and an array of non-sporting footage and stockshots. These include Rugby World Cup, ITF, AELTC (Wimbledon), the Nobel Foundation, the PGA European Tour, the Ruppersberg Collection of American History and many more.

557 ULSTER FOLK AND TRANSPORT MUSEUM

National Museums and Galleries of Northern Ireland, Cultra, County Down, Holywood, Northern Ireland BT18 0EU
Email: uftmphotoarchive@talk21.com
Web: http://www.uftm.org.uk
☎ 02890 428428 **Fax**: 02890 428728
Contact: Kenneth Anderson, Head of Photographic Archive
Access: Generally, material is available for educational and research use

Founded in 1958, the museum holds a sizeable audio-visual archive which includes film and videotape material. Material from BBC Northern Ireland is also held in the collection. Northern Ireland's new Digital Film Archive includes newsreel footage of the Belfast-built *Titanic*, World Wars I and II, aviatrix Amelia Earhart's accidental landing at Derry in the 1930s, and the reconstruction years of the 1950s. Television footage includes the Beatles interviewed on UTV in the early 1960s, documentaries, television news, drama and feature films. The Digital Film Archive is available free of charge on PCs to six educational centres around Northern Ireland.

558 ULSTER TELEVISION FILM LIBRARY

Ulster Television Limited, Havelock House, Ormeau Road, Belfast BT7 1EB
Email: ddoherty@utvplc.com
Web: http://www.u.tv
☎ 028 90 262147 **Fax**: 028 9024 6695
Contact: Declan Doherty, Archives Supervisor
Access: Film Library staff will try to answer queries from any source

Ulster Television holds the Independent Television Commission's franchise to broadcast on Channel 3 in Northern Ireland. A selection of material has been kept since the inception of the station on 31 October 1959.

559 UNDERCURRENTS

Old Telephone Exchange, Pier Street, Swansea, Wales, SA1 1RY
Email: archive@undercurrents.org
Web: http://www.undercurrents.org
☎ 01792 455900
Contact: Paul O'Connor, Director
Access: Limited. Access for disabled

UNDERCURRENTS is an alternative news video magazine distributed via VHS and the Internet. Since 1993 Undercurrents has distributed and archived environment and social justice news of direct action protest which have been recorded by both activists and video journalists on camcorders. Many of the 'micro documentaries' have won international awards. The perspective comes from the direct viewpoint of the community in struggle. Undercurrents the organisation also offers video training and archives all tapes on Betacam SP.

560 UNITED SOCIETY FOR THE PROPAGATION OF THE GOSPEL (USPG)

Partnership House, 157 Waterloo Road, London SE1 8XA
Email: archive@uspg.org.uk
Web: http://www.uspg.org.uk
☎ 020 7928 8681 **Fax**: 020 7928 2371
Contact: Catherine Wakeling, Archivist
Access: USPG's film collection is deposited with the National Film and Television Archive (qv)

There are fifty-six films – all 16mm. Researchers should contact the NFTVA to view the material. Films date from the 1920s to the 1970s. Films were produced by the Society for the Propagation of the Gospel in Foreign Parts (SPG) and the Universities' Mission to Central Africa (UMCA), which merged in 1965 to form USPG. Films were produced to educate supporters about the work of the societies and to assist in raising funds. The subject matter reflects the diversity of work undertaken around the world.

561 UNIVERSITY COLLEGE CHICHESTER

Learning Resources Centre, College Lane, Chichester,
West Sussex PO19 4PE
Email: marketing@ucc.ac.uk
Web: http://www.ucc.ac.uk
☎ 01243 816089 **Fax**: 01243 816080
Contact: Learning Resources Centre Staff

The book collection supports the teaching of modules and includes standard undergraduate text books, introductions and readers on film theory, film history and film studies. Other areas include: the development of Hollywood and its politics, sexuality as portrayed in films, national cinemas, popular television in Britain, television comedy, soap operas, children and television, Bakhtin theories, etc. The collection of films and videos is also closely related to what is taught and thus is a mixed one.

562 UNIVERSITY OF ABERDEEN

Aberdeen Campus, Hilton Place, Aberdeen AB24 4FA
Email: c.munro@abdn.ac.uk
Web: http://www.norcol.ac.uk
☎ 01224 273321 **Fax**: 01224 273956
Contact: Carole Munro, Senior Librarian

The collection comprises mainly off-air recordings of educational television broadcasts. Formerly the Northern College of Education.

563 UNIVERSITY OF BIRMINGHAM
BARBER MUSIC LIBRARY

Edgbaston, Birmingham B15 2TT
Email: j.a.gray@bham.ac.uk
Web: http://www.is.bham.ac.uk/barbermusic
☎ 0121 414 5851 **Fax**: 0121 414 5853
Contact: Jules Gray, Manager

Holdings include: books, periodicals, manuscripts, correspondence, programmes, videos/films/DVDs, scores/libretti/music, sound recordings/ CDs, production material.

564 UNIVERSITY OF BIRMINGHAM LIBRARY

University of Birmingham, Main Library, Edgbaston, Birmingham B15 2TT
Email: l.c.priestley@bham.ac.uk
Web: http://www.is.bham.ac.uk
☎ 0121 414 5817 **Fax**: 0121 471 4691
Contact: Lydia Priestley, Language & Media Resource Centre
Access: By arrangement for non-University members

The Language and Media Resource Centre was established to support the multimedia needs of students and staff.

565 UNIVERSITY OF BRIGHTON, DEPARTMENT OF
INFORMATION SERVICES

G4b Cockcroft Building, Lewes Road, Brighton BN2 4GJ
Email: B.Beresford@brighton.ac.uk
Web: http://library.brighton.ac.uk
☎ 01273 642 769 **Fax**: 01273 606 093
Contact: Barbara Beresford, Media Librarian
Access: Ring to confirm opening hours

The Department of Information Services has four libraries which are open to the public. Each library has a substantial video collection as part of its subject resources. Although the majority of programmes are off-air recordings, there is a large number of commercially available specialist programmes in each library. Three of the libraries are located in or near Brighton town centre: St Peter s House Library, Aldrich Library and Falmer Library. The fourth, Queenswood Library, is in Eastbourne. Each library has a telephone line for enquiries and it is recommended that visitors phone the relevant site in the first instance or search the library catalogue online.

566 UNIVERSITY OF BRISTOL, DEPARTMENT OF DRAMA – THEATRE, FILM, TELEVISION

Cantocks Close, Woodlands Road, Bristol, Avon BS8 1UP
Email: jacqueline.maingard@bristol.ac.uk
Web: http://www.bristol.ac.uk/drama
☎ 0117 928 7833
Contact: Jacqueline Maingard, Lecturer, Film and Television Studies

Established in 1947, ours was the first department at a British university dedicated to the study of drama in performance. We were also the first to introduce the practical and theoretical study of film and television. Our resources include the Wickham Theatre, an adaptable space where its productions are presented and practical theatre teaching takes place; the Brandt Cinema and video viewing complex which serve the study of film and television; and the internationally recognised Theatre Collection which is both a theatre archive and a reference library. The department has broadcast-standard film and video making equipment.

567 UNIVERSITY OF BRISTOL, DEPARTMENT OF RUSSIAN

17 Woodland Road, Bristol BS8 1TE
Email: Birgit.Beumers@bris.ac.uk
Web: http://www.bris.ac.uk/Depts/SML/Russian
☎ 0117 928 7596
Contact: Birgit Beumers
Access: 09.00–17.00

The department has its own material resources room which is equipped with live television (currently linked to NTV International), two designated computer work-stations for use with Russian and Czech, and a collection of resources relating to Russian and Czech language and culture. It is located near to the Arts Faculty Library, which has a large Russian holding built up over many years and also a collection of films on VHS and DVD.

568 UNIVERSITY OF CAMBRIDGE FACULTY OF EDUCATION

184 Hills Road, Cambridge CB2 2PQ
Email: library@educ.cam.ac.uk
Web: http://www.educ.cam.ac.uk
☎ 01223 767700 **Fax**: 01223 767602
Contact: Angela Cutts, Faculty Librarian

Audio-visual holdings include radio programmes on education and related subject areas.

569 UNIVERSITY OF CENTRAL LANCASHIRE LIBRARY & LEARNING RESOURCES SERVICE

St Peter's Square, Preston, Lancashire PR1 2HE
Email: aturner-bishop@uclan.ac.uk
Web: http://www.uclan.ac.uk/library/index.htm
☎ 01772 892 2285 **Fax**: 01772 892960
Contact: Adrian Turner-Bishop
Access: Library opening hours

Large collection of feature films on video from early years compilations to latest blockbusters. Small but growing collection of video art. Fashion collection videos.

570 UNIVERSITY OF DERBY
LIBRARY & LEARNING RESOURCES

Kedleston Road, Derby DE22 1GB
Email: j.robinson@derby.ac.uk
Web: http://www.derby.ac.uk
☎ 01332 591282
Contact: Jane Robinson

Materials cover books, journals, videos, DVDs, and slides. Indexes include
FIAF International Film Archive, International Index to the Performing Arts.

571 UNIVERSITY OF EXETER BILL DOUGLAS CENTRE

The Old Library, Prince of Wales Road, Exeter EX4 4SB
Email: M.L.Allen@exeter.ac.uk
Web: http://www.centres.ex.ac.uk/bill.douglas/menu.html
☎ 01392 264321 **Fax**: 01392 263871
Contact: Michelle Allen, Curator
Access: Galleries open Mon-Fri, 10.00–16.00. Research Centre Mon-Fri,
10.00–13.00 and 14.00–17.00

The Bill Douglas Centre collection consists of all types of artefacts, books
and archival material relating to the history of the cinema and pre-cinema.
The Centre itself does not collect films, but does acquire anything relating
to them. Within those materials which relate to the history of cinema,
there are important collections of sheet music from films, biographies of
film stars and directors, film annuals, fiction connected to the film industry,
film stills, postcards, posters and cigarette cards. Other items include toys
linked to films, a good library of technical film books (especially from the
early years of the century), film scripts, academic histories and critical
studies, and a wide range of periodicals.

Bill Douglas Centre

Cinematographe

572 UNIVERSITY OF GLASGOW MEDIA SERVICES

64 Southpark Avenue, Glasgow G12 8LB
Email: B.A.Farmer@udcf.gla.ac.uk
Web: http://www.gla.ac.uk/media
☎ 0141 330 4908 **Fax**: 0141 330 5674
Contact: Barbara Farmer, Head of Production
Access: By prior permission

Subjects relate predominantly to the teaching in all eight faculties, ranging from lab techniques to documentaries and promotional videos.

573 UNIVERSITY OF GREENWICH LIBRARY

Woolwich Campus, Beresford Street, London SE18 6BU
Email: K.B.M.Marshall@greenwich.ac.uk
Web: http://www.gre.ac.uk/lib/index.html
☎ 020 8331 8197 **Fax**: 020 8331 8464
Contact: Kate Marshall, Humanities Librarian
Access: Mon-Thu, 09.00–21.00. Fri-Sat, 09.00–17.00 during term time

The University of Greenwich library service is spread out over six campus libraries. All comments and statistics relate to Woolwich campus library only. The teaching of the 'Media and Communication' and 'Media and Society' courses takes place at Woolwich and the materials detailed will cater for these courses. Although the collections are modest at present, we will be developing them over the next few years, especially in the field of film and media studies.

574 UNIVERSITY OF KENT AT CANTERBURY, THE TEMPLEMAN LIBRARY

Canterbury, Kent CT2 7NX
Email: d.whittaker@kent.ac.uk
Web: http://library.kent.ac.uk/library
☎ 01227 764 000 **Fax**: 01227 475 495
Contact: Derek Whittaker, Subject Librarian
Access: Mon-Thu, 09.00–22.00. Fri, 09.00–20.00, Sat, 12.00–19.00, Sun, 14.00–19.00. Reduced hours in vacations (all on Internet site)

The book collection is very broad based and reflects teaching and research interests. It includes: History and Film, Film and Philosophy, Film analysis, Documentary interpretation and criticism, British Cinema, American Cinema, European Cinema, Gender, Narrative Cinema, Experimental and Fantastic Cinema.

575 UNIVERSITY OF NEWCASTLE UPON TYNE SCHOOL OF MODERN LANGUAGES

Newcastle Upon Tyne NE1 7RU
Email: ann.davies@ncl.ac.uk
Web: http://www.ncl.ac.uk/crif
☎ 0191 222 7441 (Secretary) **Fax**: 0191 222 5442
Contact: Ann Davies
Access: By prior permission

VHS/DVD collection of mainly off-air recordings of main national cinemas. Library holdings of books (not periodicals) in all areas of film.

576 UNIVERSITY OF READING, FACULTY OF LETTERS AND SOCIAL SCIENCES

Whiteknights, Reading RG6 6AA
Email: a.w.e.phillips@reading.ac.uk
Web: http://www.rdg.ac.uk/libweb/
☎ 0118 931 8878 **Fax**: 0118 931 8873
Contact: A.W.E. Phillips, Head of Department
Access: Limited access for children under ten at Main Library, Whiteknights. Restrictions on loan of software and AV material and access to special collections

The Department of Archives and Manuscripts is responsible not only for a large body of university archives and records but also for around 150 major collections of historical and literary papers and over 1,500 other items. These include: Vernon Bartlett (1894–1983), author, journalist and broadcaster; the Beckett Collection is the world's largest collection of Samuel Beckett resources, including audio-visual material, photographs and ephemera; papers of Elinor Glyn, playwright and novelist (1864–1943), who was chiefly known for popular romantic fiction and for Hollywood film scripts; correspondence of David Lean (1908–1991), and others.

577 UNIVERSITY OF SALFORD, DEPARTMENT OF MEDIA & PERFORMING ARTS

Adelphi Campus, Peru Street, Salford M3 6EQ
Email: g.palmer@salford.ac.uk
Web: http://www.salford.ac.uk/mmp
☎ 0161 295 6044
Contact: Gareth Palmer, Head of Division

Contemporary Documentary Archive: the collection consists of mainly documentaries dealing with crime and the police (e.g. CRIMEWATCH UK, MERSEY BLUES etc). The collection also includes fly-on-the-wall documentaries and programmes which use 'hidden cameras', (e.g. NEIGHBOURS FROM HELL, BEADLE'S ABOUT). However, the collection is expanding to include documentaries in general and will perhaps branch out to include current affairs programmes and drama.

578 UNIVERSITY OF SALFORD ISD

Adelphi Campus, Peru Street, Salford, Manchester M3 6EQ
Email: A.Callen@salford.ac.uk
Web: http://www.salford.ac.uk/ais
☎ 0161 295 6183 **Fax**: 0161 295 6083
Contact: Andy Callen, Liaison Officer
Access: External users should apply in writing to the Campus Manager

A collection of books and videos to support the media and performance courses at the Adelphi Campus. Subjects covered include performance, drama, film, television, radio, culture, mass media, broadcast industry, and computing (Internet/multimedia). Areas of special interest are: film scripts; off-air recordings, including many examples of films, documentaries, drama productions and other television programmes. Videos cover a good selection of world cinema. CDs of BBC sound effects and background music.

579 UNIVERSITY OF STRATHCLYDE ARCHIVES

University of Strathclyde, McCance Building, Richmond Street, Glasgow G1 1XQ
Email: archives@strath.ac.uk
Web: http://www.strath.ac.uk/Archives
☎ 0141 548 2497 **Fax**: 0141 552 0775
Contact: Margaret Harrison, Archivist
Access: 09.00–13.00, 14.00–17.00 (appointment advisable)

Small collection relating to university activities, development of campus, etc. Chiefly 1960s and after but includes film of Edward VII unveiling foundation stone of Royal College building in May 1903.

580 UNIVERSITY OF STRATHCLYDE LIBRARY

Jordanhill Campus, 76 Southbrae Drive, Glasgow G13 1PP
Email: l.r.emery@strath.ac.uk
Web: http://www.lib.strath.ac.uk
☎ 0141 950 3309 **Fax**: 0141 950 3150
Contact: Linda Emery, Media Librarian
Access: Library opening hours

The media collection covers a broad spectrum of subjects, age-levels and physical formats. The collection therefore covers most subjects taught in schools from pre-school to secondary, further and adult education and higher education. There are also media resources supporting the teaching of social work, speech and language therapy, music, sport and all education courses. The physical formats include sound recordings (audio cassettes, compact discs and jazz records), video-recordings (commercial and off-air), slides, wallcharts, multimedia packs and a range of software.

581 UNIVERSITY OF SUNDERLAND INFORMATION SERVICES

Chester Road, Sunderland SR1 3SD
Email: julie.archer@sunderland.ac.uk
Web: http://www.library.sunderland.ac.uk
☎ 0191 515 2900 **Fax**: 0191 515 2904
Contact: Julie Archer, site librarian

This is a university library collection which includes all subject areas. The University has four site libraries; Chester Road Library, St Peter's Library, Hutton Library and Ashburne Library.

582 UNIVERSITY OF SURREY, ROEHAMPTON – INFORMATION SERVICES

Roehampton Lane Learning Resources Centre, Roehampton Lane, London SW15 5SZ
Email: S.Clegg@roehampton.ac.uk
Web: http://helios.roehampton.ac.uk:8001/www-bin/www_talis
☎ 020 8392 3053
Contact: Sue Clegg, Director of Information Officer
Access: Not currently

Roehampton has two Learning Resource Centres which between them house 370,000 books and other material to support the academic needs of its users. The Roehampton Lane Learning Resources Centre in particular houses a strong collection of performing arts material in the areas of drama and theatre, dance, film and television. In line with the modules taught at undergraduate level the college has good collections of material on film and video productions, audience studies, film history, narrative, criticism and theory, European cinema, Shakespeare on film, and social and political aspect of cinema.

583 UNIVERSITY OF SUSSEX LIBRARY

Falmer, Brighton BN1 9QL
Email: library.specialcoll@sussex.ac.uk
Web: http://www.sussex.ac.uk
☎ 01273 678 157 **Fax**: 01273 678 441
Contact: Dorothy Sheridan, Head of Special Collections
Access: Prior arrangements must be made for weekends and evenings. Opening hours weekdays. Mon-Fri 10.00–17.00. Borrowing only permitted with a University of Sussex library card

Special collections include: The Mass-Observation Archive and the Frank Muir and Denis Norden Archive: over 600 radio and television scripts by two of the foremost British comedy writers of the 1950s and 1960s. Printed in-house catalogue available in the library for film and television productions and audio items (holdings of film and television productions only on the website). Sound recordings include over 12,000 items (mostly University of Sussex lectures).

584 UNIVERSITY OF THE ARTS LONDON: CAMBERWELL COLLEGE OF ARTS LIBRARY

Peckham Road, London SE5 8UF
Email: r.creamer@camb.linst.ac.uk
Web: http://www.linst.ac.uk/library
☎ 020 7514 6350 **Fax**: 020 7514 6324
Contact: Ruth Creamer, Head of Learning Resources
Access: Prior permission necessary. Opening hours term time: Mon, Wed, Fri, 1000–1700; Tue, Thu, 10.00–20.00. Other times: Mon-Fri, 10.00–17.00

The London Institute comprises five constituent colleges: Camberwell College of Art, Central St Martin's College of Art and Design, Chelsea College of Art and Design, London College of Fashion and the London College of Printing. Holds 900 videos and the Thorold Dickinson book collection comprising some 2,500 titles.

585 UNIVERSITY OF THE ARTS LONDON: CENTRAL ST MARTIN'S COLLEGE OF ART AND DESIGN, MUSEUM AND STUDY COLLECTION

Southampton Row, London WC1B 4AP
Email: s.backemeyer@csm.linst.ac.uk
Web: http://www.csm.linst.ac.uk/textsite/collection.asp
☎ 020 7514 7146 **Fax**: 020 7514 7024
Contact: Sylvia Backemeyer, Head

Film, video and photography have become core media for artists and designers and are integrated into our fine art and graphic design courses and research. Central Saint Martins has both contemporary and historical collections of works of art and design. We have a number of historical collections which are available for research and study purposes. Holdings include thirty-seven German UFA posters from the 1920s conserved; eighteen unconserved.

586 UNIVERSITY OF THE ARTS LONDON: CENTRAL ST MARTIN'S COLLEGE OF ART AND DESIGN LIBRARY

Southampton Row, London WC1B 4AP
Email: j.ingram@csm.arts.ac.uk
Web: http://www.arts.ac.uk/library
☎ 020 7514 8123 **Fax**: 020 7514 7033
Contact: Joan Ingram, Media Librarian
Access: During library opening hours

University of the Arts London consists of five internationally renowned colleges, Camberwell College of Arts, Central Saint Martins College of Art and Design, Chelsea College of Art and Design, London College of Communication and London College of Fashion. Drawing upon more than 150 years of experience, we are Europe's largest university for art, design, fashion, communication and the performing arts. Library includes nearly 100 video tapes and DVDs.

587 UNIVERSITY OF THE ARTS LONDON: LONDON COLLEGE OF COMMUNICATION

Elephant & Castle, London SE1 6SB
Email: s.mahurter@lcc.arts.ac.uk
Web: http://www.lcc.arts.ac.uk
☎020 7514 6638 **Fax**: 020 7514 6597
Contact: Sarah Mahurter

Formerly known as the London College of Printing. A rapidly expanding collection of off-air and pre-recorded videotapes and DVDs, covering a broad range of film styles and genres. Growing number of avant-garde and experimental films on video. All material held is in support of the undergraduate and postgraduate courses taught in the LCP Media School. In July 2005, the London College of Communication in partnership with Ealing Institute of Media achieved Screen Academy status, tasked with educating and training the new generation of filmmakers. The LCC is actively seeking to increase its film archives holdings and make its collections available to the Academy Network, a community of over 1,500 practical film making students for research and study purposes.

588 UNIVERSITY OF THE ARTS LONDON: LONDON COLLEGE OF FASHION

20 John Prince's Street, London W1G 0BJ
Email: k.baird@lcf.linst.ac.uk
Web: http://www.fashion.arts.ac.uk
☎ 020 7514 7410 **Fax**: 020 7514 7580
Contact: Katherine Baird, Special Collections Librarian
Access: Open to London Institute staff and students only during library opening hours

The London College of Fashion Library holds a range of video recordings covering the subjects studied at the college. These include fashion, clothing and textile history and design, marketing and management, beauty therapy and health, hairstyling and make-up, cultural studies, art and design. The video collection consists of off-air recordings, commercially-produced videos and college productions.

589 UNIVERSITY OF THE WEST OF ENGLAND, BOLLAND LIBRARY

Frenchay Campus, Coldharbour Lane, Bristol BS16 1QY
Email: maggie.shrubshall@uwe.ac.uk
Web: http://www.uwe.ac.uk/library/info/frenchay
☎ 0117 965 6261 **Fax**: 0117 976 2509
Contact: Maggie Shrubshall, Assistant Librarian
Access: Library open to the public for reference use. Limited borrowing facilities available on subscription – phone for details. Usual copyright restrictions apply to all materials

There are eight libraries on different UWE campuses. Off-air recordings and bought-in videos reflect the subjects taught at each campus, e.g. health and social care, humanities, engineering. At Frenchay the Faculty of Languages and European Studies runs a European Cinema Module so this library's book and video stock includes material for this subject. The Bower Ashton campus includes material for film and media studies.

590 UNIVERSITY OF ULSTER ART & DESIGN LIBRARY

York Street, Belfast, Northern Ireland BT15 1ED
Email: m.khorshidian@ulster.ac.uk
Web: http://www.ulster.ac.uk
☎ 028 9026 7269 **Fax**: 028 9026 7278
Contact: Marion Khorshidian
Access: Staff and students

As this is a general art and design library, mainly undergraduate, there is no specialist collection. This is only one of four libraries in the university. See also Department of Humanities, Coleraine Campus (qv).

591 UNIVERSITY OF ULSTER AT COLERAINE LIBRARY

University of Ulster, Cromore Road, Coleraine, Northern Ireland BT52 1SA
Email: cp.ballantine@ulster.ac.uk
Web: http://www.ulst.ac.uk/library/craine/special.htm
☎ 02870 324546 **Fax**: 02870 324357
Contact: Kay Ballantine, Sub-Librarian Humanities

The moving image collection in the library is designed to support teaching and research in media studies at the university. It contains published material only: books, journals and videos relating to film, video, television and radio, and does not contain any unique material.

592 UNIVERSITY OF ULSTER AT COLERAINE, THE FILM AND SOUND RESOURCE UNIT

Cromore Road, Coleraine, Northern Ireland BT52 1SA
Email: c.harrison@ulster.ac.uk
Web: http://www.ulst.ac.uk/library/craine/special.htm
☎ 028 7032 4058 **Fax**: 028 7032 4952
Contact: Christine Harrison
Access: Weekdays, 09.15–16.45. Disabled access

The collection was established in 1970 to locate and collect local archive films and film relating to course teaching, primarily in the Faculty of Humanities. Attention has increasingly focused on the acquisition of audio-visual material relating to the history of the last thirty years in Northern Ireland. Amateur, documentary, feature film, news and current affairs material is included. There is also over eighty-five hours of programme material from Ulster Television reflecting its range of output from 1959. In addition there are sound broadcasting tapes on history and current affairs.

593 UNIVERSITY OF WALES ABERYSTWYTH – THOMAS PARRY LIBRARY

Llanbadarn Fawr, Aberystwyth SY23 3AS
Email: ajc@aber.ac.uk
Web: http://www.inf.aber.ac.uk/tpl
☎ 01970 622417 **Fax**: 01970 622190
Contact: Alan Clark, Site Librarian
Access: By arrangement

16mm films have been collected since the college's inception in 1964. Video (VHS) has been added more recently. Some film is acquired for archival purposes. The earliest film dates from 1922.

594 UNIVERSITY OF WALES, BANGOR – MAIN LIBRARY INFORMATION SOURCES

Main Library, College Road, Bangor, Gwynedd LL57 2DG
Email: library@bangor.ac.uk
Web: http://www.bangor.ac.uk/is/library
☎ 01248 382971 **Fax**: 01248 829 79
Contact: Einion Wyn Thomas, archivist
Access: Restricted to UWB patrons

The main part of the collection at UWB consists of videocassette copies of motion pictures (both bought and off-air recordings) for the film studies course. The book (including film scripts) and serials collection related to this course is being developed. In addition to the film studies collection, there are hundreds of videocassettes, mostly off-air recordings, relating to psychology. There are small video collections relating to Wales and the Welsh language and some education videos for children.

595 UNIVERSITY OF WALES COLLEGE, NEWPORT

Library and Learning Resources, Caerleon Campus, PO Box 179, Newport NP18 3YG
Email: lesley.may@newport.ac.uk
Web: http://lis.newport.ac.uk
☎ 01633 432103 **Fax**: 01633 432108
Contact: Lesley May, Deputy Head, Library and Learning Resources

We provide a single point of contact for students' learning support needs, including library services, computing facilities, study skills support, printing and copying. We also provide a full range of library, IT, printing and audio-visual services to staff, as well as promoting pedagogical practice and innovation in learning and teaching through the Centre for Learning Development.

596 UNIVERSITY OF WESTMINSTER LEARNING RESOURCES CENTRE

Harrow Campus, Watford Road, Northwick Park, Harrow HA1 3TP
Email: kyffine@westminster.ac.uk
Web: http://www.wmin.ac.uk/page-611
☎ 020 7911 5000 ext 4112 **Fax**: 020 7911 5952
Contact: Eleri Kyffin, Librarian

The Learning Resources Centre houses a videotape collection comprising off-air recordings, commercially produced tapes, pop music videos and feature films. A particular strength is animation and printed guides are available to this part of the collection. Books and periodicals support undergraduate and postgraduate courses.

597 VALENCE HOUSE MUSEUM & ARCHIVES

Becontree Avenue, Dagenham, Essex RM8 3HT
Email: mark.watson@lbbd.gov.uk
Web: http://www.barking-dagenham.gov.uk/4-valence/valence-menu.html
☎ 020 8270 6865 **Fax**: 020 8270 6868
Contact: Mark Watson, Acting Museum Curator
Access: By appointment only

The majority of the collection belongs to the two film societies operational in the borough from the 1940s to the 1970s. The Dagenham Co-operative Film Society produced drama and documentary films in the borough of Dagenham during the late 1940s and 1950s after the merger of Barking and Dagenham boroughs in 1965. The Fanshawe Film Society operated as a film club but shot some documentary footage in the 1960s and 1970s.

598 VALLEYS RADIO

PO Box 1116, Ebbw Vale, Wales NP23 8XW
Email: admin@valleysradio.co.uk
Web: http://www.valleysradio.co.uk
☎ 01495 301116 **Fax**: 01495 300710
Contact: Emma Thomas, Head of News

The radio station holds forty-two days' output to meet legal requirement.

599 VALLEYSTREAM: ALEXANDER ARCHIVE

Plas y Graig, Iolyn Park, Conwy, Conwy LL32 8UX
Email: avpro@valleystream.co.uk
Web: www.valleystream.co.uk
☎ 01492 572614 **Fax**: 01492 584287
Contact: Steven Bate, Producer
Access: By appointment

Seventy-eight reels of original 16mm cinefilm taken by one woman (Miss Marjorie Alexander) from about 1931 to 1962. It includes footage of Hitler at Nuremberg, military parades in the UK during the 30s, celebrations for George V's Silver Jubilee celebrations in 1935, HMS *Conway*, and the filming of THE INN OF THE SIXTH HAPPINESS; scenes of horse-drawn ploughing and steamships; plus family life filming of her relatives in Wales, Liverpool, the Wirral, Cumbria, Suffolk and New Zealand. The archive is complemented by still photographs, letters, certificates, etc, from those times, plus recent video and television interviews with the Alexander family.

600 VALLEYSTREAM: GWILYM DAVIES COLLECTION

Plas y Graig, Iolyn Park, Conwy, Conwy LL32 8UX
Email: avpro@valleystream.co.uk Web: www.valleystream.co.uk
☎ 01492 572614 **Fax**: 01492 584287
Contact: Steven Bate, Producer
Access: By prior appointment only

The collection consists of approximately 30,000 original photographic negatives, mostly in full-colour medium format (some 35mm) and covering the years 1974 to 2001. The majority are aerial images of North Wales and were taken from a small Cessna aircraft by amateur photographer Gwilym Davies. They include towns, mountains and countryside from Anglesey in the west to Deeside in the east, from the northern coastline to Aberdyfi in mid Wales. Of historic interest are aerial video footage plus stills of the construction of the A55 expressway along the north coast during the 1980/90s.

601 VICKERS ARCHIVES FILM COLLECTIONS

Cambridge University Library Archives, West Road, Cambridge CB3 9DR
Email: jdw1000@cam.ac.uk
Web: http://www.lib.cam.ac.uk/Handbook/D8.html
☎ 01223 333000 **Fax**: 01223 333160
Contact: John Wells, Assistant Under-Librarian
Access: Limited access to video material only, by appointment. Access for disabled

The collection is that of the former Photographic Department of Vickers plc, which was based at the company's headquarters in London. Papers, photographic negatives, and cine film formerly stored in the head office of Vickers Plc on Millbank chart the rise and post-war metamorphosis of what was once one of the largest armaments companies in the world. The bulk of this collection covers the period 1870–1970, and includes records of Vickers' former rivals Armstrong Whitworth of Newcastle, taken over in 1928.

602 VIEWTECH EDUCATIONAL MEDIA

7–8 Falcons Gate, North Avon Business Centre, Dean Road, Yate BS37 5NH
Email: sales@viewtech.co.uk Web: http://www.viewtech.co.uk
☎ 01454 858055 **Fax**: 01454 858056
Contact: Simon Littlechild, Manager
Access: Limited

Viewtech's library of over 3,000 titles forms a comprehensive range of educational programmes, many from which footage may be supplied for broadcast and non-theatric purposes.

603 VIRGIN RADIO

No 1 Golden Square, London W1F 9DJ
Email: paul.jackson@virginradio.co.uk
Web: http://www.virginradio.co.uk
Contact: Paul Jackson, Programme Director

Virgin Radio went on-air at 12.15pm on 30 April 1993.

604 VOICE OF THE LISTENER AND VIEWER (VLV)

101 King's Drive, Gravesend, Kent DA12 5BQ
Email: info@vlv.org.uk
Web: http://www.vlv.org.uk
☎ 01474 352835 **Fax**: 01474 351112
Contact: Linda Forbes, Administrator
Access: By appointment

VLV has an extensive archive of its own with records of all its conferences since 1984, plus a reference library of books and magazines, etc, some from overseas consumer groups which are not likely to be replicated elsewhere in Britain. There is also an archive of the former Broadcasting Consortium (of charities which lobbied around the 1990 Broadcasting Bill and subsequently for a few years). The strength of the VLV collection lies in its perspective of the listener and viewer, representing the citizen and consumer interest.

605 WALSALL LOCAL HISTORY CENTRE

Local History Centre, Essex Street, Walsall WS2 7AS
Email: localhistorycentre@walsall.gov.uk
Web: http://tinyurl.co.uk/5tub
☎ 01922 721305
Contact: Stuart Williams, Photographic Service
Access: Tue and Thu 09.30–17.30, Wed 09.30–19.00, Fri 09.30–17.00, Sat 09.30–13.00. Access for disabled

The Centre is the archive repository and local studies library of Walsall Metropolitan Borough Council and as such accepts donations and deposits of film/video material which relates to the local area. Film is transferred to video for easier access by researchers. This is only a small collection which does not represent a large part of the overall Centre holdings.

606 WAR ARCHIVE

Images of War Ltd, 31A Regent's Park Road, London NW1 7TL
Email: derek@dircon.co.uk
Web: http://www.warfootage.com
☎ 020 7267 9198 **Fax**: 020 7267 8852
Contact: Derek Blades
Access: By appointment only

The War Archive is a collection of original film footage from both the First and Second World Wars and the preceding periods. The archive consists of almost 200 hours of footage from Great Britain, Germany, Russia, the USA and Japan, and covers all aspects of these important periods in recent history.

607 WARRINGTON COLLEGIATE LEARNING RESOURCE CENTRE

Padgate Campus, Crab Lane, Warrington WA2 0DB
Email: l.crewe@warr.ac.uk
Web: http://www.warr.ac.uk/links/155-learning_resource_centre.php
☎ 01925 494494 **Fax**: 01925 816077
Contact: Lorna Crewe, Assistant Librarian, Visual Resources Media & Performing Arts

Resources include books, talking books and large print books, journals, magazines, newspapers, CDs and DVDs, videos with viewing facilities, music CDs, and online databases.

608 WAVE 96.4 FM

PO BOX 964, Victoria Road, Gowerton. Swansea SA4 3AB
Email: steve.barnes@swanseasound.co.uk
Web: http://www.thewave.co.uk
☎ 01253 304965 **Fax**: 01253 301965
Contact: Steve Barnes, Station Controller

The radio station holds forty-two days' output to meet legal requirement. Does not maintain an archive but holds a private music library.

609 WELLCOME LIBRARY FOR THE HISTORY AND UNDERSTANDING OF MEDICINE – ICONOGRAPHIC COLLECTIONS

210, Euston Road, London NW1 2BE
Email: icon@wellcome.ac.uk
Web: http://library.wellcome.ac.uk
☎ 020 7611 8489 **Fax**: 020 7611 8703
Contact: Reader Services Librarians
Access: Mon, Wed, Fri 09.45–17.15; Tue, Thu, 09.45–19.15; Sat, 09.45–13.00. Staff are available to assist. Access for disabled. By prior arrangement

The first surviving in-house film was made in 1912, the first recorded purchase in 1928. The library was founded by Sir Henry Wellcome and reflects his interest in documentary techniques. Most items have been acquired since World War II. The library holds original archive material of which copies on videotape are available for viewing in most cases. Some films are also available for viewing on laserdisc and DVD. Three separate departments of the Wellcome Library hold moving image materials; the Iconographic Collections, including over 200 documentary films; Archives and Manuscripts including about forty films; and the Medical Film and Video Library (*see below for separate entry*).

610 WELLCOME TRUST MEDICAL FILM AND VIDEO LIBRARY

The Wellcome Trust, 210 Euston Road, London NW1 2BE
Email: mfvl@wellcome.ac.uk
Web: http://library.wellcome.ac.uk/mfac.html
☎ 020 7611 8766 **Fax**: 020 7611 8765
Contact: Angela Saward, Curator of Moving Image and Sound
Access: During office hours in the department by appointment or in the library (extended opening hours)

The Moving Image and Sound Collections are home to around 3,000 moving image and 2,000 sound items on the subjects of human and animal health and welfare. The 'jewels in our crown' are the approximately sixty films made or commissioned by the Wellcome Foundation in the 1940s, 1950s and 1960s on contemporary and historical aspects of tropical diseases and medicine. Key donations are from the British Medical Association, British Pharmacological Society, British Dental Association, the maternity unit of Queen Charlotte's Hospital, the Institute of Neurology, the Royal College of Surgeons and the Royal Society of Apothecaries and the University of London Audio-Visual Centre. We are receiving new material regularly.

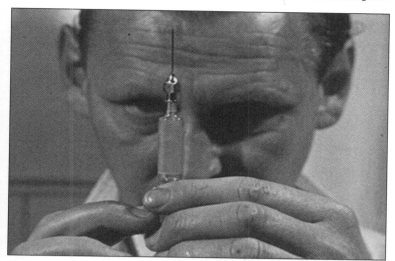

Doctor prepares vaccine injection from FUNDAMENTAL PRINCIPLES OF IMMUNIZATION (1961)

611   WESSEX FILM AND SOUND ARCHIVE

Hampshire Record Office, Sussex Street, Winchester SO23 8TH
Email: david.lee@hants.gov.uk
Web: www.hants.gov.uk/record-office/film/index.html
☎ 01962–847742 **Fax**: 01962–878681
Contact: David Lee, Film and Sound Archivist
Access: Mon-Fri 09.00–17.00. Staff are available to assist. Access for disabled

The Wessex Film and Sound Archive was established in February 1988. The material dates from 1890 to the present. Particular subject strengths are the military; merchant shipping, including shipbuilding and technical material; amateur films; British Powerboat Company (Scott-Paine films); the seaside; local radio, including BBC Radio Solent, Radio Victory, Ocean Sound and Radio 210; oral history; towns like Southampton, Portsmouth, Bournemouth and Winchester; Bournemouth orchestras; off-air recordings of classical music performances on the radio in the 1960s. WFSA also holds master and viewing copies of documentaries made by BBC South, Meridian, TVS and Southern Television.

612   WEST GLAMORGAN ARCHIVE SERVICE

County Hall, Oystermouth Road, Swansea SA1 3SN
Email: westglam.archives@swansea.gov.uk
Web: http://www.swansea.gov.uk/westglamorganarchives
☎ 01792 636760 **Fax**: 01792–637130
Contact: Kim Collis, County Archivist
Access: Digitised material will be available for reference without prior booking. Access for disabled. Detailed catalogue in searchroom. See www.archivesnetworkwales.info for collection level information

The Archive Service holds still photographs relating to West Glamorgan from a variety of sources, including personal photographic collections and photographic records made by Swansea Council of building works and road improvements. From the 1930s, the Council began to make films of important civic events. At first the films were shot by contracted commercial firms, but in the late 1940s, a small film-making unit was set up in the central library. The surviving films in the archives date from the 1950s onwards: they are in the process (2005) of being digitised onto DVD for accessibility.

613   WEST SUSSEX RECORD OFFICE

County Hall, Chichester, West Sussex, PO19 1RN
Email: records.office@westsussex.gov.uk
Web: http://www.westsussex.gov.uk/RO/home.htm
☎ 01243 753600 **Fax**: 01243 533959
Contact: Richard Childs, County Archivist

Since 1992 the Record Office has been a founding partner of the South East Film and Video Archive (qv) and is its repository and conservation centre. The archive seeks to locate, collect, preserve and promote moving images made in or relating to the South East of England. There are now over 1,000 items in the archive including newsreels, corporate documentaries, promotional material, and feature films from the Shoreham Film Studio. Of equal importance are the home movies and local footage from private collections.

614   WESTMINSTER CITY ARCHIVES

City of Westminster Archives Centre, 10 St Ann's Street, London SW1P 2DE
Email: archives@westminster.gov.uk
Web: http://www.westminster.gov.uk/archives
☎ 020 7641 5180 **Fax**: 020 7641 4879
Contact: John Sargent, Archives Centre Manager
Access: By arrangement, Tue, Thu, Fri, 09.30–19.00. Wed, 09.30–21.00. Sat, 09.30–17.00. As much notice as possible required, especially for 16mm films

There is no special collection of films and videos. Covering dates are 1935–1990, but Liberty plc is likely to deposit videos regularly. Holdings include: footage of Visit of King George V and Queen Mary to St Marylebone Town Hall in 1935. ALL ON A WINTER'S DAY; VIEWS OF ST. MARYLEBONE (c.1950); films of Paddington; Langham Hotel publicity video (1990). Audio holdings include: two reminiscences of elderly Paddington residents recorded by the Paddington Society (1960–1961); over twenty interviews with women who worked in domestic service in Westminster between the wars (part of a project begun in 1997); interviews with two former Metropolitan policemen serving at Cannon Row police station (c.1920s-1940s).

615 WESTMINSTER MUSIC LIBRARY

Victoria Library, 160 Buckingham Palace Road, London SW1W 9UD
Email: jsargent1@westminster.gov.uk
Web: http://www.westminster.gov.uk/libraries/special/music/index.cfm
☎ 020 7641 4286 **Fax**: 020 7641 4281
Contact: John Sargent, Acting City Archivist
Access: Free for any member of the public during library opening hours.
Registered users unrestricted. Orchestral sets service limited to permanent orchestras

The full subject strength of the Music Library's collection is as follows: 16,117 Books; 450 periodicals; 50,989 printed music, 536 manuscripts of which about 500 are by Emanuel Moor. The Edwin Evans (1871–1945) collection holds press cuttings, mainly from 1930s and 1940s, and about 500 letters from musicians of the same period. Oriana Madrigal Society collection of sets of past songs and madrigals. Extensive collection of collected editions/Denkmaler available for loan. No audio-visual materials for loan. (There is a small sound collection of CDs available for loan administered by the Victoria Library on the same site.)

616 WILTSHIRE AND SWINDON RECORD OFFICE: COW AND GATE COLLECTION

Libraries and Heritage HQ, Wiltshire County Council, Bythesea Road, Trowbridge BA14 8BS
Email: johnd'arcy@wiltshire.gov.uk
Web: http://www.wiltshire.gov.uk/heritage/html/wsro.html
☎ 01225 713136 **Fax**: 01225 713515
Contact: John D'Arcy, Principal Archivist
Access: Mon, Tues, Thurs, Fri 9.15–17.00; Wed 9.15–19.45

Cow and Gate, infant food manufacturers, 1893–1959, thereafter known as Unigate PLC. This collection includes a variety of video materials mainly but not exclusively from the 1970s and 1980s. Includes advertising materials and corporate productions. Materials are mainly held on U-matic tape.

617 WINCHESTER SCHOOL OF ART

Park Avenue, Winchester, Hants S023 8DL
Email: wsaenqs@soton.ac.uk
Web: http://www.wsa.soton.ac.uk
☎ 0238 059 7013 / 6984,
Contact: Linda Newington, Librarian

Winchester School of Art Library is a specialist art and design library comprising books, exhibition catalogues, special collections, journals, slides and videos. It has been developed primarily as a teaching collection and, as a result, reflects the academic disciplines taught within the school.

618 WIRRAL ARCHIVES

Wirral Museum, Birkenhead Town Hall, Hamilton Square, Birkenhead, Merseyside CH41 5BR
Email: archives@wirral-libraries.net
Web: http://www.wirral.gov.uk
☎ 0151 666 3903 **Fax**: 0151 653 7320
Contact: Emma Challinor, Archivist
Access: Open Thu and Fri 10.00–17.00, Sat 10.00–13.00

Wirral's Archives Service collects, preserves, stores and catalogues all types of historical documents relating to the Wirral area, its people, businesses and institutions. The archives include ledgers, newspapers, photographs, maps, plans, films, title deeds, legal and business papers and microfilms. A small collection of films of local interest are held as part of the archive's service.

619 THE WOLF 107.7 FM

10th Floor, Mander House, Wolverhampton WV1 3NB
Email: info@thewolf.co.uk
Web: http://www.thewolf.co.uk
☎ 01902 571070 **Fax**: 01902 571079
Contact: Richard Dodd, Programme Controller

The radio station holds forty-two days' output to meet legal requirement.

620 WOLVERHAMPTON ARCHIVES & LOCAL STUDIES

42–50 Snow Hill, Wolverhampton, West Midlands WV2 4AG
Email: wolverhamptonarchives@dial.pipex.com
Web: http://www.wolverhamptonarchives.dial.pipex.com
☎ 01902 552480 **Fax**: 01902 552481
Contact: David Bishop, City Archivist
Access: Film and U-matic material by arrangement only. Unrestricted access to the video collection: Mon, Tue, Fri, 10.00–17.00 Wed, 10.00–19.00. 1st and 3rd Sat of each month, 10.00–17.00. Disabled visitors should contact the archivist prior to visiting

Films and videos have been acquired as an incidental part of the Borough Archives collection policy.

621 WOLVERHAMPTON COLLEGE

Westfield road, Bilston, Wolverhampton WV14 6ER
Email: bigfordv@wolvcoll.ac.uk
Web: http://www.wolverhamptoncollege.ac.uk
☎ 01902 821116
Contact: Val Bigford, Learning Resources Manager

Wolverhampton College was known as Bilston Community College until it merged with Wulfrun College. Now known as City of Wolverhampton College. Holds 1,200 video titles.

622 WOMEN IN JAZZ

Rooms 1–3 Queen's Buildings, Cambrian Buildings, Swansea,
Wales SA1 1TW
Email: enquiries@womeninjazzswansea.org.uk
Web: http://www.jazzsite.co.uk/wja
☎ 01792 456666
Contact: Jen Wilson, Director

Formerly known as The Women's Jazz Archive, this was established in
Swansea in 1986 by pianist and historian Jen Wilson. The jazz collection
comprises many thousands of audio/visual records, photographs, journals
and periodicals, a growing library, paintings, stained glass windows, stage
gowns etc. Donations have come from the estates of the broadcaster Dr
Barry Stern and vocalist Beryl Bryden. Beryl Bryden who was presented with
both Louis Armstrong and Billie Holiday awards, is also part of the Women
in Jazz oral history collection. A selection of stage gowns was presented by
Blanche Finlay, together with her oral history.

623 WORLD BACKGROUNDS

Millennium Studios, Elstree Way, Borehamwood, Herts WD6 1SF
Email: ralph@worldbackgrounds.com
Web: http://www.worldbackgrounds.com
☎ 020 8207 4747 **Fax**: 020 8207 4276
Contact: Ralph Rogers, Director
Access: Limited, preferably sending clients VHS copies

World Backgrounds is now one of the UK's leading video library portals,
serving the film and television industry with quality stock footage for the
last fifty years. We specialise in scenes for features, television commercials,
television productions, pop promo's and corporate videos. Our film
footage originates from Vistavision, 70mm, 35mm or 16mm negatives.

624 WORLD IMAGES

8 Fitzroy Square, London W1T 5HN
Email: info@world-images.org
Web: http://www.world-images.org
☎ 020 73888 555 **Fax**: 020 73878 444
Contact: Claudine Ellis, Film Library Manager
Access: Limited, available by arrangement with archive staff

World Images is an international archive management service and a stock
footage library. Our collections include the video archives of leading non-
governmental organisations NGO and several specialised collections, such
as Amnesty International, Greenpeace UK, International Fund for Animal
Welfare (IFAW), and WWF. Smaller collections include In Depth Solutions
and Farm Animal Welfare Network (FAWN). The archive represents one of
the most comprehensive collections of environment, animal welfare and
human rights footage in the world.

IFAW International Fund for Animal Welfare

625 WPA FILM LIBRARY

c/o National Geographic Film & Television Library, First Floor, National House, 60/66 Wardour Street, London W1F 0TA
Email: psmith@ngs.org
Web: http://www.wpafilmlibrary.com
☎ 020 7734 9159 **Fax**: 020 7287 1043
Contact: Patrick Smith, Sales Manager

The WPA Film Library, founded by independent producers in 1987, began as a repository of archival and contemporary stock footage for documentaries. In 1989, the company merged with the MPI Media Group, one of the country's oldest independent home video labels and the producer of hundreds of documentaries. Since its inception, the WPA Film Library has grown into one of the world's leading footage sources, offering tens of thousands of hours of high quality, vintage and contemporary images, and a leading online stock footage resource.

626 WWF VIDEO LIBRARY

World Images, 8 Fitzroy Square, London W1T 5HN
Email: info@world-images.org
Web: www.world-television.com/worldimages/wwf
☎ 020 73888 555 **Fax**: 020 73878 444
Contact: Claudine Ellis, Film Library Manager
Access: Limited, available by arrangement with archive staff

Well-known for its wildlife coverage, the WWF video library is a varied and extensive footage resource. Images cover species, oceans, forests, environment, scenic locations, industries, people of the world. The collection comprises about 1,000 hours of footage on BetaSP, DigiBeta and DV.

627 YORK MINSTER ARCHIVES

Dean's Park, York YO1 7JQ
Email: archivist@yorkminsterlibrary.org.uk
Web: http://www.yorkminster.org
☎ 01904 611118 **Fax**: 01904 611119
Contact: Peter Young, Archivist
Access: By arrangement with archive staff

Haphazard from 1942, but more systematic since the 1980s. Holdings include films relating to York Minster including enthronements, special services and television programmes.

628 YORKSHIRE FILM ARCHIVE

York St John College, Lord Mayor's Walk, York YO31 7EX
Email: nfo@yorkshirefilmarchive.com
Web: http://www.yorkshirefilmarchive.com
☎ 01904 716 550 **Fax**: 01904 716552
Contact: Sue Howard, Director
Access: Staff are available to assist. Access for disabled

The Yorkshire Film Archive exists to locate, preserve and show film made in, or about the Yorkshire region. Material dates from 1897 and includes newsreels, documentaries, advertising and amateur films.

Child monk

629 ZURICH FINANCIAL SERVICES (UKISA)

UK Life Tower, Montpellier Drive, Cheltenham GL53 7LQ
Email: susannah.mogg@uk.zurich.com
Web: http://www.zurich.com
☎ 01489 561559
Contact: Susannah Mogg, Media Relations Manager

The Zurich Financial Services (UKISA) Ltd archive comprises three films. *Note: Eagle Star is now part of the Zurich Financial Services Group. The Group Archives were closed in 2003. Records were transferred to the Guildhall Library, London.*

The Researcher's Guide: Film, Television, Radio & Related Documentation Collections – Republic of Ireland

630 ANNER INTERNATIONAL – DIGITAL, POST PRODUCTION

50 Upper Mount Street, Dublin 2, Ireland
Email: bookings@annerinternational.com
Web: http://www.annerinternational.com
☎ +353–1-661 2244 **Fax**: +353–1-661 2252
Contact: Andy Ruane, Managing Director
Access: Limited

The company started in 1975. The collection has been built up since, and includes some material dating from before that year. It is being added to on an ongoing basis. The collection is very strong on news footage of the Northern Ireland Troubles and holds footage of many prominent Irish politicians including Gerry Adams and Charles Haughey. News footage of Sinn Fein Ard-Fheises and IRA kidnappings is also held.

631 EMDEE INTERNATIONAL PRODUCTIONS

42 Cross Avenue, Blackrock, Dublin, Ireland
Email: emdee@indigo.ie
Web: http://www.scorpiotvcommercials.com
☎ +353–1- 2881399 **Fax**: +353–1- 2881399
Contact: Larry Masterson
Access: Limited. Not open to the public

Emdee Productions has been in operation since 1986 specialising in 16mm documentary films in addition to television and cinema commercials. The company has a large aerial collection.

632 FOYNES FLYING BOAT MUSEUM

Foynes, County Limerick, Ireland
Email: famm@eircom.net
Web: http://www.flyingboatmuseum.com
☎ +353–69–65416 **Fax**: +353–69–65416
Contact: Margaret O'Shaughnessy, Curator
Access: Research facilities very limited. By arrangement only

The museum is a non-profit making community-funded institution. The collection comprises material from 1937–47 relating to the beginnings of Atlantic passenger travel. It is the only museum of its kind in the world. The collection is still being added to.

633 GUINNESS ARCHIVE DIAGEO IRELAND

Guinness Storehouse, St James's Gate, Dublin 8, Ireland
Email: sue.garland@guinness.com
Web: http://www.guinness.com
☎ + 3531 471 4557 **Fax**: + 3531 408 4737
Contact: Eibhlin Roche, Archivist
Access: Limited, by appointment. Mon-Thu 9.30–17.00; Fri 9.30–16.30

Guinness company films and videos produced for internal training and communication, for visitors, for trade promotions and advertising commercials. Mostly British, some Irish and overseas. The material relates to the brewing company and its beer brands, dating from mid-1950s to the present day.

634 IRISH FILM ARCHIVE

Film Institute of Ireland, 6 Eustace Street, Dublin 2, Ireland
Email: archive@ifc.ie
Web: http://www.fii.ie
☎ +353–1-679 5744 **Fax**: +353–1-677 8755
Contact: Sunniva O'Flynn, Archive Curator
Access: By appointment made by phone or mail. Staff are available to assist. Researchers can apply to the Curator for information about the archive's holdings

The Irish Film Archive has been located in custom-built premises in the Irish Film Centre since 1992. Collections of Irish and Irish-related materials are preserved and freely accessed by researchers, programme makers and members of the public. It has been a provisional member of FIAF since 1989.

635 IRISH FOLKLIFE FILM ARCHIVE

Irish Folklife Division, National Museum of Ireland – Country Life,
Turlough Park, Castlebar, Co Mayo, Ireland
Email: tpark@museum.ie
Web: http://www.museum.ie
☎ +353 94 9031773 **Fax**: +353 94 9031583
Access: For established film personnel only

Film on crafts in rural Ireland; shot in the 1950s, 1960s and 1970s.

636 IRISH TRADITIONAL MUSIC ARCHIVE

73 Merrion Square, Dublin 2, Ireland
Web: http://www.itma.ie
☎ + 353 1 661 9699 **Fax**: + 353 1 662 4585
Contact: Treasa Harkin, Melodies & Images Officer
Access: Mon-Fri 10.00–13.00, 14.00–17.00

Established in 1987, the archive is the first body to be exclusively concerned with the making of a comprehensive collection of materials – sound recordings, books, photographs, videos – for the appreciation and study of Irish traditional music. The archive currently holds over 24,500 sound recordings, 16,000 books and serials, 2,700 programmes, 3,200 ballad sheets, 10,000 photographs and paper images, 3,200 items of sheet music, 1,100 videotapes, and a mass of ephemera. Special collections include the RTÉ Television Collection, a cooperative television project covering RTÉ's television archive of Irish traditional music film and video recordings, from the 1920s to the present.

637 LIMERICK FILM ARCHIVE

c/o Belltable Arts Centre, 69 O'Connell Street, Limerick City, Ireland
Email: filmclub@eircom.net
Web: http://www.belltable.ie/index.html
☎ +353–61–341435 or 319866. Mobile: 087 2983180. **Fax**:
+353–61–418552
Contact: Declan McLoughlin, Coordinator
Access: By prior arrangement only. Access for disabled

Formed in March 1992, to locate and acquire film, video and cinema material of Irish interest, with particular emphasis on fifty items relating to the mid-West region (Limerick and Clare counties). Since its inception, the Archive has been successful in acquiring over thirty film titles (both 35mm and 16mm), over 500 hours of video material, a large file on local and national cinemas (their history, photographs, programmes and related memorabilia, etc.). The archive also has the largest collection of data and stills on Irish film players in Ireland. All archive holdings were purchased or donated.

638 NATIONAL ARCHIVES OF IRELAND

Bishop Street, Dublin 8, Ireland
Email: mail@nationalarchives.ie
Web: http://www.nationalarchives.ie
☎ +353 1 407 2300 **Fax**: +353 1 407 2333
Contact: Ken Hannigan, Keeper
Access: Mon-Fri 10.00–17.00

Very small collection of video recordings of official conference proceedings, but it is likely to grow. At present, only recordings of the National Education Convention, October 1993, are available for inspection.

639 OLLSCOIL EDUCATIONAL EXPERIENCES

Audiovisual Centre, University College Dublin, Belfield, Dublin 4, Ireland
Email: Helen.Guerin@ucd.ie
Web: http://www.ucd.ie/avc/html/homepage/main_fra.htm
☎ +353–1-7167038 **Fax**: 353–1-2830060
Contact: Heken Guerin, Director
Access: Limited. Mon-Fri 9.30–13.00 & 14.00 to 17.00

The collection comprises adult educational series covering: Archaeology; Science; Economics; Women's Studies; Animals; Irish Expression; Psychology; Reading; Computers; Philosophy. The role of the Audio Visual Centre is to promote and develop the use of educational media and technology in furthering the university's mission.

640 RADHARC FILMS ARCHIVE

43 Mount Merrion Avenue, Blackrock, Ireland
Email: peterkelly@esras.com
Web: http://www.radharcfilms.com
☎ +353–1-288 1939 **Fax**: +353–1-283 6253
Contact: Peter Kelly, Managing Director of Esras Films Ltd and Management Company of Radharc Archive
Access: Limited, on application

Thirty-seven years of religious documentary production for Irish television. Produced by Ireland's oldest independent production company, and Ireland's longest running television series – RADHARC. The archive comprises over 400 titles from all over the world, including: Biafra, El Salvador, Chile, The Phillippines, Nicaragua, Poland, Northern Ireland, Vietnam, Haiti, Burma, etc.

641 RTE RADIO LIBRARY SALES

Radio Telefis Eireann, Donnybrook, Dublin 4, Ireland
Email: tapes@rte.ie
Web: http://www.rte.ie/libraries
☎ +353 1 208 3326 **Fax**: +353 1 208 2610
Contact: Malachy Moran, Manager of RTÉ Libraries and Archives
Access: By prior permission, Mon-Fri, 09.30–17.30

RTÉ Radio Libraries and Archives holds a selection of news, sports, arts, traditional music, documentaries and drama. The collection of recorded music dates from the founding of 2RN in 1926. Spoken word archiving began a decade later. The oldest sound recordings date from before 1930 but the bulk of the collection is from the last quarter of the twentieth century. Since 1996 live daytime radio programmes transmitted on a daily or weekly basis have been recorded, catalogued and stored digitally. RTÉ now holds over 100,000 hours of music and spoken word recordings. Every year over 5,000 hours of spoken word and 2,000 hours of commercial music recordings are added to the collection.

642 RTE STILLS LIBRARY

Radio Telefís Eireann, Donnybrook, Dublin 4, Ireland
Email: keoghe@rte.ie
Web: http://www.rte.ie/libraries
☎ +353 1 208 3127 **Fax**: +353 1 208 3031
Contact: Emma Keogh, Stills Librarian
Access: By prior permission, Mon-Fri, 09.30–17.30

RTÉ Stills Library holds an estimated 2.8 million photographic images acquired from a number of sources. Photographs taken by RTÉ photographers include images of presenters, guests and the staff involved in the production of RTÉ Television and Radio programmes. Alongside this material, RTÉ Stills Library holds a number of historically important collections that date from the early twentieth century. Original images are held in different formats including glass plates, lantern slides, negatives, 35mm slides, digital, and both colour and black-and-white prints. Digital images are stored in either JPEG or TIFF formats. Over 50,000 of these digitised images have been catalogued so far.

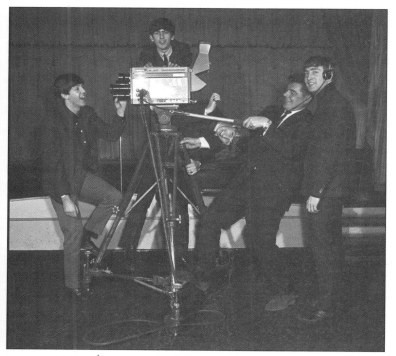

The Beatles with RTÉ cameraman Bill Robinson, 1963

643 RTE TELEVISION ARCHIVES

Radio Telefís Éireann, Donnybrook, Dublin 4, Ireland
Email: razib.chatterjee@rte.ie
Web: http://www.rte.ie/laweb/sales/sales_index.html
☎ +353–1-208 3369 **Fax**: +353–1-208 4354
Contact: Razib Chatterjee, Manager of Television Library Sales
Access: By prior permission, Mon-Fri, 09.30–17.30

RTÉ Television Libraries and Archives hold material produced or commissioned from 1961 to the present day. This footage contains news, current affairs, programmes in the Irish language, documentaries, features, entertainment, sport, drama, art, literature, music and a wide variety of stock shot material. As well as broadcast archives RTÉ has over the years acquired Irish interest newsreels dating from c.1913. A growing number of smaller film and video collections are deposited with RTÉ Television Libraries and Archives for preservation, restoration and digitisation.

644 UNIVERSITY COLLEGE DUBLIN, DEPARTMENT OF IRISH FOLKLORE

University College, Belfield, Dublin 4, Ireland
Email: seamus.ocathain@ucd.ie
Web: http://www.ucd.ie/irishfolklore
☎ +353–1-706 8216 **Fax**: +353–1-706 1144
Contact: Séamas O' Catháin
Access: Mon-Fri 14.30–17.30. By arrangement only for video and sound

Built up from 1935, since the foundation of the Irish Folklore Commission. In 1971, the commission was transferred, staff and holdings, to University College Dublin, where it became the Department of Irish Folklore. The material has been collected from various sources – field work, loan, gift, etc. All of the collection deals with some aspect of folklore and folk life. Most of it relates to Ireland.

Research organisations and services

Arts and Humanities Data Service (AHDS)

http://ahds.ac.uk

The Arts and Humanities Data Service preserves digital data in the long term, promotes good practice in the use of digital data, provides technical advice to the research community, and supports the deployment of digital technologies.

British Film Institute (*bfi*)

http://www.bfi.org.uk

The British Film Institute promotes understanding and appreciation of Britain's rich film and television heritage and culture.

Federation of Commercial Audiovisual Libraries International (FOCAL)

http://www.focalint.org

The Federation of Commercial Audiovisual Libraries International Ltd, is a not-for-profit professional trade association providing networking and marketing opportunities for content industry professionals.

Film Archive Forum

http://www.bufvc.ac.uk/faf

The Film Archive Forum represents all of the public sector film and television archives which care for the UK's moving image heritage. It represents the UK's public sector moving image archives in all archival aspects of the moving image, and acts as the advisory body on national moving image archive policy.

Footage.info

http://www.footage.info

The footage industry's talking shop.

Footage.net

http://www.footage.net

The stock, archival and news footage network.

The International Association for Media and History (IAMHIST)

http://www.iamhist.org

The International Association for Media and History is an organisation of filmmakers, broadcasters, archivists and scholars dedicated to historical inquiry into film, radio, television, and related media.

Joint Information Systems Committee (JISC)

http://www.jisc.ac.uk

The JISC supports further and higher education by providing strategic guidance, advice and opportunities to use Information and Communications Technology (ICT) to support teaching, learning, research and administration.

Media, Communication & Cultural Studies Association (MECCSA)

http://www.meccsa.org.uk

MeCCSA is the UK national subject association for its field in higher education. The Association exists to represent the field of Media, Communication and Cultural Studies.

Moving History

http://www.movinghistory.ac.uk

An online research guide to the United Kingdom's twelve public sector moving image archives.

The Museums, Libraries and Archives Council (MLA)

http://www.mla.gov.uk

MLA was launched in April 2000 as the strategic body working with and for museums, archives and libraries, tapping into the potential for collaboration between them. The new organisation replaces the Museums and Galleries Commission (MGC) and the Library and Information Commission (LIC), and now includes archives within its portfolio.

The National Archives (TNA)

http://www.nationalarchives.gov.uk

The National Archives, which covers England, Wales and the United Kingdom, was formed in April 2003 by bringing together the Public Record Office and the Historical Manuscripts Commission. It is responsible for looking after the records of central government and the courts of law, and making sure everyone can look at them.

National Council on Archives (NCA)

http://www.ncaonline.org.uk

The National Council on Archives was established in 1988 to bring together the major bodies and organisations, including service providers, users, depositors and policy makers, across the UK concerned with archives and their use. It aims to develop consensus on matters of mutual concern and provide an authoritative common voice for the archival community.

Oral History Society

http://www.ohs.org.uk

The Oral History Society is a national and international organisation dedicated to the collection and preservation of oral history.

Radio Academy

http://www.radioacademy.org

The Radio Academy is the professional body for people working in the radio industry and provides neutral ground on which the whole subject of radio can be discussed.

Radio Studies Network

http://www.radiostudiesnetwork.org.uk

The UK's network for researchers and teachers of sound broadcasting.

Research Information Network

http://www.rin.ac.uk

The RIN is a new organisation set up in 2005 to lead and co-ordinate the provision of research information in the UK. Its ambition is to serve the research community by helping to cut paths through the ever-growing and increasingly-complex mass of information that underpins the work of all researchers.

Royal Television Society

http://www.rts.org.uk

The Royal Television Society is the leading forum for discussion and debate on all aspects of the television community.

Society of Archivists Film and Sound Group

http://www.pettarchiv.org.uk/fsg

Aims to develop the exchange of views and information and the encouragement of good practice among those concerned with the acquisition, preservation and arrangement of film and sound archives.

Stock Footage Online

http://www.stockfootageonline.com

Stock Footage Online is the indispensable resource for buyers and sellers of digital and film stock footage.

Vega Science Trust

http://www.vega.org.uk

Vega is a not for profit trust which broadcasts science programmes for free over the internet.

British Universities Film & Video Council research services

The BUFVC promotes and supports the use of moving images and related media in UK higher and further education, and the use of moving images in research generally. It publishes a number of online databases ideal for academic and commercial footage researchers.

British Universities Newsreel Database – BUND

http://www.bufvc.ac.uk/newsreels

A database of British newsreel and cinemagazine production from 1910 to 1979. It delivers over 170,000 records and a large collection of digitised documents.

HERMES

http://www.bufvc.ac.uk/hermes

A database of nearly 30,000 audio-visual materials in current UK distribution, selected for their value in UK higher and further education and research.

Moving Image Gateway – MIG

http://www.bufvc.ac.uk/gateway

A subject-classified guide to websites that relate to moving images and sound and their use in higher and further education.

Radio Research Database – RRDB

http://www.bufvc.ac.uk/databases/rrdb.html

A guide to current radio-centred academic research in the UK.
http://www.bufvc.ac.uk/databes/rrdb.html

Researcher's Guide Online – RGO

http://www.bufvc.ac.uk/rgo

The online version of this publication, with extended descriptions of collections and services. For further details, see next section.
http://www.bufvc.ac.uk/rgo

Television and Radio Index for Learning and Teaching – TRILT

http://www.trilt.ac.uk

An extensive database of British radio and television from 1995 onwards, enhanced by the BUFVC with additional information for selected programmes of educational interest. The data accumulates at a rate of 1.3 million records a year. Available to BUFVC members only.

TV Times Project – TVTiP

http://www.bufvc.ac.uk/tvtip

Comprehensive ITV and Channel 4 programme content from the TV Times 1955–1985. Available to UK higher and further education users (Athens password) and BUFVC members only.

This Week

http://www.bufvc.ac.uk/thisweek

Comprehensive data for the ITV documentary series THIS WEEK (1956–1992). Available to UK higher and further education users (Athens password) and BUFVC members only.

Subject Index

Numbers refer to collection numbers, not page numbers.